More Praise for *Girl in Glass*

A *Washington Post* Book Club selection

A *Public Books* Favorite Book of 2015

"The author has spun a profound work of philosophy and sewn it into the shell of an exquisite memoir." —**Jennifer Senior,** *The New York Times*

"In this courageous and passionate book, Deanna Fei tells the story of delivering a medically fragile child at twenty-five weeks. Even those who know the outcome will be gripped by the novelistic depiction of oscillating hope and despair. But the real accomplishment of this book is that it takes memoir as a jumping-off point for pondering the obligations attached to scientific progress and collective wealth. In addressing the issue of how much a human life is ultimately worth, it becomes a deeply moving work of moral philosophy." —**Andrew Solomon,** *New York Times* **bestselling author of** *Far from the Tree*

"Deanna Fei has written three gripping tales in one—her transcendent journey as the mother of a child born way too soon; her plunge into the harsh realities of corporate greed and bumbling when a certain CEO publicly labeled her daughter a 'distressed baby'; and her hard-won understanding of what society owes its most fragile beings. Readers will fall in love with Fei's daughter, and come to see that she is all of our children." —**Lisa Belkin, author of** *Life's Work* **and former columnist for the** *New York Times's* **Motherlode Blog**

"Luminous. An unflinching testament to the improbable miraculousness of life." —**Thrity Umrigar, bestselling author of** *The Space Between Us* **and** *The Story Hour*

"Fei grippingly details her dread, anxiety, and wonder with her second-trimester delivery . . . An urgent call for corporate compassion by a woman with a baby in peril." —*Kirkus Reviews*

"[Fei] critiques . . . the entire American health-care system. Yet this is not a fire-breathing polemic or a policy tract. It's most effective, and affecting, as a mother's memoir of how her life changed the day her daughter came into the world far too soon . . . Moving and persuasive."
—*The Washington Post*

"A heartbreaking yet beautiful story of motherhood and love . . . Fei is a gifted writer with a courageous tale to share. This memorable book belongs on the shelf of every library."—*Library Journal* (starred review)

"[Fei] writes with precision, grace, and a devastating honesty."
—*The Boston Globe*

"This memoir is so starkly, poignantly written, so smart and wrenching, and I just had a truly visceral response to both the story and to Fei's fierce, plain mother love throughout."—*The Millions*, "Year in Reading 2015"

"Everyone must read this book." —**Melissa Harris-Perry, MSNBC**

"Honest and clear-eyed . . . Mesmerizing." —*Yahoo! Parenting*

"Somehow finding immense bravery amid her turbulent experience, Fei has written a memoir, *Girl in Glass* . . . She's able to construct a scene with just a few details and go straight to its emotional heart . . . Her writing immerses readers through intimate vignettes: the first time she was able to embrace her daughter; the daughter's first feedings achieved painstakingly for months; her daughter's first unassisted breaths . . . It's amazing how she's able to ask so many of the hard questions . . . about the value of one fragile human life. Anyone who recognizes or questions the idea that human life has a price tag will want to read this book." —**Tamiko Nimura,** *Hyphen Magazine*

"Dramatic . . . Argue[s] eloquently against corporate greed and the bottom line of profit and loss." —*The Catholic Reporter*

"One of 2015's most important and moving books." —*Largehearted Boy*

GIRL IN GLASS

Dispatches from the Edge of Life

DEANNA FEI

BLOOMSBURY

NEW YORK · LONDON · OXFORD · NEW DELHI · SYDNEY

For Leo and Mila

Bloomsbury USA
An imprint of Bloomsbury Publishing Plc

1385 Broadway	50 Bedford Square
New York	London
NY 10018	WC1B 3DP
USA	UK

www.bloomsbury.com

BLOOMSBURY and the Diana logo are trademarks of Bloomsbury Publishing Plc

First published 2015
This paperback edition published 2016

ISBN: HB: 978-1-62040-991-6 / ePub: 978-1-62040-993-0 / PB: 978-1-62040-992-3

LIBRARY OF CONGRESS CATALOGING-IN-PUBLICATION DATA HAS BEEN APPLIED FOR.

2 4 6 8 10 9 7 5 3 1

Typeset by RefineCatch Limited, Bungay, Suffolk
Printed and bound in the U.S.A. by Berryville Graphics Inc., Berryville, Virginia

To find out more about our authors and books visit www.bloomsbury.com. Here you will find extracts, author interviews, details of forthcoming events and the option to sign up for our newsletters.

Bloomsbury books may be purchased for business or promotional use. For information on bulk purchases please contact Macmillan Corporate and Premium Sales Department at specialmarkets@macmillan.com.

PREFACE

My first child, my son, arrived in the world as the most ordinary kind of miracle: the radiant perfection in the birth of a baby. Thirteen months later, my second child exited my body much too soon and was rescued by doctors, encased in glass, and attached to machines. This baby, my daughter, seemed fated to be a tragic outcome—unless, by an act of divine intervention, she turned out to be a miracle child.

Her odds overshadowed her existence. Her life was suspended between birth and death, hope and fear, nature and science. Each moment that she survived carried her not toward a promised future, but further into limbo.

One year after I brought my daughter home from the hospital, just as I allowed myself to believe that she had defied the odds, the CEO of a large American company—my husband's employer—publicly blamed her for his decision to cut employee benefits. He used an unlikely phrase that soon generated countless headlines and became a social media meme: "distressed babies." A phrase that exposed everything I had tried to forget.

Amid a media firestorm, I came forward to tell my daughter's story for the first time, to defend her right to the care that saved her life. The story went viral; the CEO issued an apology, and I forgave him; the news cycle turned anew.

Yet in the wake of the controversy, as I found myself reading an outpouring of messages from strangers across the country, I realized I'd only just begun to understand how my daughter had made her way home.

Many of those who wrote to me to embrace the story of my daughter's birth also entrusted me with stories of their own. Stories of being targeted by employers for needing medical care, of suffering similar exposure without having drawn attention from the media, of navigating their own precarious journeys at the edge of life. Stories that called upon me to seek a measure of recognition for them, too.

Thus began an unexpected journey of my own to explore the broader sweep of my daughter's story—and what it means to save a life. From the front lines of neonatal intensive care units to the spreadsheets wielded by cost-cutting executives; from the insidious notions of risk surrounding modern pregnancy to the imperiled state of our right to medical privacy; from decades of medical innovation to the question of how we care for our most vulnerable; and finally, to the potent force of a child's will to live. Above all, this is a story of how love takes hold when a new life defies all expectations.

PART I

Lay your sleeping head, my love,
Human on my faithless arm;
Time and fevers burn away
Individual beauty from
Thoughtful children, and the grave
Proves the child ephemeral:
But in my arms till break of day
Let the living creature lie,
Mortal, guilty, but to me
The entirely beautiful.
—W. H. AUDEN, "LULLABY"

1

THE SECOND NIGHT after my baby daughter arrives—I still struggle to say *she was born*—she comes to me in a dream. I'm curled up in the hospital bed, sleeping in a fetal position, when I feel a tiny hand between my palms.

In reality, my baby is not with me. I can't hold her at all. Her bed lies one floor above mine, behind a locked steel door, walled in glass, obscured by a tangle of tubes and wires and machinery.

What little there is of her to look at, I can hardly bear to see. When I manage to look, the thought that grips me is this: *She isn't meant to be here. Let her go.*

She weighs one pound nine ounces. She can't cry or nurse or breathe. Her head is too large, her ears barely formed. Her legs look like those of a decrepit old woman or a starving child, the skin shriveled and sagging over twigs of bone.

Her skin is purplish red, bloody and bruised. One doctor, visibly shaken, describes it as "gelatinous."

Why shouldn't it be? No part of her is supposed to function out here. She is still supposed to be part of me.

Just two nights ago, I went to bed at home, still pregnant. Twenty-five weeks into a perfect pregnancy. Until four thirty A.M., when I woke up in acute pain.

I swallow a handful of antacids. My husband leaves for the airport. I try to go back to sleep. Only when I hear myself gasp "God help me" do I pick up the phone.

My obstetrician tells me to head to the hospital. I say that I can't leave my baby—meaning Leo, my one-year-old son—home by himself.

Leo is just waking up, talking to his reflection in the crib mirror. When I open his door, he beams his exuberant, roguish grin. I unzip his sleep sack, kiss his fat cheeks, change his diaper. He plunks himself on my lap to guzzle a sippy cup of milk. The pain is escalating, punctuated by waves of tremendous pressure. I stifle a cry into my baby boy's thick hair.

After call upon call, our babysitter is still half an hour away. Peter's cousin on the fourth floor, roused from bed, runs down the stairs. Leo's grin fades to a bewildered sob as I put him back in his crib with a bowl of Cheerios and grapes.

In a cab on my way to the hospital, alone in the backseat, my mouth clamped shut and my feet braced against the floor, I will myself to hold it in: the pain, my pregnancy, this life I'm supposed to be nurturing.

Then I see the blood, and I know I'm failing.

My baby girl. She's not going to become a baby. She's slipping away, and there is nothing I can do to hold on to her. This is a sudden, primal knowledge, one that steels me through each red light, the driver's sidelong glances, another red light, and another.

I'm having a miscarriage, I tell myself. *I don't know this baby yet. Miscarriages happen.*

Through the sunlit lobby, the leisurely elevator, each turn of the long white corridors. Past myriad impassive faces and swinging doors. Through the masked introductions. The blur of fluorescent ceiling lights. The probing of gloved hands. The yanking of curtains.

I know that it's over. The first sonogram, that tiny upside-down gummy bear. Those first little flutters morphing into impassioned jabs and kicks. The anatomy scan: the pulsating heart, the primitive profile, the ten fingers and toes, Peter's exultation, my mother's tears of joy when I told her the news: a girl.

A girl who took us by stealth. A girl who'd hold her own against Leo, the fiercest creature I've ever known. A girl who would arrive just in time for the tail end of the year of the dragon. A beautiful girl who would complete our family. Our baby girl.

All that is over. Now I'm just waiting for the ordeal to end.

This isn't the worst thing in the world, I tell myself.

The long, sharp slice. The glowing orange cave of anesthesia. I'm grateful to enter that cave. I'm not sure I ever want to come out.

The ticking of a clock in a quiet room. The hand of my husband. It takes us a while to ask what happened to the baby.

An incomprehensible situation becomes surreal. My obstetrician, Dr. Bryant, shows up with a jaunty manner. An attendant leads Peter off, with a perky command to have a camera ready. I'm wheeled into the postpartum wing—the same place where I presented my honey-gold, lush-haired son thirteen months ago, receiving congratulations at every turn.

This time, my arms are empty. Yet people smile at me and say, "Congratulations!"

I try to smile back and say thank you. They seem to be performing an elaborate charade for my sake, and since I can't sit up or walk or swallow a sip of water on my own—since the smallest unadvised movement threatens to rip me open at the seams—I do my best to play along.

But then there's the doctor visibly shaken by my daughter's skin. There's this admission from Dr. Bryant: "Twenty years ago, this would have been a miscarriage."

Then, in a clear, modulated voice, the head neonatologist, Dr. Kahn, explains that my baby might not survive one month, or one week, or one day. That she has roughly a one-third chance of dying before we can bring her home. That she also has a one-third chance of being seriously disabled, unable to ever lead an independent life, survival aside.

At the same time, Dr. Kahn calls my daughter "amazing": she is initiating most breaths on her own, maintaining her oxygen levels with a little help from the ventilator, even responding well to her feedings.

When I'm wheeled to the neonatal intensive care unit for the first time, I will myself to be brave and positive. For now, my daughter is alive.

She has eyes that blink, the finest brushstrokes of hair. These appear to be the only unharmed parts of her. She lies very still, tethered to more devices than I can count. I look past the tubes, the wires, the bandages, the skin—my God, her skin—to take stock of all the parts that new mothers do: the cheeks, the toes. None of her should be seen except through the fuzzy green magic of ultrasound.

"Congratulations!" we're told, again and again.

Peter and I attempt to respond appropriately. We call our families. We calculate that we have a one-third chance that our daughter will somehow be okay.

I'm instructed to start pumping every two hours, to get my breast milk flowing. Even though my baby might not survive the day. Even though, as far as my body knows, she slipped away that morning.

At dusk, Peter goes home to Leo. It's the first night I've ever spent away from my son.

My sister Michelle, who is nine months pregnant, stays with me in the hospital. Her condition confuses everyone: obviously, she should be the one who just had a baby, not me. I give her my dinner. She helps me to the bathroom and back. With pain medication still dripping into my veins, I manage to fall asleep.

Attendants wake me to check my vitals every few hours. I pump and go back to sleep. In the eerie hospital twilight, nothing is too real. Until morning, when my hand instinctively settles on my belly to feel my baby moving.

I feel dazed, knifed, on the verge of vomiting what remains inside me. I force myself to pump again. In response to the hard, dry, mechanical suctioning, my breasts seem to shriek *Are you joking?*

Peter returns with his best approximations of the items I've asked him to bring: my pumping bra, my nursing nightgown. I wouldn't have been able to find them, either. Just the other day, in preparation for a renovation that was planned a lifetime ago, we set aside clothes to last the next few months and packed everything else away.

The purpose of the renovation is to convert our closet and reading nook into a baby room and a kids' bathroom. The demolition is scheduled to start today.

While I pump, Peter grapples with the renovation, child care for Leo, our health insurance, his paternity leave. Each practicality hinges on the question of our daughter's survival.

When we visit her again, the dim room feels like a crypt. The only sound is the heavy breathing and gurgling of machines.

She's splayed on her back, her eyes scrunched tight. Her head appears to be held by the ventilator hoses at an unnatural angle. Her tiny, shriveled limbs jerk and flail. Her hands bat against the bandages and tubes that mask her from nose to neck.

She looks as if she's writhing against the instruments that have been jammed into her one-pound-nine-ounce body. As if she's suffocating amid all this state-of-the-art technology.

The nurses and doctors are working heroically to keep her alive. I'm superfluous to that mission. All I can do for her, I'm told again and again, is pump.

When Dr. Kahn comes to my room, I'm pumping. Peter and I act upbeat and friendly. We can't help hoping that getting this doctor to like us will improve our daughter's chances.

Dr. Kahn sits down. The pump heaves and my legs shake as she speaks.

A follow-up head ultrasound. The one yesterday was clear. The one today shows an intraventricular hemorrhage. Bleeding in the right ventricle of my daughter's brain. Blood seeping into the surrounding tissue. Brain damage.

This is the worst thing, a voice in my head jabbers.

I can hardly hear Dr. Kahn. At last I reach over to shut off the pump.

The bleeding is the aftermath of the injury. The injury already occurred. There is nothing to be done. The question now is how far the bleeding will spread. There is a risk of brain swelling and inflammation that can lead to death within days or minutes. If she survives, the extent of the damage will remain unknown for months or years.

I try to speak. At last Peter articulates a question.

Do we still have that one-third chance that our daughter will somehow be okay?

Dr. Kahn has worked here for decades. She has seen thousands of babies come and go. This is plain in the stoop of her shoulders, the twitch of her nose, the pallor of her kind, peaked face.

"Well," she says, "when you have a birth as catastrophic as this—"

And then, as she gazes at us, she starts to cry.

I'm grateful for her tears. Even more grateful for her choice of words. Here, finally, is the raw truth against the relentless farce of *"Congratulations!"*

Catastrophic.

This confirmation allows us a measure of calm. We ask more questions. We learn the gradations of severity of intraventricular hemorrhages, with grade IV being the worst. The first assessment of our daughter's bleed is grade IV.

We learn the term *comfort care.* If our daughter were disconnected from the machines, she would pass away within one hour.

Dr. Kahn does not discuss whether or when this might become an option. But for me, simply hearing the phrase seems to hold out the possibility of relief.

I know the feel-good, inspirational version of this story. A blessing in disguise. A miracle child. An angel who will teach me more than I ever thought I could learn about life and love.

But I don't believe in angels. I don't believe in calling a catastrophe a blessing. I don't want a miracle child. What baby should have to bear such a burden? I only want my child, my baby girl, unharmed. I want the ordinary miracle of that.

I know that I can't have it. So I would like to grieve and go home to take care of my son.

Babies die every day. Why not mine?

Dr. Kahn takes her leave, but not before asking if our daughter has a name.

A name?

I wait until her footsteps recede.

If either my husband or I were faced with an end-of-life decision for the other—which is to say, if one of us were rendered, like our daughter now, unable to breathe or eat or utter a sound—we've always assumed we'd know what the right choice would be.

Still, the thought that grips me is one that I haven't voiced to him, until now.

Let her go. She isn't meant to be here. She doesn't belong in this world.

For the first time, Peter breaks down.

Between my own sobs, I tell myself, *This can't be. I have to find a way to wake up pregnant again, with my baby girl safe inside my body.*

Eventually, the sobs subside. My husband brings me water. It's time to pump again. This time, I produce a few drops of colostrum.

At my daughter's bedside, I use a swab to collect the colostrum, which the doctors and nurses call liquid gold. The drops vanish into the swab before I can dab them to her lips.

For the first time, I reach into the incubator and touch her hand. Her fingers are so tiny that they're less like fingers than like the fins of a minnow, the tendrils of a pea. But they grasp at my finger.

All at once, I know that I can't help but love her, because she is mine, because I am her mother. But I don't think I can bear it. She needs a braver mother, a selfless mother, a heroic mother. A mother who could never wish to let her go.

That night, she comes to me in a dream. I'm sleeping in a fetal position when I feel a tiny hand between my palms. The hand is tiny, but warm and steady. I look at it for a moment before I know whose hand it is. I close my eyes again and hold on.

We hold on.

2

I FORGET WHERE I AM, why I am here. I forget that I ever saw her.

In moments—drifting off to medicated sleep, discussing my sister's pregnancy, watching Peter send a work e-mail—nothing could feel less real than that tiny creature encased in glass.

"How's your baby?" people ask—a hospital attendant, a nurse.

I forget. I burst out in a smile, I start to say, "He's great—" before I catch myself, before I remember. I mean Leo, of course. My irresistible, strapping, wiseass, romantic, indomitable baby boy. Thirteen months ago, he was born down the hallway. Seven pounds ten ounces, twenty-one inches long. Somehow he'd timed his arrival to his actual due date—and Labor Day, the little showoff.

How can he be at home when I am here? Since his birth, the umbilical cord never seemed severed, only stretched: to the distance from my skin to his. Not across a bridge and up the West Side Highway; not a day and a universe away.

Now my previous life seems surreal, too.

My days at home with Leo. His twice-daily plundering of every cabinet and drawer. His hurtling from wall to wall of the bathtub, attempting to gain toeholds on the faucet. His habit of galloping up to strangers in the park and demanding food like a celebrity hailing a valet. His newest predilection for dancing to James Brown's "(Call Me) Super Bad."

My three days a week to write, scrabbling to finish my second novel before the arrival of my second baby, the hours away from my son both woefully inadequate and much too long.

My evenings with Peter, hasty catch-ups over hasty dinners, then collapsing on the couch to watch TV while he scratches my head or my feet.

All of it seems golden and precious. Every moment of that life, every single one until the moment I woke up in pain at four thirty A.M., seems idyllic.

Yet I complained. I thought I had real worries. I've always been a worrier, but never more so than when I found myself unexpectedly pregnant with a second baby before I felt convinced that I would survive my first.

I was worried about time and space and money and just one pair of hands. I was worried that I couldn't possibly manage to be a good mother to both of my babies without sacrificing all of myself.

Thinking people space out their children because you need time to forget, just enough, the soul-crushing exhaustion of life with a newborn. It's not the pain of childbirth, as I once assumed. It's every single day and night after. My babies would be—were supposed to be—less than one and a half years apart, and I had not forgotten anything yet.

Also, for much of his young life, my son was a ruthless tyrant. Insatiable in his appetites, ferocious in his demands, unable to contain his contempt for the peons scurrying around him, especially me.

From the day I brought him home, I'd suspected that he was actually a grown man somehow trapped in an infant's body. Not just any man, but a warrior king, a master of the universe, maybe the last maharajah, maybe Leonardo DiCaprio or Jay Z. Every time he opened his mouth, this is what he seemed to be shrieking: *How dare you! Don't you know who I am?*

So I was worried about how I'd keep up with him for the rest of my pregnancy. I was worried about how I'd chase him and soothe him and snatch him back from various precipices as my belly swelled.

I was worried about Leo having less of me. That he was sensing something amiss. Already, something about the pregnancy had propelled him to self-wean. And in the last few weeks, uncharacteristically, he'd been waking up crying in the middle of the night and insisting on being carried all day.

Peter brought home a book called *Mama, What's In There?*—the only book on the subject of becoming a big sibling he could find that was written for a baby. Each page had a different family of animals—bears, dolphins, elephants—with a youngster asking its pregnant mother, "Mama, what's in there?" Each mama had a flap on her belly you could open to find a baby, or a whole litter of them, happily floating inside. I found the concept grisly, but Leo loved books with flaps, tabs, anything he could yank.

Except for this book. Every time I tried to read it to him, he shrieked and smacked it away. We never made it to the final page: a human family.

I was worried about how I'd help my sister with her first baby, who was due in early October. Throughout Leo's first year, Michelle was like a second mother to him—one whose patience and resourcefulness often outstripped mine. Would it be too galling to ask her to return all the baby gear I'd just given to her, or should I simply buy everything all over again?

I was worried about how to get through the winter without a maternity coat. The baby—my baby girl—was due to arrive at the end of January. The last months of my first pregnancy had been in late summer, which was its own form of torture, but at least I'd had only to slip on a flowy dress.

The morning I woke up in pain, the date was October 9. Winter is still months away.

I was worried about my marriage.

From the time Peter and I became a couple, eight years earlier in Shanghai—he was a newspaper correspondent, I was researching my first novel—we'd edited each other's work, brushed our teeth side by side, held hands during every plane takeoff and landing. We'd vowed to remain that kind of couple even if the day ever came when we touched down from our whirlwind life and started a family together.

But once Leo arrived, I became the primary caregiver, Peter the primary breadwinner. During the scant hours we had to ourselves, we seemed to be encased in moon suits, unable to hear much but the sound of our own complaints, our own labored and repetitive breathing. We wanted to come together, but the drift was hard to fight, and we were so tired.

Then Leo became a little more manageable. I gradually returned to my writing. Peter and I instituted date nights. We were finally finding a new equilibrium as a family when we found out I was pregnant again.

I was worried about pouring more money into our house, the lower half of the scruffy, spacious brick town house in Brooklyn that had felt like home at first sight. We didn't know then about the nests of mice in the kitchen, the blocked vents in the bathroom, the rotted pipes in the basement. Or that soon the house would swallow most of our monthly income, both of our book advances, multiple maxed-out zero-interest credit cards, loans and gifts from family—and plunge us deeper into debt with every flare-up of its creaky organs.

Our house was the main reason Peter had recently given up his perch as a *New York Times* correspondent to become an editor at a new media company. With his augmented salary, we'd only just managed to pay off our outstanding debts. Yet after we found out I was pregnant again, we became frantic to fix up our nest.

I was worried about the disruption, the dust. The workmen hammering and drilling during Leo's naps. The impending months of haggling with the contractor over a chipped tile, a crooked outlet. I was worried about whether the job would be finished before my daughter was born.

It never occurred to me that she would arrive the day before the work was scheduled to start.

I was worried about my work. I'd hoped to finish my second novel before Leo was born, but I hadn't bargained for what pregnancy did to my brain the first time around. Once Leo showed up, he only extended his dominion.

I hadn't managed to carve out my three days a week to write until Leo was eight months old. Once I found out I was pregnant again, I told myself it was now or never. If I didn't finish my novel before my second baby arrived, the characters would never forgive me for abandoning them yet again.

The morning I woke up in pain, as implausible as it already seems, I was about to start writing a pivotal scene in which my main character suffers a miscarriage.

One thing I wasn't worried about was my pregnancy. It was an untroubled pregnancy, an easy pregnancy, a pregnancy so smooth that for nearly three months I hadn't even noticed it.

My first pregnancy and birth were smooth, too, but like all first-time mothers, I had worried. An ectopic pregnancy, a blighted ovum. Down syndrome, Tay-Sachs, spina bifida.

Gestational diabetes, a prolapsed cord, a stillbirth. Every checkup, every benchmark had become a chance to find out the next worry.

This time I had perspective. At every checkup, the obstetricians breezed in and out. The heartbeat was strong, the ultrasounds looked perfect, my weight and my blood pressure and the size of my belly were textbook. At one point, my doctor said, "You're one of the patients we never have to worry about."

When I was pregnant with my son, I'd worried about his future personality and strength of character. Whether he'd grow up too removed from the immigrant struggles of my parents, too entitled. The fact that he would be born in the year of the rabbit, that soft, trembling creature. As a countermeasure, Peter and I took to calling him "Tiger Cub," and then just the Cub. We joked that he would have to prove his mettle on his very first test: the Apgar scores to evaluate his physical health upon delivery.

With my daughter, I wasn't worried. Not only because she would be born in the year of the dragon, but because I knew the women in my family. I knew that my daughter would grow up, in her own way and in her own right, to be a fierce, passionate, bold, loving girl who would fight every good fight but also be unashamed to daydream, to eat chocolate in bed, to stay up gossiping with girlfriends, to twirl before me in a dressing room, to cry on her daddy's shoulder.

She would be my kind of girl.

In those moments before the hazy golden Before has evaporated, before my Now has reassembled around me in all its stark solidity, I pray. I wasn't raised to pray. I don't know how to pray, but now I pray.

Please let me wake up at home again. With my baby boy down the hall and my baby girl safe inside me. Please let me keep her safe until she can feed, until she can breathe, until her brain can withstand life outside the womb. I'll do anything to go back. I will never, ever, ever complain again.

3

SHE LIES INSIDE WHAT IS CALLED an *isolette*, a glass-walled bed on a base with numerous switches and buttons. The enclosure has two windows on each side that click open to allow a person's hands inside. Ports at either end allow the tubes and wires to connect her body to the machines.

Isolette. It's just the name of this high-tech kind of incubator, and *incubator* has a cozy, warm sound, bringing to mind fuzzy baby chicks. But every time I hear *isolette*, it sounds like a compound of *isolated* and *desolate*.

My daughter's isolette is labeled with a pink name tag: IT'S A GIRL! The blanks are filled in with black marker or blue pen, all clearly written in haste.

NAME: *Fei Girl*
DATE OF BIRTH: *10-9-12*
TIME OF BIRTH: *8:00 A.M.*
WEIGHT: *705 grams / 1 lb. 9 oz.*

Taped to this name tag is the ID bracelet that matches the ones attached to both my and Peter's wrists. Her own body appears too encumbered to bear this strip of paper, the only physical link to us.

At one end of her isolette is the ventilator, the machine that gives my daughter breath. A bulky stand that gurgles, connected to hoses that reach to her mouth, with a monitor that shows the oxygen saturation level, the number of breaths per minute, and other numbers I don't understand. This machine plugs into an outlet with an ordinary plug. If you wanted, you could probably knock it over.

At the other end of her isolette are more screens, with oscillations and more numbers that tell me she is alive while my body tries to tell me something different.

Her feet are no more than two inches long, yet they look disproportionately large against her withered legs. A red-lit electronic sensor is secured to the sole of one foot. Her heel is wrapped in bloody gauze.

Her legs are bent outward like a frog's. The skin looks vaguely reptilian, too, hanging thinly over the meager bones, not made for this air, not yet. There are no dimples or folds of flesh; there is no roundness or softness at all; there is no flesh.

Her diaper is no bigger than a handkerchief, yet it hangs off her body in a sagging bulk. At first, I register it as another medical device rather than a familiar household item. It hasn't occurred to me that any part of her might function like that of a normal newborn: if she can't cry or nurse or breathe, why would she pee? Also, the diaper is plain white, unlike any other diaper I've seen: no brand or design or logo, as if no company wanted to be associated with a baby like this.

Where her belly button should be is a tangle of tubing, held in place by layers of bandages. The reddish purple skin over her torso is covered with so many abrasions that I can't tell whether it is wounded or has never been intact.

The widest part of her arm is no bigger than my pinkie finger.

Both arms are flopped out, palms up, in the manner of a victim surrendering.

Her shrunken chest is obscured by more wires and adhesives. Her rib cage appears to cave in with each breath. Each rib looks liable to rupture her skin. The left side of her chest is punctured by a thick white tube. This must be the central line that feeds into a large artery, extending nearly to her heart.

Hoses connect from the ventilator to the mouthpiece that props her lips open, one white and one blue, each hose thicker than the biggest part of her arm. They look like a terrible weight for her head to bear. The mouthpiece is secured to her face with long strips of adhesive tape that stretch, one above her mouth and one below, across her face from ear to ear.

Her ears are soft, stunted swirls, tiny organs interrupted midflower. They look unearthly, like the orifice of a deep-sea creature.

She wears the hospital-issued newborn hat, white with alternating pink and blue stripes, a fixture of delivery rooms across the nation. Even with the brim folded over several times, the fabric yawns over her head.

Her tendrils of hair appear to have been painstakingly painted, one by one, with the finest brush. She has the beginnings of eyebrows, fawn-colored fuzzy arches. Her skull looks as if it could break open the skin over her forehead. Veins strain there. The skin strains to stay in one piece.

Her lips are slivers of flesh that look much too delicate to encircle those ventilator hoses. Her little nose appears to be pushed upward by the thick white tape.

When her eyes are closed, they look like tiny wet nicks in her gaunt, raw-skinned face. When they open, they shine a quiet, stoic light. They have the look of someone very solitary, the look of unspeakable suffering.

As I sob in my wheelchair in my bloodstained hospital gown,

I'm dimly aware of other people. The nurses' muted bustle and conversation, the sleep of other babies, the waveforms on other monitors, the coming and going of other parents.

Yet around my daughter's isolette, there seems to be a dark shroud. People look over, then look away. When the nurses hover, they are sober, silent, focused, hands working quickly. Most of the time, no one is by my daughter's side as she struggles on the edge of life and death.

When my vision clears, I try to gaze into her eyes, but in the panes of her isolette, I see the reflection of the flickering numbers on the screens that surround her, and my own wrecked face.

4

WHAT HAPPENED?
      There is a simple answer: A preterm birth. A premature baby.

My daughter is a preemie. That sounds common enough, even kind of cute.

I was a preemie, too. My mother can't recall how early, maybe four or five weeks. Early enough that as she was being rushed into the delivery room, she was so distraught that a nurse told her not to worry, that her own child had been born early, too, and was just fine.

Then comes the laugh line: My mother sobbed, *But—is your kid smart?*

At this point in the storytelling, my mother would shake her head. "Can you believe it? That nurse should've slapped me."

And we would laugh. There I stood, sound of body, brain apparently intact.

What happened?
Five and a half months into my second pregnancy, I woke up in labor—sudden, unexplained labor—and my daughter was delivered via emergency cesarean.

In recent years, I think I've read in passing about a mysterious increase in the incidence of premature births, in the level of prematurity. I think I've read about the astronomical costs and extraordinary interventions involved in caring for such babies. I probably wondered to myself, without dwelling on it for long, whether all of them truly ought to be saved.

I've heard of babies so tiny they can fit in the palm of your hand. I've seen those photos somewhere. The NICU here has one taped to the door: a baby nestled in a cupped palm, sepia-toned, serene and perfect. Just like a regular baby, only in miniature.

My daughter looks nothing like that. She's pre-premature. She's pre-alive.

Then again, the books displayed in the NICU list a category for a baby like her: "extremely premature." These books chart the probabilities of outcomes for each category of preemie, from "mildly premature" to her category: the odds of death, of major complications, of serious disability.

Her official gestational age is twenty-five weeks and three days. In terms of her odds, every one of those days matters. But we never had any certainty about her due date.

One of the books has no row for cases more extreme than hers. It notes that, until recently, a preemie like her had virtually a zero percent chance of survival. This book distinguishes itself from other books for parents of preemies as the one with "a positive approach."

Most of the charts list 1,000 grams as the lowest cutoff. My daughter has already dropped below her birth weight of 705 grams, and she is dropping lower by the hour.

Eventually, I find charts that include rows for babies born at twenty-four weeks, twenty-three weeks, even twenty-two weeks and under, but then there are no statistics, only words in parentheses: *poor outcome, insufficient data, N/A.*

Or blank spaces.

5

THE WORD *MIRACLE* SEEMS to hover around me like a shiny helium balloon: there's *It's a Miracle!* bobbing alongside *Congratulations!* These words seem so implausible that I can't register their proximity, I can't imagine their utterance, until yet another person comes along to say, in a chipper tone, something like:

She's a miracle.

You have a miracle baby.

She'll be your little miracle, just you wait and see.

I try to appreciate the sentiment, the kindness, the hope that these people are attempting to convey.

But what if your apparently healthy husband collapsed at work, or your son got hit by a car? What if you found yourself rushing to the hospital while your loved one was rendered unable to eat or breathe or utter a sound? Would you call that a miracle?

My daughter should still be a fetus. She shouldn't have to live up to a word like that.

If she doesn't make it, if she can't surmount all the challenges heaped at her tiny feet, will she lose that mantle of miraculousness? What will you call her then?

An angel, I guess.

It's not that I don't want a miracle. I've never wanted anything more.

But a miracle is not a person. A miracle is an outcome you can pray for. A miracle would be my daughter's brain bleed reversing course. A miracle would be her making her way back into my womb. A miracle would be her growing up to be a healthy, happy girl.

But she shouldn't have to be a miracle in order to simply exist.

I'm her mother, and I need to cherish her for who she is, for however long she lives, not for some vision of what I pray might happen. I need to see her clearly. I need to learn her eyes, the bend of her toes, the grip of her hand. I can't fall in love with a mirage.

6

EARLY ON THE SECOND DAY, when the sky is still bluish black, I drift out of sleep and my hand settles upon my belly, once again, to feel my baby move. Then I remember.

I'm alone in my postpartum room. Peter is home with our son. I press the call button and ask for my pain medication. I'm overdue for my dose. The attendant says a nurse will come.

With each passing minute, I feel more distinctly the stitches, the bleeding, my hollowed womb contracting. I press the button again, then again. No one comes.

I'm told the unit is understaffed. I understand that my situation does not qualify as an emergency, yet I know that my condition is acute. The pain itself is not unbearable. What I don't think I can bear right now is feeling anything at all.

One day ago, my husband left me alone in the dark and the walls of my body gave way.

When I came to in the recovery room and grasped for his hand, we were just grateful that we still had each other. We were like survivors of a shipwreck, stunned and adrift.

The ticking of that clock. I will never know how many minutes elapsed before I murmured, "Is she alive?"

He said, "I don't know."

But we both thought we knew. That must be why my husband, a journalist, hadn't asked.

I whispered, "Go ask."

He said, "Okay," and he went.

After Dr. Kahn tells us about the brain hemorrhage and leaves the room, after I voice the thought that has gripped me ever since I first laid eyes on my daughter and my husband finally breaks down, this is what he says, once he can speak again:

"If they take her off the machines—if it comes to that—we wouldn't be there."

My tears evaporate. Yet the room sways.

Is my husband saying that if our daughter were disconnected from life support, we would leave her to die alone?

I think of her quiet, shining eyes. Her tiny hand holding mine.

My husband is trying to rescue me. He thinks that he can airlift us out of this disaster zone. He is still in one piece.

Ever since we arrived at the hospital, he has projected optimism with all his might. I'm the one who broke him down.

Let her go. She isn't meant to be here. She doesn't belong in this world.

But I never meant to let her go alone.

Maybe I don't really know my husband. After all, there are many things I didn't know until now. For instance, that a perfect pregnancy could end like this.

I'm gasping for air, my limbs giving out, watching my husband seize a lifeline and float away from me.

But he's speaking out of love—for me and for our child at home. He's guarding the family he knows.

Something gathers deep inside me, knits my spine upright, steadies my voice.

"We're her parents," I say. "However long she lives, whatever her life turns out to be. We're the ones who have to hold her. She's our baby."

Peter sits up and nods, blinks until his eyes are dry, repeats my words until they ring with conviction.

I'm breathing hard, as if I've managed to swim to some promise of safety. I know what to do for my daughter in the event of a quick and merciful release.

I don't know how to be the mother she needs if she lives.

7

WHAT'S HER NAME?" the nurses have started to ask. "Mommy, did you pick a name?" The next time we see Dr. Kahn, she asks us again.

I think of other cultures, ancient traditions, that dictate some kind of waiting period before the heralding of a new baby. The Chinese custom of celebrating at one hundred days. The Jewish custom of holding the baby shower after a healthy baby is born.

On all the identification tags, my daughter is FEI GIRL. When the doctors and nurses talk to one another, she is "Baby Fei."

Her arrival has seemed so wholly a catastrophe that happened to my family that it hasn't occurred to me that the professionals tasked with keeping her alive have something at stake in her name.

After all, what is a name? It's not only a statement of who we are as parents, of our particular aspirations for our child: how earthy, how ethnic, how literary, how different, how classic, how hip, how solid, how whimsical.

A name is an announcement of a person's existence. It establishes her as an individual within a society. It enters her into the public record. It makes her real.

Even if she won't exist for long, she exists now. Even if she never leaves the hospital, she is here now. She needs a name.

Peter and I agree on the kind of name we want for our daughter: simple and easily pronounceable, slightly unusual but unpretentious, pretty but not flowery. We started looking through a book of girl names just last week. I found a few that I kind of liked, he found a few that he kind of liked; there wasn't much overlap. He jotted a provisional list into his phone, and we went to bed.

If we had one name that we'd cherished for years, the perfect name for the daughter we'd envisioned, would we give it to her? I'm thankful the question is moot.

Now one name comes to me. I don't know anyone personally by the name. It has no specific connotation to me. It just stays with me.

When I mention it to Peter, he's noncommittal.

We run through the list again. We brainstorm variations. I try to come to terms with giving my daughter a name I don't mind.

As if she hasn't been dealt enough setbacks in life already.

I mention that one name to Peter again. This time, he pauses and pronounces it slowly. What does it mean?

We find just two relevant websites. The first lists the most common meaning as "rival; emulating"—not exactly auspicious. The secondary meaning is "friendly, soft, pleasant." These qualities are not high on our list of priorities for our daughter.

The next website lists only one meaning: "miracle."

We dismiss the name.

8

B Y THE SECOND DAY, my daughter has already undergone
more procedures and received more diagnoses than I can
track, and the list keeps growing.

The insertion of breathing tubes into her windpipe that attach
to the ventilator. The flow of oxygenated air through the hoses,
the mechanical supplementation of her breaths, the artificial
pressure to open her airways and air sacs. The insertion of the
umbilical catheter, the IV, the central line. A feeding tube that
snakes into her mouth and down her esophagus, delivering her
first drops of breast milk directly to her stomach from a syringe
and a pump. Head ultrasounds, chest X-rays, heel sticks. Blood
transfusions to replace her blood cells—which, left to their own
devices, simply disintegrate.

She has the intraventricular hemorrhage, which is irreversible. She has severe respiratory distress syndrome, due to the
prematurity of her lungs. Hypotension: low blood pressure.
Hypothermia: low body temperature. Anemia: a low blood
count due to blood loss and her inability to produce sufficient red
blood cells. Jaundice: a buildup of bilirubin due to the rapid
breakdown of her red blood cells and the immaturity of her liver.

Bradycardia: the slowing of her heart rate. Apnea: the cessation of breathing.

She is at constant risk of infection, given the condition of her skin, her ineffectual blood, the numerous lines puncturing her body. All the devices keeping her alive—the breathing tubes, the feeding tubes, even the tape on her skin—are also prime targets for dangerous bacteria. Any disruption to her bodily functions could snuff out the little life she has.

Each time we enter the NICU, we pull clean gowns over our clothes—in my case, another gown over my gown. We scrub our hands with harsh pink soap and scalding hot water. We clean our nails with a special pick. We dry our hands, every stray droplet. We apply a gel designed for surgeons to use pre-op. Then we douse our hands with sanitizer before we lift a finger toward her isolette.

If she survives, she'll probably stay in the NICU until she reaches her full-term gestational age in late January. If she survives, she will graduate to being at risk for certain outcomes that were mentioned to us in much the same way that, thirteen months ago, we were advised to keep Leo's umbilical stump dry. They include, but are not limited to: blindness, deafness, chronic lung disease, cerebral palsy, mental retardation, the inability ever to lead an independent life.

Right now, the starkest metric is her weight: below seven hundred grams and still falling. This is the measure of her tenuous hold on this earth.

Sometimes all of the medical terms sound like absurdly specific ways of saying something simple: nothing is wrong with her, except that she is out here. If she were still inside me, she would breathe through the umbilical cord. Her lungs would be perfectly adequate for the function they were meant to serve: growing and developing, with more than three months left to mature.

Her skin would be just fine gelatinous, because she would be bathed in fluid. Her blood would be sustained by my blood. Her brain would be cushioned from any blow.

There is nothing wrong with her, except that she is out here. There is nothing wrong with her, except everything.

9

THREE DOCTORS, ALL WOMEN, have become my deities. Not in the sense of an Almighty Creator, but more like the gods in Chinese myths: far more powerful than ordinary mortals, yet still prone to human weakness—bad luck, infighting, pride, error.

They can't wave a hand and save my daughter. But compared to me, they're omnipotent.

Dr. Kahn is the main deity. Her thin shoulders are stooped exactly as you'd imagine for someone hunched over an isolette day after day. Her skin has the pallor of someone whose natural habitat is the windowless, breezeless rooms of the NICU. Her glasses twitch on the bridge of her nose exactly like those of someone charged with the most fragile human lives in the world.

You might mistake her for a nun who just ventured out of her convent for the first time in decades, or a warmhearted German headmistress from the earlier part of the last century. You would not imagine her to have a husband or children of her own.

I've never been so awed by any woman before.

* * *

Dr. Bryant is a preternaturally poised African American woman with a crisp, understated way of speaking and elegant, careful hands. One of the four female obstetricians who rotate in my practice, she was also the one who happened to see me thirteen months ago, on Leo's due date.

In this new era, Dr. Bryant feels almost like an old friend. Someone who knew me as something other than a failure of a mother.

Since the delivery, she has been the prototype of cheery professionalism. "She's looking good," she says of my daughter. She inspects my incision and pronounces it "beautiful."

Even when she learns about the intraventricular hemorrhage, she manages to seem concerned yet unfazed. "Well, when they're so little, their brains are more elastic," she says.

Peter and I echo these words to each other. *Elastic, her brain is elastic, maybe it will bounce right back.*

The next time we see Dr. Kahn, we quote Dr. Bryant, reframing her formulation as a tentative question.

Dr. Kahn's voice is as measured as ever, but her lip is slightly stiff. She tells us that Dr. Bryant has repeatedly stopped by our daughter's isolette looking "absolutely stricken." That she, Dr. Kahn, has felt the need to reassure Dr. Bryant that our daughter "will probably survive." She explains that obstetricians see it as their job to keep the baby safe through those nine months. When that doesn't happen, as in this case, it's hard for them not to feel they didn't do their job.

I struggle to comprehend that another person, faced with my daughter's condition, might contemplate a failure other than my own. That Dr. Bryant's matter-of-fact positing about the resilience of a baby's brain is less a scientific insight than a reflection of her own emotions. That her jauntiness in my presence might be a cover for her own distress.

"I let her do her job," Dr. Kahn says. "Now let me do mine."

Finally, Dr. Haber is our pediatrician and the personification of a conscientious medical provider—a woman who, at sixty, is also distinctly cool: fashionable, sassy, blunt.

The last time I saw her, at Leo's one-year checkup a month ago, my belly was too obvious for us to ignore. When Dr. Haber congratulated me, I fretted about the timing.

Dr. Haber declared, "It's perfect! They'll grow up together. They won't have any sibling rivalry. It'll be perfect."

On the second day, we call her office and Peter summarizes the salient facts: twenty-five weeks, odds of death, odds of disability, severe brain bleed.

There is a brief silence.

"Wow," Dr. Haber says. "Wow."

In that silence, in those flat syllables, we know she understands.

Peter tries to articulate what we haven't been able to tell anyone else. "Look, we're not religious. We're not sentimental. We don't want life for the sake of life. For us, the worst-case scenario would be—"

"For her to survive and ruin everyone else's lives," she says. "I get it."

She asks practical questions and offers practical advice. To make ourselves known to every doctor, nurse, and staff member who will tend to our daughter. To compel them to humanize the care as much as possible. To have one central point of contact for our updates and questions.

Dr. Haber says that she will also make herself known to Dr. Kahn. She will find out any details that might not have been shared with us. She will translate anything we don't understand.

"Use me," she says. "Just use me."

Then she says that she will call us again that night, and every single day from now on.

"You don't have to do that," we say hastily.

"I want to," Dr. Haber says. "She's my patient, too."

Much later, I will notice that the realm of each deity roughly corresponds to past, present, and future. But for now, past and present are still inseparable, and the future seems purely hypothetical.

What happened?

Maybe it's an unproductive question, an unseemly question. As patiently as they can, the doctors attempt to dispel it from their higher realm.

If I'd arrived at the hospital sooner, wouldn't my daughter have been safe?

"You were fully dilated when you got to triage," Dr. Bryant says.

But if I'd arrived twenty minutes earlier, one hour, three hours—

"The baby was coming out," she says.

Peter fixates on the grimy suitcases he hefted up from the basement in preparation for the renovation. All evening, I was overtaken by fits of sneezing, but it had already been a terrible allergy season.

"It wasn't the suitcases," Dr. Bryant says. "It wasn't the sneezing."

Then was it that my pregnancies were so close together?

Dr. Bryant says that an interval of less than six months between pregnancies is considered risky. The interval between mine was at least eight.

Was it that Peter and I made love that night?

Gently, firmly, Dr. Bryant shakes her head.

Then what happened?

"It happens," Dr. Bryant says. "In my decades of practice, I've known this to happen."

When we ask Dr. Kahn, she says, "Well, someday someone will win a Nobel for figuring out the answer to that."

The general prevailing theory, she says, is that, for some reason, the baby needed to come out.

Something went wrong and we all missed it. Something so wrong that my daughter needed to be rescued from my body before her skin could hold itself together, before her brain could withstand the trauma, before she could nurse, before she could breathe.

What happened?

Did I deliver a child or lose one?

Do I keep holding on or do I prepare to let go?

10

B Y NIGHTFALL ON THE SECOND DAY, Peter and I have decided on a name. The name that stayed with me earlier. We found another definition: "dear one."

We filled in her paperwork. We haven't said the name to anyone but each other. Now it's time to tell the doctors and nurses.

We named her Mila, with the same hyphenated last name as our son. She is the only person in the world who shares a last name with our son.

In the dark, hushed room, the nurse on duty greets us with a sparkling smile that seems like the first genuine smile I've seen since my daughter's arrival.

I reach to shake her hand, then stop short. So does Peter. Hanging on this nurse's chest is an ID card, with a name printed in all caps: MILA.

We stammer.

The nurse peers at us curiously, then introduces herself. Her name is Mila, which is short for her given name, one that is not uncommon in the Philippines, where she was born and raised. Her given name is Milagros.

The meaning of Milagros: *miracle*, of course.

11

ON THE THIRD DAY, my daughter is still alive. The third day is a significant milestone, according to Dr. Kahn—as is, I suppose, every day, every hour.

"She's feeding at an almost unbelievable level," Dr. Kahn says: absorbing 2 milliliters of breast milk per session—two drops, more or less—that help to protect her body from infection and stimulate her digestive system to mature.

The brain hemorrhage remains confined to one side, the right ventricle, and so far it has not spread farther. Also, the hemorrhage has been downgraded from grade IV to grade III: from the worst level of severity to the second-worst.

All of this is good news. Good news that extinguishes hope for a quick release from this agonizing uncertainty.

Dr. Kahn leads us into a small conference room, where she arranges the images of our daughter's brain on a backlit display. With great care, she traces the fluid-filled chambers that cushion the developing brain and spinal cord.

In Mila's case, a rupture occurred in the blood vessels of the germinal matrix, the delicate nests of cells that line the ventricles and, in a normal pregnancy, disappear by thirty-four weeks of gestation. Blood filled the right ventricle, causing it to swell. The blood also appears to have seeped past the borders of the ventricle to the actual brain tissue: brain damage. How far it trespassed is the question that Dr. Kahn and her colleagues have debated. Dr. Kahn hints at the complex, painstaking process by which a consensus on the downgrading of the hemorrhage was achieved.

There are the two ventricles, the left chamber dark and clear, the right chamber filled with a billowing white cloud. There is the border of the right ventricle. There is the brain tissue on the other side of the border. All along this border, the picture is blurry and gray.

Here, before us, are the same images upon which the specialists based their diagnosis. Is the blood on or over the line?

Soon the billowing cloud will disappear without a visible trace. The question that remains is how much damage that cloud will leave in its wake.

If Mila survives her stay in the hospital, an MRI will be performed upon discharge, but that procedure won't give us any clearer predictions of her future. The severity of the injury will reveal itself only as she reaches or fails to reach each milestone. Smiling, sitting, eating, crawling. Walking, talking, running, jumping. We might begin to fathom the damage when she turns six months old, or one year, or two, or later still.

Again and again, Peter presses Dr. Kahn for a clearer breakdown of our daughter's chances of somehow being okay. Like him, I'm desperate for the simplicity and solidity of numbers.

Again and again, Dr. Kahn maintains that all that we know is all that we can know.

On the third day, my IV stand has been rolled away, my catheter removed. With Peter's help, I stagger down the corridor to the elevator that takes us up one floor, around a corner, and down another corridor, and I enter the NICU to see my daughter on my own feet. The wheelchair gets rolled away, too.

I begin to understand that life will continue outside the hospital. Tomorrow, once I'm approved for release, I will go home. To my son, to my old life as Leo's mama, but also to a new life as the mother of a baby on life support in the NICU.

In the three days that our daughter has stayed alive, Peter and I have already made a few decisions that seemed to mock our circumstances—irrelevant in the scope of life and death, yet hinging on that question.

Peter is taking a week off from work, but not his two-week paternity leave. That he will save for when—if and when—our daughter comes home.

The renovation of our apartment: the five-figure deposit check already cashed by the contractor, the workmen and their heavy equipment at the ready. If our daughter lives, we will need that baby room and the kids' bathroom. If she dies, I guess we won't.

How could I ever have another baby after this? How could I hold on to it? How could I sleep one night of another pregnancy?

But how could our daughter's death serve to complete our family?

Peter has given the go-ahead. The demolition is under way.

The world outside the hospital seems too wide, too exposed, too bright.

Where I now sit, the walls are thick, the curtains opaque. The window doesn't open. I haven't attempted to raise the shades. This is a closed world, with its own denizens and rules and supplies. It's the only place where people understand what happened, where they're equipped to deal with the eerie limbo in which my daughter exists.

This is a hospital, after all: a place where misfortune and tragedy are routine, where the stricken seek care, where the sick and injured stay.

12

ON THE FOURTH DAY, I finally allow myself to anticipate holding my baby boy. I'm desperate to snatch him up in all his bouncing, iron-willed, overabundant vitality. To squeeze his luscious cheeks, his ham-hock thighs, his plum of a rear end. To bury my face into the softest part of his neck and never look up again.

My daughter's weight has continued to drop, along with the oxygen levels in her blood, necessitating multiple increases in the level of oxygen delivered by the ventilator.

She doesn't seem to register my presence. Her hand doesn't reach for my finger. I'm afraid to touch any other part of her body. I whisper words of reassurance, but they get lost against the walls of her isolette.

I won't be able to pick up my son. This is all I can hear of my discharge instructions. For six weeks, I'm prohibited from lifting anything above the weight of a normal newborn. Leo is three or four times that weight.

I'm already ducking the reality of how I'll take care of Leo given my relentless pumping schedule. The NICU doctors and nurses have told me to pump every two hours, fifteen to twenty minutes each session, including overnight, at least ten to twelve times a day.

It was only two months ago that I stopped pumping for Leo. Nothing could feel more unnatural than pumping milk for my daughter now. My body still presumes that she slipped away that first morning. She might not live to drink the drops of milk I'm wringing out.

But pumping milk for her is the one task I've been assigned by the professionals keeping my daughter alive. How can I fail at this, too?

Next, I learn that I'm also prohibited from taking buses and subways, because of the stairs and the crowds and the jostling. Our house is an hour-long commute from the hospital. We don't own a car. I can't think ahead anymore.

For the first time, I change out of my hospital gown. The contents of the bag that I was given at triage are relics from another era: clog boots, a black sweater, my skinny maternity jeans with a soft, stretchy waist panel.

The denim is dark and doesn't show the blood. Only I can feel the stiffness, the weight.

An attendant wheels me through the long corridors, down the leisurely elevator, into the sunlit lobby.

Waiting by the revolving doors, we watch another family pass by in the proper version of the parade: the beatific new mother like royalty in her wheelchair, the exultant new father with a bounce in his stride, their soft-cheeked baby bundled into the plush car seat for the first time.

Before I became a mother, I found the sight of newborns unsettling, when I noticed them at all: those scrunched faces, puny bodies, limp necks. Now this newborn looks, to me, hulking in size and strength, obscenely plump, freakishly ready for the outside world.

Of course, he's perfectly ordinary. We're the odd ones here. We have no car seat, no receiving blanket, no baby. Only the ID bracelets on our wrists, and our daughter's tiny footprints in a plain black folder.

I want to rush back to the NICU, to tell her that we won't be gone for long, that she won't be alone. To touch her hand one more time. But the corridors between us already seem impassable.

PART II

I lay in the dark, waiting for the night to end.
It seemed the longest night I had ever known,
longer than the night I was born.

I write about you all the time, I said aloud.
Every time I say "I," it refers to you.
—LOUISE GLÜCK, "VISITORS FROM ABROAD"

13

IN NOVEMBER 2010, PETER and I embarked on his dream trip: a month in India. He'd just given up his career at the *Times* for a job at the *Huffington Post* that would enable us to pay our mortgage. We planned the trip during his time between gigs as some amalgam of celebration and consolation.

We considered ourselves pretty well traveled, both of our passports thick with extra visa pages, but nothing had prepared us for the sensory overload of this trip. Every stop seemed to present the grandest, the dirtiest, the shiniest, the oldest, the most extreme experience of its kind. Every must-see seemed like a once-in-a-lifetime opportunity, except that we had four more lined up that day.

By the time we arrived in the Hindu pilgrimage town of Pushkar, amid the desert castles and fortresses of Rajasthan, I longed for a shower that was partitioned from the toilet. For loose, long-sleeved tunics and large shawls to shield me from the catcalling and ogling that seemed a little more menacing here than in any other country I'd visited. For closed shoes—preferably knee-high boots—instead of flip-flops, which left my feet wide open to the feces and trash we often stepped through on the paths to touristed monuments.

Pushkar seemed, to my overwhelmed eyes, strangely dull. The main attraction was a murky brown lake surrounded by little temples. In the center of town, unflappable cows slowly ambled the steep alleys, backpacker cafés advertised banana pancakes, and vendors hawked cushion covers and hookah pipes.

Local etiquette required bare feet as we circled the lake, sidestepping mean-eyed birds pecking at litter and emaciated stray dogs depositing excrement in our path. Before we'd made a complete circle, the soles of our feet were tar-black.

For dinner, after a week of curries at every meal, we went to a backpacker café and ordered a pizza. Of course, it was terrible.

But the next morning, at sunrise, the lake shimmered under a pearlescent pink sky. Birds swooped and dove, exquisite in flight. At every ghat, families chanted, made offerings of coconuts and geraniums, and undraped their bodies to bathe in the holy water.

Hindu priests approached us to ask if we wanted a blessing. This was, of course, their livelihood. We politely declined, again and again. Yet each time, we hesitated a moment longer.

Soon the pink glow faded. The dawn worshippers dispersed. After breakfast, we would leave Pushkar for the next stop on our itinerary.

One last holy man approached us. He was older, kindly, relaxed. We chatted a little about what we'd seen of India, what he knew of America. He offered to show us his temple.

Peter and I reached for each other's hands and followed him. We both knew what the other was thinking: if the gods happened to be listening, there was something we might as well ask.

Six years earlier, when Peter and I met in Shanghai, I was wrapping up a fellowship and set to move back to New York. It was easy to open up to him, to go back to his high-rise bachelor pad on our first date. The date stretched into a weekend, at the end of which I remembered to tell him that my time in China was nearly done. He was about to embark on a ten-day reporting trip down the Mekong River. By the time he returned to Shanghai, I'd be gone.

He persuaded me to float down the Mekong with him. We were halfway down the river when he suggested moving in together. By the end of the trip, he was saying he loved me. If I'd had to decide right then whether he was my future husband or a high-functioning type of crazy, my reply would not have boded well for our future.

When I told my friend Mika about him, framing the relation-ship (I thought) as a fling, her reaction surprised me. "You know, this is the first time I've heard you talk about a guy without making fun of him," she said.

It was true that from the day I met Peter, I'd felt a strange sense of warmth and well-being in his presence. That he could intuit whole tangles of meaning from a few inarticulate mumbles from me—about my writing, or my relationship with my mother, or my sense of place in China. That I was transfixed by his dedic-ation to his work. That when I sat down bleary-eyed to a hotel breakfast he'd ordered for me or binge-watched *The Sopranos* with my cheek against his chest, I felt I'd known him much longer than a few weeks.

In lieu of a third date, I moved in with him, but I told myself it was a temporary arrangement. While I researched and wrote my novel, he filed features about inept contractors in postinva-sion Iraq, makeshift morgues in the aftermath of the Indian Ocean tsunami, Chinese-made weapons and oil pipelines in southern Sudan, child abduction rings in southern China with links to American adoption agencies.

Between junkets, we trekked the remote Tibetan peaks of Sichuan province, motored through the Kurdish countryside where Turkey bordered Syria, ate soft-shell crabs at every meal in Vietnam, vacationed at a beach resort nestled between fishing villages in Trivandrum, India. All the while, he maintained the imperative to strive for a "blame-free" relationship, in which there was no such thing as one person winning and the other losing, an ideal that seemed preposterous to me until, day by day, he showed me what he meant.

We'd been together for more than a year by the time I started to understand his vision of our future together—not just a couple, but someday a family. We were in a cab in Guilin, China, speeding from yet another airport to yet another hotel as dusk descended. I was fighting a cold and weary of travel as we hurtled past karst hills and banyan trees.

I thought he was focused on the scenery when, out of the falling darkness, he said my name, first and last, so quietly he might have been talking to himself.

He said he would love me forever. I started to make a lighthearted rejoinder.

He said: "I love generations before you and generations after. I love your children. I hope to be their father."

Soon we moved back to our mutual hometown of New York City and found the house that seemed like the perfect place to put down roots together. We married in Brooklyn Bridge Park on a pebble beach with kids playing in the surf of the East River by our heels and the Q train rumbling by overhead.

Still, every time he brought up the subject of babies, I laughed it off, postponed the thought. I didn't want to give up my autonomy, my submersion in my work, my propensity to daydream. In this respect, I wasn't much different from one of the main characters in my first novel, *A Thread of Sky*: "The prospect of pregnancy had always terrified her. An alien hatching inside her, diverting her nutrients, deforming her body. No way to expel it except by letting her own flesh rip. And then this permanent burden, the rest of her life compromising between her dreams and its needs."

In taking my characters on their fictional journeys, I explored a lot of my fears—about independence and romance, strength and vulnerability, failure and success, love and fear of loss. Now I was thirty-one, married, published. Wasn't it time?

I didn't tell anyone we were trying to have a baby. In my mind, we just weren't trying not to have one.

Months passed, each one punctuated with a period. I started to think it would be nice to have a cuddly baby. I started to fret there might be something wrong with me. Still, I wondered whether I was bothered less by the nonappearance of a baby than by the anxiety of not succeeding at this particular task—that is, the fear of failure, even in this most biological of endeavors.

By the time we planned our trip to India, I was feeling an undeniable ache. Our lives felt perpetually busy and yet weightless. At heart, we were waiting for our baby.

Traveling around India, I felt jet-lagged, unprepared, vulnerable. Just before we arrived in Pushkar, I had an urge to tell Peter about the time, more than ten years ago, when I was date-raped.

He already knew the broadest contours of the episode. He also knew that it had come upon the heels of an adolescence during which I frequently experienced some form of sexual violation on my way to school and back: men surrounding me on a crowded train, sliding a hand up my skirt, masturbating at a deserted bus stop, accurately betting a young girl in those circumstances wouldn't speak up.

I didn't consider myself particularly traumatized compared to most people on this planet. Still, I spent much of my dating years getting back at men, I guess. Even when I fell into serious relationships, I rarely let down my guard. Those relationships only started every time I was about to move.

All those years that Peter had worked to convince me of his vision of our future, he'd also tried to persuade me to open up to him about the date rape. Now, in Rajasthan, I did.

There wasn't much to tell. The guy and I were in my dorm room. We were unprotected. I said stop. He didn't stop. Somehow it felt safer to give in. I started to float outside my body, which was trapped beneath his. I gazed down at us from above. Suddenly I knew I needed to make him stop. I shouted. I shoved him off. He seemed to be in shock, too. He swore he hadn't heard me.

I would never know the truth. I never really forgave him, but I never really forgave myself, either.

While Peter held me and listened, I floated above myself again, curled up on a lumpy mattress in a guesthouse in western India.

Afterward, there seemed a newly freed space inside me. The only pang I felt was that I'd waited so long to let my husband in.

We repeated what the priest told us to say, the syllables in Hindi and English sounding equally foreign to two unbelievers. Yet we closed our eyes and bowed our heads. We accepted the offerings the priest pressed into our palms and tossed them into the water. He smudged vermilion powder on our foreheads and tied red strings around our wrists.

Then the priest signaled that a monetary contribution would help our chances. Peter and I looked at each other. We wanted to give just enough money that our gesture felt significant and sincere, enough that the priest wouldn't be insulted, enough that the gods above Pushkar might appreciate it. We handed over three thousand rupees: about fifty dollars.

We refrained from washing our foreheads for days. We wore the strings on our wrists until they unraveled and slipped off undetected, weeks later.

By then, we were back in Brooklyn, where Flatbush Avenue now looked as clean and calm as a country road. My string fell off first. Peter started his new job with his fraying red threads conspicuous below his shirt cuffs. When the string disappeared, he panicked. But then we understood: it had lived out its fate.

Outside, passersby charged through the blasting dark cold of the new year. Inside, I was already heavy and warm and slow, snuggled deep in this new, pervasive sensation: a baby was growing inside me. I didn't even glance at the test.

Peter pumped two victory fists in the air. He picked me up and twirled me around and kissed me. Then he laid his cheek against my belly and whispered to our baby.

How big was Leo then? An orange pip, a sesame seed, the dot at the end of this sentence.

Months passed before either of us mentioned Pushkar. One day, in a burst of irreverent glee, Peter said, "We bought our baby. No one can take him away from us. We bought him fair and square."

By then, the life force of our son, the solid, protruding, kick-boxing bundle of him, seemed beyond reasonable doubt.

Someday, we joked, we'd deploy this portion of our child's biography—say, when he became a sullen teen. *Watch your mouth, kid. We paid good money for you. Fifty bucks—you better believe it.*

14

I WAKE WITH A start on a bobbing raft on a black sea. It's womblike here. I must be safe.

Then an icy wave crashes over me. I gasp and choke. The next wave looms.

My baby girl is no longer inside me. She's in the NICU. It's the middle of the night, my first night back home. Outside are passing cars, rustling leaves, the gathering autumn winds.

Peter is asleep beside me, our mattress on the floor. Our bedroom upstairs is a demolition site. Entire swaths of our apartment are boarded up, shrouded in plastic, covered in dust, marked off with tape.

Yesterday, on the drive home from the hospital, everything looked eerie: the West Side Highway, the Brooklyn Bridge. Our stoop, our green door, our wedding photo on the wall. How could everything still be here, just the way it was before?

Leo looked baffled at the sight of me. No tackling, no kissing, not even a smile. He'd adapted to my four days' absence, I suppose. In any case, I couldn't pick him up, so I kept my distance.

He reached for Peter. He wanted to dance to James Brown: "Papa Don't Take No Mess." Perched high up in Peter's arms, pumping his right fist, keeping time with his chunky legs, bopping his head, squealing with delight.

After we put him to bed, Peter hefted our king-sized mattress from our bedroom upstairs to this drafty space on the ground floor, the only space it could fit. The arrangement felt strangely cozy. No sharp corners, no hard edges, nowhere to fall. I took a Percocet and drifted to sleep, feeling gratitude for small blessings.

By then, everything that had happened felt like a bad dream, from the moment I woke up at four thirty that morning to the sight of that tiny reddish-purple creature entangled in tubes and wires.

Now I fumble in the dark for another pill.

The October morning is blindingly bright, with a fresh chill in the air. My steps are slow and shaky, my midsection throbbing and weak. I'm layered against the wind; still, I feel cold and rickety.

Inside the playground gates, we release Leo from his stroller and he's off, galloping on all fours. He practices his drunken fat man's walk, then topples and gallops off again.

With his eyes glinting, he makes as if he's about to eat a handful of muddy leaves—then claps his other hand, the empty one, to his mouth and pretends to chew. At the top of the jungle gym, he bangs on the slide until everyone is watching. Then he launches himself down headfirst, arms outstretched: my baby Superman.

Every time I laugh, my stitches strain. I sink gingerly onto a bench, where I spot an old classmate. We're friendly; we're not friends.

He asks me how old Leo is now.

Thirteen months, I say.

The guy seems confused. He thought Leo was older, he says.

I smile and shrug. This is a common reaction. Some people take one look at Leo and pronounce him a "man-baby."

But my classmate still looks perplexed. "Do you have another kid?"

He must mean a kid older than Leo.

"No," I say. "I mean—yes, but she—she just arrived."

"Oh. Wow." The guy glances at Peter, chasing after Leo; back at me, alone on this bench. "Who's home with her?"

"She's still in the hospital," I say. "She came really early."

"How early?" This poor guy has no idea what he's asking.

"Really early," I say.

Still he peers at me, perplexed.

"Really, really early," I say. My face tries to form a reassuring, sheepish smile.

"Oh," he says.

I shield my eyes from the sun and conspicuously scan the playground for Leo.

My old classmate starts after his own daughter. Then he pauses and turns back. "Congratulations," he says.

What else can I say? "Thanks."

We're making our way home when my phone rings. It's the NICU. Dr. Kahn is careful not to let an extra beat elapse before she says, "Mila's doing okay." She relays Mila's weight, her fluid intake, her ventilator settings, her blood gases.

My daughter is still alive.

I hasten to assure Dr. Kahn that Peter and I will be at the hospital later today, as soon as we have child care for our son. Am I imagining a new reserve in her voice? While we've been laughing in the playground with Leo, while I've been trying to deny my daughter's existence, Dr. Kahn has been busy keeping her alive.

Before we left the hospital, Dr. Kahn gave us tips on

navigating life as NICU parents. No news is good news: that's rule number one.

Rule number two is that there will be bad news—a patient like my daughter is bound to have bad days—but we have to focus on the big picture.

I assume the big picture means survival. Given how little leeway my daughter has, I'm not sure what kind of bad news could have no bearing on the big picture. Still, I have to heed Dr. Kahn's sensible advice.

Over the next weeks, I will try. Every time that number appears on my phone, I try to sound upbeat and friendly, like someone whose baby the NICU staff would particularly like to save. I ask the doctors how they're doing. I thank them, no matter what they have to say.

Against the tide of these calls, I build my storm wall. I build it to barricade myself from the one that could destroy everything I own. My wall is scrawled with slogans, as blustery and crude as any street graffiti.

I don't know her yet.

She's not really a baby.

I love her, but not the way I love my son.

If she doesn't make it, it's for the best.

I tell myself that call will never come. I tell myself it is bound to come. I tell myself that if or when it comes, I will be prepared.

15

As a child, I never believed in gods or religion or any other higher order, but when I became a mother, my view of creation underwent a small yet dizzying shift. How could I gaze upon the face of my first child without seeing some form of destiny?

Everything that led to my son's radiant presence seemed preordained, a fortune written in the stars, the consummation of the threads of our lives.

Thirteen months ago, he was born, tunneling into my arms as if it were the most predestined journey of all time. Here was my son, exactly the way he was meant to be.

Every touchstone in his life since then has been a continuation of that story. It's not an extraordinary story, just the most fundamental story we can tell. A story of genesis. A birth story.

On the Night You Were Born is a book that sits on the shelf in Leo's room, either a gift or a hand-me-down. A few months ago, when I read it to him for the first time, I cringed at the way it seemed less a children's tale by the end than a paean to the self-regard of modern parents. (The caged bears at the zoo were dancing all night for this specimen of man? Heaven blew *every* trumpet and horn?)

But when I read aloud the first lines as I cradled my boy in my lap, my voice began to quiver.

On the night you were born,
the moon smiled with such wonder
that the stars peeked in to see you
and the night wind whispered, "Life will never be the same."

By the time I joined the wind and the rain in whispering his name, as the book instructed, I could hardly turn the pages because I was swiping at my tears before they dripped into his hair.

I must have been pregnant with my daughter already, but at the time, I had no idea.

Both my son and my daughter began their exodus from my womb in the inky hours before dawn. A rainy morning in late summer, a sunny morning in early fall.

Forty weeks, twenty-five weeks. Seven pounds ten ounces, one pound nine ounces. *Congratulations, catastrophic.*

On the night you were born . . . On the day you were born . . . Ever since you were born . . . You were born . . .

Every mother tells this story to her child. Every child knows that's how the story of the universe begins.

My daughter might never live to hear her story. To feel the wind or see the moon or be held in my arms.

And everything that led to her tenuous presence now seems ill-fated. Did I miss the warning signs? Was there a bolt out of the blue? A smiting by the gods? Was she doomed from the start?

My baby boy, my baby girl. How did their journeys take such opposite turns?

16

WHEN I FIRST RESEARCHED the experience of miscarriage for my novel in progress, I couldn't help wondering
how some women who lost pregnancies in the earliest stages
could mourn as if they'd lost actual babies. At the start of 2011, I
began to understand.

My primary obstetrician, Dr. Flores, gave me and Peter the
feeling that she had all the time in the world to address every
question. Together, the three of us took our first look inside my
belly. What was in there, causing such a fuss?

A kernel, just hanging out against one wall of that cozy dark
cave. Dr. Flores measured its length and pronounced it perfect,
along with every other measurable feature of my pregnancy.

I was bursting with an earthshaking secret—one that could
still dissipate at any moment. Nothing reassured me more than
obsessively checking a week-to-week pregnancy calendar and
seeing how precisely my symptoms matched the official predictions: the tenderness, the forgetfulness, the fevered dreams about
tiny aliens and fragile dolls.

I was hostage to the howling demands of my body: ravenous,
drowsy, needing to pee, all of the above simultaneously. I

sleepwalked from meal to meal, gorging on nachos, double cheeseburgers, pork bone ramen, brownie sundaes.

I could almost feel the minute yet revolutionary developments inside my belly. The baby growing to the size of a blueberry, a raspberry, an olive. The formation of its face, arm and leg buds, kidneys, mouth and tongue, eyelids.

At my next checkup, the baby was a gingerbread man standing perfectly upright. As we peered at its outlines, it waved its right arm. Then it jumped. Then it performed a full-body jig.

Peter and I might have thought we'd hallucinated, but Dr. Flores looked a little startled, too.

"Wow," she said. "That's a very active baby. It's unusual for it to be quite so active already."

"Unusual—in a good way, right?" we asked.

"Yes," Dr. Flores said, "a definite sign of a healthy baby."

Meanwhile, at his new job, Peter's head was spinning from the plunge from newspaper newsrooms to this new frontier of sponsored content, listicles, and search engine optimization. I was accustomed to him being submerged in his reporting, but now he received calls from Arianna Huffington at all hours about PR and personnel crises: charges of plagiarism, corporate shilling, nepotism.

"We need Peter. He has integrity," she would say, as if calling for a dash of seasoning.

All of our plans were subject to cancellation when she called upon him to accompany her to galas and book parties. I quickly lost track of his hobnobbing: from Barbara Walters to Cory Booker to every other tech billionaire. From a jar of "Spitzer Family Jam" in our fridge to a slap on the shoulder from President Obama. It made for titillating conversation at our kitchen counter, but it wasn't exactly what we discussed when Arianna first gazed at him across a dinner table and asked if he had a dream.

*   *   *

A few months before, Peter had met Arianna at an economics conference and sent her copies of our books. She invited me to blog for her site and personally tweeted my posts. The openness and immediacy of the forum were intoxicating, as was the sense that someone as prominent as her might be interested in anything I wrote—albeit for free.

When Peter mentioned that we were in L.A.—a reporting trip for him, with me tagging along on a mileage ticket—Arianna immediately invited us to her Brentwood home. As mystified as we were flattered, we wondered if she'd confused us with some other, more fabulous couple.

At the awe-inspiring gates to her mansion, we spoke to the disembodied voice of some minion, and then the gates swung open. I was nervously scratching at the price tag remnants on the bottle of wine we'd just bought when Arianna herself opened the door, tall and glamorous and beaming.

She handed us a copy of her latest book, in which she'd quoted Peter's work. Every surface of her house seemed upholstered in cream and gold. She gave the convincing impression of having read our books. She quoted lines of my blog posts that she'd found witty. She wanted to know how Peter and I met.

We mentioned that Peter was considering returning to China for the *Times*, but we didn't explain the primary reason: we could no longer afford to stay in our home. Short of playing the lottery, our last-ditch plan was to rent it out while living in subsidized expat housing for a few years and saving enough money that, upon returning to the city, we might be able to pay our mortgage. Of course, we also didn't tell Arianna that every time I imagined having a baby so far away from my family, I wanted to cry.

Yet she seemed dismayed at the prospect of our moving to China. She suggested we continue our conversation over dinner at an Italian restaurant in town. The next thing we knew, Arianna

Huffington stood gamely beside our rental car while Peter and I raked water bottles and food wrappers out of the passenger seat.

We'd known our share of brilliant and influential people, but we'd never known anyone to dazzle us like Arianna. We knew the rap against her, the oil heir's wife turned Republican gubernatorial candidate turned liberal media mogul. How her site aggregated off the backs of the original reporting done in newsrooms like Peter's, sandwiched it between Lindsay Lohan's side boobs and Jenny McCarthy's antivaccine diatribes, and reaped the clicks. We'd heard that she treated employees like personal assistants, that she was first and foremost a publicity machine for herself.

But at dinner, she struck me as an utterly fascinating woman who seemed to find me and Peter equally fascinating. I'd started to wonder if she just wanted new friends when she paused dramatically and fixed her gaze on my husband.

"Pee-*terrr*," she purred, in that famously thick accent. "Do you ever dream big?"

Peter hesitated, then earnestly said that he might like to write a column, maybe another book one day.

"No, I mean *big*," Arianna said. "Like, really, really big."

Peter seemed at a loss.

I figured it was time to cut to the chase. "Do you have a dream in mind for him?" I asked.

In fact, she did. She wanted to take the *HuffPost* to the next level, and she envisioned a major role for Peter. She considered the story that had become Peter's métier at the *Times*—how the national economy had stopped functioning for most ordinary citizens—the biggest story of our day, and she wanted her site to own it. At the *HuffPost*, Peter would oversee all business and tech news, supervise his own team of reporters, write a column and make TV appearances in his own voice, and continue to report features whenever he chose.

She also mentioned that she could double his salary.

Once Peter could talk again, he explained that he was a newspaper guy to the core, but he'd give some thought to her offer.

Over the next days, as we stumbled in a daze under the profligate Southern California sun while the bills piled up in the house in Brooklyn where we'd envisioned raising our babies, we considered the future of print journalism. The prospect of joining a burgeoning new media company. The money. We couldn't help wondering if Arianna had tapped our private conversations to craft a proposition we couldn't refuse.

17

OUR SECOND NIGHT BACK HOME, Peter is hard at work building our temporary nest, tunneling through sheets of tarp, wooden beams, hanging wires, layers of dust, when he stops short.

"What did I cook us for dinner that night?" he asks. "The night before everything happened. Before you went into labor. What did I cook us for dinner? What did we eat?"

What did we eat? Blue cheese, smoked fish?

A lettuce salad and a sausage pizza. Sausage has nitrates. That must have been it.

In the next moment, we both shake our heads.

When we lay down on our mattress on the floor, I press my eyelids to the nape of his neck, as if the particular darkness I can find there might blot out everything else. I adhere my body to each bend of his, as if I might merge us and never be alone again.

In the middle of the night, I jolt awake from my drug-induced oblivion with a sudden, unshakable conviction. *The renovation ended my pregnancy.*

The smell of sawdust and plaster is thick in the air. My ears are still ringing from the hammering and drilling that resounds through our hours at home. Those bedroom walls that enclosed us for six years have been laid to waste by sledgehammers and wrecking bars. How could my baby girl have withstood such destruction?

I refrain from waking Peter. I swallow another pill.

In the morning, when I ask, he reminds me of the sequence of events. Still, as the workmen start their commotion, I have to talk myself out of begging them to stop.

The central task that shapes each day now is visiting our daughter, though Peter and I almost never say *visit* out loud. Instead, we talk of going to the hospital. How should we go, when will we go, how long can we stay at the hospital?

Not long. Never for long.

Since I can't take the subway, we rent a car or call a taxi. I've never been more conscious of our privilege, that we can spend such sums of money on transportation to and from the NICU every day and feel reasonably certain that this alone will not ruin us.

At night, with little traffic, we might make the trip in forty minutes. In the daytime, it takes at least an hour. One afternoon, the Brooklyn Bridge is closed for repairs and there's a parade we've never heard of in midtown, and we crawl through traffic for more than two hours while the meter on our child care for Leo ticks away. We barely settle down beside our daughter before we have to leave again.

We are always getting there, and then leaving again.

Every time I enter the NICU, I fumble and trip through the sequence. Washing and sanitizing my hands. Depositing bottles of breast milk into the freezer. Hanging up my coat, signing in, donning a hospital gown from the laundered stacks folded on a high shelf that I can't reach without straining my stitches.

Checking in with the doctors. Getting a drink of water; with all the pumping, I'm constantly parched. Pumping once again, especially if the commute has taken more than an hour. Washing and drying and storing the equipment. Washing and sanitizing my hands again.

By the time I reach my daughter's isolette, I'm desperate to see her. No matter what I've told myself to get through the night, the love wells up of its own accord, though it is always accompanied by fear.

If there is only good news, the fear might be only a hum. The same volume as the gurgling of the ventilator, the intermittent beeping of the machines. In moments, I can focus on her the way any mother focuses on a new baby.

The little ski jump of her nose. The way her eyes twitch beneath her eyelids when they're closed. The gleam of her eyes when they open. Each delicate brushstroke of hair.

I let her hand encircle my finger. I caress the soles of her feet. The rest of her is too fragile to touch.

I see her yawn: the most wondrous movement on earth. Her eyes seem to turn in my direction, she seems to recognize my voice. Then a voice in my head hisses, *Don't get too attached.*

Sometimes she lies beneath phototherapy lights to treat her jaundice. Under the unforgiving glare, with tiny silver shields over her eyes, she looks like the fantastical subject of a dystopian lab experiment.

Other times, when she is peacefully bathed in darkness, she might look as though she is truly my baby, a baby I will one day bring home.

Then the voice hisses, *But—her brain.*

Peter whispers, "She stretches like the Cub. Her eyes look like yours. Her hair will be so pretty."

The experience of admiring her, the parts of her that aren't completely obscured by medical devices, is also the saddest feeling in the world.

She would have been beautiful, I think. *She would have been perfect.*

Then I castigate myself. How can I mourn my own daughter who lies before me struggling to live?

The bad news might be that her weight has dropped yet again, or that she has a low platelet count, or that she needs another blood transfusion—or any other news that I can't imagine hearing even once about my son, but now issue forth about my daughter like weather reports. Then the fear is a loud drone that might rise to a thundering roar.

Even on the good days, it's never long before the calm breaks. Sometimes she "desats": the level of oxygen saturation in her blood, which should hover above 95 percent, plummets to 85, then 70, then lower, while a red light flashes and the alarm beeps faster and louder.

The nurses might look up, then walk over. They might fiddle with the connections and turn the knobs. They might simply wait, while I wait to see if my daughter will expire before my eyes. Her body is often so motionless that I know only from the numbers and waveforms on the screens that she is still alive.

Touch and go. This is a phrase that someone has probably said out loud to us in the last few days. A phrase that never struck me as quite literal until now.

Sometimes she appears agitated, flailing against the tubes and wires, struggling to move her head. One nurse says this is simply her moving the way she might move inside the womb. Another says it's a sign of how "feisty" she is.

If my daughter were trying to signal with every muscle in her body that I should let her go, would her movements look any different from this?

I arrive with murmurs of comfort, but within minutes, I run out of words. I sing a lullaby through her porthole, hoarse and barely audible above the machines, until the song starts to sound like a dirge.

I tell myself not to make too much of her grasp on my finger: it's only a reflex, after all.

The truth is, each time I visit my daughter, it feels like a return to the scene of the disaster. If my first days with my son were spent celebrating new life, this is communing with death: its constant proximity, its heavy shadow.

There is no life without death: this I know. But the arrival of a new baby is generally an occasion when the separation between the two realms might be contemplated as a wide river, a rolling plain, the stretch of decades. Not the unplugging of machines and less than one hour.

The only way to brave this limbo is simply to bear witness. To bear witness is to know her as she is, no more and no less. To know her is to love her, because she is mine, because I am her mother. The more I love her, the harder it gets.

18

JUST INTO THE SECOND TRIMESTER of my first pregnancy, I hunkered down to work on my second novel—thankfully, my main character had become pregnant, too. But I'd sit down to write, and then find myself feverishly researching nursing pillows and baby carriers until the day was gone.

I ventured to my first prenatal yoga session and found myself immediately soothed by the teacher's slow, gentle voice, the Brahmari bumblebee breathing, even the pelvic exercises. The class consisted of me and two hugely pregnant women who looked as if standing and breathing required considerable exertion.

One evening, they paused in their ongoing chats about midwives and birthing centers to ask about my own birth plan.

In truth, I was mystified by how the culture around me emphasized planning every detail of the delivery as if that was the end rather than the means. And apparently a natural birth was the exalted end. As if a woman's level of pain tolerance or her ability to deliver without medical intervention was a statement of her strength, her politics, her very love for her child. Of course, nothing would be spared to procure for that child the most coveted pediatricians and lactation consultants, the most technologically advanced car seats and strollers, the latest machines that most closely mimicked maternal shushing and swaying—all of which added up, I couldn't help thinking, to a particular definition of natural.

As offhandedly as I could, I mentioned the name of my hospital and the fact that I hadn't ruled out an epidural. There was silence. Both women stared at me as if I'd said that I might eat my baby.

And yet those yoga sessions still seemed the only hours of the week I was among my new species. When my brain and my body seemed to work in concert toward a profound purpose.

My belly swelled in earnest just as spring thawed the city. Everywhere I went, strangers smiled at me on the street and gave me seats on the subway. Everyone was so nice that I didn't mind when they offered unsolicited opinions on how I carried the pregnancy or the gender of my baby.

The vote was unanimous: a boy. I never wavered in this conviction myself.

Yet when the doctors confirmed it, I couldn't help worrying. I pored over the fuzzy green ultrasounds: the defiant nose and fists and feet. The definite protuberance between those irrepressible legs, with the official pronouncement in all caps: BOY.

What would I do with a boy? When I told my mother the news, she blurted the same question. We knew how to talk among girls, shop for girls, play with girls. We knew the strength of girls.

Peter had just started to get his bearings at the *HuffPost* when Arianna confided that they were about to merge with AOL. Peter would become a senior executive, overseeing dozens of sites and hundreds of employees he'd never heard of, on top of his original job description, which had never seemed manageable.

The night he came home charged on her bullish talk, I couldn't help asking a few questions. When had he ever wanted to be a corporate manager? What about his own reporting and writing? Also, even to Peter's old newspaper colleagues, the *HuffPost* now had an undeniable cachet. How would its brand mesh with dial-up Internet?

But we'd already tied our fortunes to Arianna Huffington, and here we sat in our house, with the Cub secure in my belly.

He'd grown to the size of a mango, a papaya, a melon. Then no more fruit comparisons, only the measurements of an actual soon-to-be baby: one pound and eight inches, two pounds and ten inches. He was developing arm and leg bones, vocal cords, the roof of his mouth. The ability to hear, to perceive light, even with his eyelids still sealed shut. Toeprints and fingerprints, eyebrows and hair. Air sacs in his lungs, fat beneath his skin.

Every time I felt the force and purpose in his pummeling and somersaulting, I suspected he'd have his own ideas about what to do with him once he pushed his way out.

19

A T NIGHT, LYING ADRIFT but not asleep, I frequently feel a little fillip inside and reach to caress my belly. *There's the baby*. But no: it's a muscle twitch, a pocket of air, my organs creaking back into place.

In the daytime, in more rational moments, I know that what happened to my daughter is not my fault. That's what the books tell me. The lists of known risk factors for a premature birth are extensive: smoking, drinking, drug abuse, obesity, poor nutrition, multiple gestation, infertility, history of kidney disease, malformation of the uterus, cervical insufficiency, lack of prenatal care, high blood pressure, diabetes, preeclampsia, bleeding, fetal abnormalities, maternal age below eighteen or over forty, previous premature delivery, miscarriage, or multiple abortions. I've scoured those pages for even one box to check.

Along with these lists, the books always include a sentence like this: "There is nothing a woman does to cause, and nothing she can do to prevent, the premature birth of her baby." In the daytime, I can recite this line, albeit without ringing conviction. After all, when our culture preaches with such energy and confidence how pregnant women can do everything right to have a healthy baby, it's hard to believe that the inverse holds no weight.

At night, I can't forgive myself anything. Something I ate, something I touched, something I thought.

I've wrestled with insomnia since I was a child. The nights have always been the time when I'm tortured by itches I can't reach, when I toss and turn over something stupid I said, when workday stresses loom like matters of life and death.

Now I recall my research on the experience of suffering a miscarriage. The sudden rush of blood, the baby-shaped blob. In most cases, a miscarriage occurs when the embryo has a fatal defect, when it never could have survived as a baby. It's a natural selection process.

What if my daughter shouldn't have been saved?

At night, she seems less like my child than like a creation of the doctors and their technology.

Peter falls asleep the moment he lays his head on the pillow—a talent I've always envied, and now seems a supernatural power. Every time I toss and turn, every minute I lie staring into the dark, I feel myself hanging together by a thread. I tell myself to get a grip, and I try, but the grip is very tenuous.

While I was still in the hospital, and my first couple of nights at home, the Percocets gave me a measure of relief. My sleep seemed void of dreams, of consciousness, of my own existence. Each time I woke, I was overcome with dread—and gratitude that I'd escaped for a while.

Now that my body is gradually recovering, my postsurgery haze subsiding, the Percocets are no longer up to the task, and in any case, my supply is out.

The only way to get through the night is to knock myself out with drugs. Except that I'm supposed to pump overnight. Every two hours, every night.

When Dr. Haber calls one evening, I blurt out the NICU pumping schedule and trail off.

After a pause, she says, "I don't see how you can do that. Do you?"

She is also a lactation consultant and a mother of two. She tells me to pump every three hours throughout the day. Only the day. I'm still stammering my thanks when she asks about Leo.

Hearing his name, I can't help but smile. "He's great. I mean— he just wants to dance."

Firmly, Dr. Haber says, "You pump. You visit her when you can. You take care of Leo. He needs you. You maintain a stable environment for him. You do what you can."

When I'm not in my daughter's presence, this logic is irrefutable: My son needs more from me than my daughter does. My daughter might not live to need anything from me at all.

Except, for now, a few drops of milk. What about the effect of drugs on those drops of milk?

Dr. Kahn says that if I take Ambien, the only risk to my daughter is a mild sedative effect, which can be averted by not pumping in the immediate hours after I take the medication. That, I readily assure her, will not be a problem. Every time I encounter another NICU doctor, I ask again. My assiduous show of due diligence is partly a cover for the fact that I've already started availing myself of an old bottle of pills to get through the night and I'm not about to stop.

Every time I open my dwindling cache, my hands tremble. Each half promises one more night of averting a breakdown.

How can I put my daughter at any risk at all for the sake of getting a little sleep?

Sometimes I think I'm hearing the voices of those women in my prenatal yoga class, who would probably be as horrified at any pharmaceutical contamination of a mother's milk as they were by the prospect of a medicated birth in a hospital—never mind an emergency cesarean.

You know what else is natural? I say to them. *A dead baby.*

But if those women were self-righteous, in my own way, I was once smug—in my smooth pregnancy, my uncomplicated delivery, the pristine appearance of my son. His effortless nursing and exponential growth on my milk, our bodies still connected in a pure loop.

In my daughter's case, a series of medical interventions rescued her from my body. But what if her continued survival is the most unnatural part?

I bite down hard on the pill, to break it cleanly. I try to swallow it fast, before the jagged edges start to dissolve, but it's never fast enough. The bitterness seeps across my tongue.

20

PETER AND I ARE in a cab on our way home from the hospital, crossing the bridge, veering into the tumult of Flatbush Avenue, when I'm suddenly making the journey in reverse: alone in the backseat, my mouth clamped shut and my feet braced against the floor, feeling the life of my daughter seeping out of me.

I reach for Peter. He's sending a work e-mail. I try to focus on the lanes of traffic, the stoplights, the setting sun.

Nearly a week has gone by, and the hours that we spent apart that morning only continue to stretch.

He left me alone in the dark. When I saw him again, I had just staggered out of an elevator onto the twelfth floor of the brightly lit, bustling hospital. I didn't know which way to go. Peter rushed out of the next elevator; his cab must have arrived not two minutes after mine. He ran to my side and caught me. By then, I could no longer stand upright.

I heard Peter tell his version of the story later that day, to my family, to his. How he was already at the departure gate, preparing to board the plane, when he got my call. How he listened to my own attempts to downplay the situation and asked me to wait ten minutes, then call again. How he sprinted for a taxi. How that taxi broke down in the middle of the highway.

While he talked, I coiled inside myself. Whatever happened had happened inside me.

I became a different person in those hours. I left him and everyone else I love far behind. The fact that he doesn't seem to realize this makes me think that I might never truly return to him again.

This could be the beginning of the end, I realize. This is how easily a marriage can start to fall apart. Just a crack: you pretend you don't see it, pretend it doesn't exist. But this crack could widen and widen until neither of us can bridge the chasm.

I reach for him again. He reaches back. I need to tell him something, but I don't know how. I start with our calls that morning. Quietly, Peter says that he'll never forgive himself for asking me to wait those ten minutes while he put off boarding his flight.

He was heading to Chicago to report on disabled people whose Social Security benefits had been cruelly curtailed: adults who couldn't work or brush their own teeth. If he'd understood what was happening, he would never have asked me to wait.

"I should've taken an ambulance," I say.

Peter says that he will never forgive himself for that, either. He called the car service for me.

I don't want to say what I need to say.

The driver's sidelong glances. Each of those red lights. More calls back and forth. My location, his location, who was home with Leo. Whether to use the hospital's main entrance or the emergency entrance.

Peter starts to reply. He's only doing what we've always done as a couple: anticipate each other's sentences, build on each other's stories. But this is not a story. We're almost home now, and if I don't make my husband understand, it will be too late.

Peter's eyes are scared, his mouth pressed shut. What I'm asking from him might be the hardest thing of all: to hear the woman he loves describe the worst moment of her life and not say a word.

Alone in the backseat. Those convulsive waves of pressure. I remembered what being in labor had felt like with my son, and these paroxysms were an altogether different beast. I had to fight them with every bit of strength in my being. The survival of my daughter depended on it.

I had to hold on to her somehow, but I couldn't. The blood was blood like I've never felt before, a deep letting, fresh and wet as water.

In Peter's breath, in his grip on my hand, I know that he has heard me.

For now, that's enough.

21

IN THE THIRTY-NINTH WEEK of my first pregnancy, Hurricane Irene was barreling up the eastern seaboard and bearing down on New York City. It was late August, and I was as sweaty and immovable as a beached whale when Peter charged in: Mayor Bloomberg had just announced that all bridges and tunnels were likely to be shut down, cutting off all crossings between the hospital and our house.

Peter taped up the windows, grabbed our bags, and ushered me into a waiting car headed for the thick prewar walls of his parents' Upper West Side apartment, just a mile from the hospital, where their bookshelves displayed every edition of a title they'd once represented as literary agents: *What to Expect When You're Expecting*.

In these last weeks of my pregnancy, I was constantly in and out of labor, gradually dilating with each excruciating wave of contractions. The Cub was already perfectly in position, head down, facing back. My obstetricians had mentioned that I might have a slightly elevated chance of delivering early because I was born early myself. I knew that the baby initiates the birth, sending out neural messages that stimulate a chain reaction of hormones in the mother's body. If the Cub was coming, he must be ready.

I'd lost count of how many times he'd pushed me to the verge of rushing to the hospital, then apparently changed his mind. Sometimes he'd give me a few playful jabs afterward: *Psych!*

Still, if my in-laws hadn't been away, I would have refused to evacuate, barometric pressure be damned. In my current condition, I couldn't stand anyone. I only tolerated Peter because I needed him.

He set out candles and matches and flashlights, filled the tub with water, checked the batteries in a transistor radio. We speculated on where the obstetricians lived. Whether there'd be taxis or buses on Broadway. Peter had already figured that if all else failed, he could carry me to the hospital in his own arms.

The next morning, Mayor Bloomberg took the unprecedented steps of ordering the evacuation of residents of low-lying areas and preemptively shutting down mass transit. The wind howled viciously at every crevice of the building. Sheets of rain battered down. The streets and sidewalks were deserted.

At the height of the storm, the wrenching waves of pain overtook my body again. I sat in a rocking chair and tried to simply let each contraction do its work, knowing the pain was both necessary and transient. Hours passed. The contractions became steadier, longer, more intense.

According to that week-to-week calendar, the Cub weighed anywhere from six to nine pounds. He'd packed baby fat beneath his skin, which was opaque and thick enough to keep him warm outside my body. He'd practiced breathing, blinking, sucking, swallowing, even dreaming. He'd grown fingernails and toenails. All of his systems—his blood, bones, muscles, brain—were ready for the outside world.

Of course, I still worried: meconium aspiration, a prolapsed cord. But by now I also knew in my core that I could deliver this baby with my own bare hands if I had to.

I hoped I wouldn't have to.

In the end, it wasn't that close a call. Neither was Hurricane Irene; the city was largely spared. Soon joggers emerged, stores and restaurants reopened, the mayor held a somewhat defensive press conference, and we headed back to Brooklyn.

At home, I scrambled to finish edits on an essay for the *Times'* "Modern Love" column, tracing my and Peter's journey from the Mekong to the impending birth of our first child. I'd submitted it months earlier, but scheduling issues had delayed its publication until Labor Day weekend.

Just as I sank to new depths in my beached-whale misery, I found myself awash in congratulatory messages from old classmates, former colleagues, total strangers, even good friends around the world who hadn't known about my pregnancy until they read about it in the *New York Times*.

Apparently, this was the splashy announcement the Cub had been waiting for.

22

ON TUESDAY, OCTOBER 16, I wake with a clear feeling of hope. My daughter has survived one week. This milestone, Dr. Kahn has told us, means a greater than 90 percent chance that one day, we will bring her home.

When my phone rings, it's not the NICU. It's my mother, her voice strained. She didn't want to trouble me. She's been trying to reach Michelle. No answer. Four days with no answer.

My sister is now past her due date, when the risk of complications can increase. My long-honed instinct is to downplay my mother's worry, but now the worst-case scenarios come to mind all too readily.

My mother has started calling area hospitals to see if my sister's name appears on their intake lists. What she doesn't know—what my sisters and I have deliberately kept from her— is that Michelle has decided to eschew the care of obstetricians and give birth in her own apartment on Roosevelt Island, where every city hospital is across a bridge.

Now it's clear to me that nothing overrides a mother's worry for the well-being of her child. I explain the home birth plan. I let my mother react. I ask her to put my sister Jess on the phone.

We'd all expected Jess's first visit home from graduate school to revolve around celebrating the birth of Michelle's baby, not coping with the arrival of my daughter. Yet Jess already pronounces Mila's name in a way that leaves no doubt that, whatever my daughter's life turns out to be, Jess will love and understand her no less than my son.

Now Jess's voice is small and nervous, as if she's holding back information in my mother's presence. I interrogate her. It turns out she received a text message from Michelle's partner Axel three days ago, stating that Michelle was in labor and asking her not to tell the rest of us—maybe to keep us from worrying. Since then, nothing.

The moment Leo's babysitter arrives, Peter and I rush out with my pump and my frozen milk in a cooler. Again and again, I call Michelle and Axel. No answer.

We're pulling on to the quiet streets of my parents' neighborhood when Jess calls: A friend of Michelle's, also worried, learned from Michelle's doorman that she left the building earlier today, presumably heading to the hospital. I call and text and leave messages; still no answer.

My mother's eyes are red and her voice is ragged, but for a moment, her face betrays only the simplest and most familiar emotion: that she is happy to see me. While her first granddaughter clings to life support in the hospital, while her first daughter labors to birth her own first child. I wrap my arms around my mother and we sit on her bed and she weeps.

At last, we hear from Axel: Michelle is still in labor, at a Manhattan hospital, and the only immediate worry is unwanted medical intervention.

I'm overdue for pumping. Peter and I have barely enough time to visit Mila. My mother decides to accompany us while Jess and my father will await further word from Michelle.

After another hour of slogging through traffic, we sit down by my daughter's isolette. Something in her face—her forehead, her brow—suddenly reminds me of my mother's father, my Gong Gong. I'm starting to ask my mother if she sees it, too, when I recall that the last time we saw my Gong Gong, he was dying in a military hospital in Taiwan. Do he and my daughter share a family resemblance? Or is it just that they're the only two people I've known this close to death?

My phone rings again. It's Michelle. Her baby, my first nephew, is here. She managed to deliver him naturally in the hospital. She's sorry for making us worry. I reassure her and ask about her baby.

Her baby! He's seven pounds nine ounces and twenty inches long, with skin the same bronze as hers and thick black hair like Leo. His name is Mateo. I ask about his eyes, his nose, his toes. I ask how my sister's feeling, though I already know from her voice: overflowing with wonder and bliss, exactly the way she ought to be.

My mother is giddy, fumbling to untie her gown, preparing to rush from this hospital to Michelle's. All that matters to her now is seeing her first daughter, now a mother, and her newest grandchild. The expression on her face—irrepressible joy, fierce determination, unthinking self-sacrifice—displays some essence of motherhood that I'm still just beginning to understand.

Peter and I are back in traffic when I erupt into racking sobs that, for the life of me, I can't stop.

It's not that I'm jealous of my sister's birth, her healthy fullterm baby. There is truly no instance of good fortune that could befall my sisters that I would wish for myself instead. And after all, I have my own baby boy, the most vigorous specimen of life I've ever seen, waiting for me at home.

I'm furious that we spent my daughter's one-week birthday neglecting her to worry about a baby with a perfect prognosis. I'm desperate for someone to blame. All I can do is sob.

The Hudson River streams past: the sanitation buildings, the piers, the cruise dock, the Circle Line. Before us lies the long, tangled road still ahead to the bridge.

23

IN MY THIRTY-FOUR YEARS, I've never been injured or sick enough to be hospitalized. Until one week ago, my Gong Gong was the only hospital patient I'd ever visited. Today, Peter's last day off, hospitals seem to be our only possible destination.

When Peter and I reach my sister's room, we run into two of her friends who are just leaving. Both women look discomfited at the sight of me. I think I hear "I'm sorry," along with "Congratulations." Also, "You look great!" in somewhat startled tones. To all of which I reply with my thanks, in a piercingly bright tone.

Michelle is bright-eyed and bubbly, popping up to offer me her bed for a seat. I decline, though at midday, I'm already exhausted. My sister, on the other hand, seems like a woman about to lead an aerobics class rather than one who just delivered her first baby after more than seventy hours of labor.

Where is the baby? Peter and I scan the room, as if a newborn might be hiding on a shelf or under a chair. It turns out Mateo was found to need a day or two of monitoring in the NICU, probably due to the prolonged labor.

In our own NICU, Peter and I have just begun to notice a few babies who are pink and full-sized, blinking and sleeping in regular bassinets, whose presence in the same room as our daughter seems like the result of a practical joke. We find ourselves glimpsing a chubby cheek, a fat toe, and quickly looking away.

Their parents stride into the room looking a little anxious but exultant. Sometimes they seek eye contact, as if we might exchange congratulatory smiles. We overhear nurses telling them what they never say to us: "Don't worry, Mommy. Your baby's doing great, Daddy. Your baby will be just fine."

Now Axel, whose face is glowing, starts to tell us about the birth—the most natural impulse in the world. The unending contractions, the doctors who wanted to perform a cesarean, my sister's heroism in fending off their interventions.

While my face attempts appropriate responses, I can't help wondering if such praise implies that mothers who need medical intervention and still deliver sick babies, injured babies, stillborn babies, mothers whose stories people might prefer not to hear, mothers to whom people don't know what to say, are somehow less heroic.

Speaking for myself, I don't want to be heroic. I just want my baby girl to be okay.

We'll have to meet Mateo another time. On our way out, we're greeted by my sister's nurse, who gathers that I just had a baby, too. She congratulates me and expresses surprise at how well I look. In the elevator doors, I stare at my own reflection. My face is pale but my lip balm is rosy, my hair flows, my belly is nearly flat. I look as garish and implausible as a kabuki actor.

At our hospital, I meet a nurse whom Peter excitedly described to me the other day: a NICU nurse whose twin girls were born at twenty-six weeks and, six years later, are doing fine. I told him that unless the uplifting tale involved a baby born at twenty-five weeks or less, with a grade III brain hemorrhage or worse, I didn't want to hear it.

Now I find myself drawn to Nurse Kerry, to her easy, no-nonsense manner. I ask her about a concern that I would never mention to the doctors: the way my daughter's nose appears to be pushed upward by the thick adhesive strip that holds the ventilator hoses in place. Kerry tells me not to worry: soon enough, Mila will be weaned off the ventilator and graduate to a CPAP, some contraption that will look even worse, pushing her nose up like a pig snout. Kerry says that's no big deal, either.

Just wait, Kerry says: one day, we'll never believe Mila was ever this small. She says we should take plenty of pictures. She suggests we put our wedding rings next to her, even on her body—say, one on her ankle, one on her wrist—and take pictures to show just how tiny she is.

A photo shoot of our daughter on life support?

Since her first day, we haven't glanced at those first pictures. We haven't taken any more. She isn't supposed to be seen yet, let alone be exposed to the flash of a camera. She should still be inside my body, insulated from the outside world.

But here she is. At eight days old, her body is a calmer red hue; her skin is no longer gelatinous. Large patches look dried, scaly, molting; this must be part of the healing process. Her intake of breast milk has steadily increased, allowing for the removal of the central line. The puncture wounds have scabbed over. Her face looks slightly more formed, her ears a little less fetal.

Kerry gazes at us expectantly. There is so very little that we can do for our daughter. If some authority mentioned that performing jumping jacks by her isolette were somehow proper and helpful, we'd probably blink and ask how many.

Peter reaches into his pocket for his phone. Gingerly, I rest my hand on Mila's stomach. The weight of my hand feels as if it could crush her. But she breathes against my palm and reaches to grasp my finger. Peter puts the lens against the glass to cut the glare. She winces from the flash. He turns it off. He places his own hand beside her face. His knuckles dwarf her head.

She stretches her arms. She gropes at the tape at her mouth, at the ventilator hoses. We take pictures.

Then, with Kerry's encouragement, we wriggle off our rings and douse them with sanitizer. We start to work Peter's ring over her right foot: her toes, the ball of her foot, then her heel. It feels as if the ring could snap her bones and rupture her skin. Even with Kerry offering reassurances, we lose our nerve. We leave Peter's ring encircling our daughter's foot and mine resting near her hand and take a dozen pictures while she lies with her eyes shut.

Maybe we'll be thankful for these photos one day. But right now, the shoot feels like a ghoulish exercise. Soon we put our rings back on, say our goodbyes, and rush home to Leo.

Ever since I returned from those four days in the hospital unable to pick him up, Leo has shown an emphatic preference for Peter. I haven't tried to win him back. I don't want him to sense my need for him. I want him to enjoy his babyhood as if nothing ever happened.

He swaggers around and pulls his pranks and shrieks his displeasure and plops into our laps with the utmost sense of entitlement, the way he always has. Every time he makes me laugh, my dry lips crack and bleed, and I feel I might tear apart at the seams.

Today it seems impossible to experience joy without a corresponding measure of grief. Everything triumphant about our son is what's tragic about our daughter. The condition of one only highlights the starkest contrast to the other.

Peter says, "It's as if he took all the life there was."

Later that night, we're curled up on the couch when contractions overtake my body, rumbling and fierce. Since my daughter's arrival, I've experienced intermittent cramping, moderate to heavy bleeding. This feels like the same merciless force that nearly took her life.

I try to ignore it. Over the years, the one daily ritual Peter and I always observe, no matter how the rest of the day goes, is the hour before bedtime when we come together to watch our show while he scratches my head or my feet.

Tonight, even as the pain escalates, I keep my mouth shut and my eyes locked on the TV. When the episode ends, I stagger to the bathroom. I'm passing huge quivering clots and more blood than I've ever seen at one time.

This is exactly the situation the doctors flagged in those post-partum talks when I was barely listening. *You might experience blah blah blah. You don't need to worry unless—*

Once again, I call the obstetricians' office after hours. At least this time, I'm not alone.

The doctor on call is Dr. Flores, sounding excessively matter-of-fact. She asks me to estimate how much I've bled, but I can't manage a clear answer. She says that if I soak another sanitary pad in the next half hour, I should go to the hospital. Otherwise, there's probably no reason to worry.

I tell Peter to turn on another episode. Within a few minutes, the pain becomes so intense that I hear myself whimper. I stagger to the bathroom again. I've already soaked a new pad, and what gushes out now is enough to soak another half dozen.

Peter runs up to the fourth floor, banging on the door to his cousin's apartment. He runs back downstairs and calls the same car service I rode to the hospital eight days ago. I stay where I am, feeling my life force dropping out of me.

Once again, his cousin runs down to stay with Leo, as he did that first morning. In the backseat of the cab, I let my head flop back. I stare at the watery light of the street lamps, the trees losing their leaves against the night sky.

When Peter reaches Dr. Flores again and I hoarsely describe the bleeding, she tells us to rush to the nearest hospital. Not our hospital, where Dr. Flores is on call, where our daughter lies in her isolette. The nearest emergency room.

Once again, we're starting and stopping in traffic, waiting for each red light to turn to green. Where is the nearest hospital? The driver doesn't know. Peter directs him toward the bridge. His pace is halting and unhurried. He misses a turn. Peter restrains himself, just barely, from flinging him out of the car and seizing the steering wheel.

Maybe this is how I will die: hemorrhaging on the bystreets of the Brooklyn Bridge in a goddamn livery cab.

Peter navigates us toward a reputable hospital in downtown Manhattan, across the bridge but miles closer than ours. It occurs to me that, eight days ago, instead of barreling the additional distance uptown, I should have gone to this hospital— which, like ours, has a well-regarded NICU. Maybe the doctors at this hospital could have kept my daughter safe. At least, maybe they could have prevented her from suffering the brain hemorrhage.

We screech up to the emergency entrance. While I struggle to stay upright, Peter fills out forms and hands over cards. I'm helped into a wheelchair and given another ID band to add to the one already on my wrist: FEI GIRL.

Peter wheels me to the triage desk, where a sympathetic young man checks my vital signs and reassures me that they are in the normal range. I don't seem to be bleeding to death just yet. I won't be seen anytime soon, either. In the waiting area, we squeeze alongside a guy who appears unconscious, reeking of alcohol, surrounded by duffel bags. Overhead, a TV blares: "*The Tonight Show* with Jay Leno." The final guest happens to be a woman who briefly worked under Peter at the *HuffPost* and was recently given her own cable news show. My husband's gaze drifts to the screen, an altogether human response, and I lash out.

Why didn't he call the car service before making arrangements for Leo? I was the one in danger. Leo was safe in his crib. Hadn't our daughter already paid the price for that oversight?

That morning, when Dr. Bryant told me to head to the hospital, I'd said I couldn't. I was home alone with my baby.

"Can you bring him with you?" she'd said.

How could I have subjected my boy to that long drive? Who would've taken care of him once I was wheeled away?

Peter and I exchanged a half dozen calls to discuss arrangements for Leo that morning before I'd finally headed to the hospital. We'd both become conditioned to putting Leo's demands before our own needs. Even after our baby girl became part of me.

Peter's lips tremble. He says he's sorry. He promises he'll do better.

He's my husband, a man, not a superhero. Except that, from the time we met, Peter has striven to convince me that no matter what, he'll always come to my rescue.

Whereas I can leave our apartment and head in exactly the wrong direction on our own block, whereas I can find myself at a subway station without my wallet or phone, Peter can land in Thailand in the immediate aftermath of an unprecedented natural disaster, talk his way onto a military cargo plane, make his way through upturned villages to a remote area where the devastation is as yet unrecorded, all while procuring food and bottled water and power for his laptop to file a story via a borrowed satellite phone before deadline.

While I worry, he takes action. In every crisis, he's my savior. And I guess that's why this childish, selfish, vicious part of me can't understand how it could be that now, when I need him as I've never needed him before, he can't rescue me or our daughter.

We're finally ushered into the crowded triage area, where I'm laid onto a bed between two curtains. By now, I have no idea how much I'm bleeding. A nurse starts me on IV fluids, checks my vitals again, performs a blood test in case I need a transfusion. I can't stop shivering. The nurse brings me another blanket, then another. The warmth doesn't penetrate my skin.

I don't know how long I lie there: ten minutes, two hours. At last I'm wheeled out of the triage area, down a corridor, up an elevator, and into a stark white room.

We wait. No one comes.

I've lost my grip. The breakdown seems quite literal. This is what it feels like to fall apart. My head is spinning out in space. My legs and my torso might still be hanging together by a single gristly string. Inside my skull, there's a constant guttural scream. *I can't take any more. I can't. I can't.*

Peter grabs the nurse. Apparently the only doctor who can treat me tonight is occupied, and all we can do is wait. He asks the nurse to please give me—something. Please. I guess I'm not dying, but I think that I wish I was.

When the nurse leans over me, her question strikes me as the kindest, most understanding question she could utter: "Something more for the pain or the anxiety?"

I pause. The anxiety, I decide. Never mind that this term doesn't quite capture the experience.

She hooks up another bag to my IV. Gradually, my head starts to return to my body, my limbs start to fuse back into place, the screaming starts to quiet.

I tell Peter that I'm sorry. That we're together and we'll somehow endure. Still, I can see from his face that tonight might surpass that morning eight days ago as the worst day of his life.

At last the doctor arrives, brisk but compassionate enough. When she hears about my daughter's delivery, she says, "It's not easy, is it?"

She examines me thoroughly, kneads my uterus, consults with Dr. Flores and Dr. Bryant. She says that she can't really find anything wrong, except for some clots near my cervix that may have precipitated the abnormal bleeding.

I've stopped expecting any rational explanations. To me, everything about the pregnancy seems blighted, down to the afterbirth.

The doctor scrapes away the clots. It's a slow, ghastly process.

I don't remember leaving the hospital or getting home. I don't remember crawling onto our mattress on the floor while Peter spends the rest of that night on the couch, fearing that our marriage is over. That he failed me in a way I will never be able to forgive. That no matter what he does from here on, he'll never be able to reach me across the chasm.

All I know tonight is that by the time I close my eyes, the sky is already turning pale again.

24

THE CUB'S OFFICIAL DUE DATE fell on a chilly, rainy, windy day in early September. Throughout the hour-long subway ride to my scheduled checkup, I was damp and shivering, clenching my jaw through another bout of contractions.

When Dr. Bryant examined me, I was four and three-quarter centimeters dilated. "You're having contractions every six minutes," she said.

"I know," I said. "Can I go home now?"

The answer was no; not yet, at least. An hour later, I heaved myself up on the exam table again. Some nearly imperceptible progress, maybe another quarter centimeter. Now could I go home?

"Well," Dr. Bryant said calmly, "it's probably not a great idea to get yourself stuck in traffic on the bridge when you're in labor." Still, it was my choice. Whatever I decided, she wanted me examined again in a few hours, either there or at the hospital.

I wasn't about to go to the hospital. I knew the Cub wasn't coming out that day. What baby arrives on his due date? Moreover, after weeks of being in and out of labor, I no longer believed he was ever coming out. He had it so good in there, why would he ever leave?

Eventually, Peter and I inched our way to a Mexican restaurant a few blocks away, the wind threatening to snap our umbrella. Over tea and chicken soup, I shivered and grimaced through another few hours of contractions. Back to the doctor's office: not even another quarter centimeter. Back to the restaurant again. Another cup of tea, another few hours of contractions.

I just wanted to crawl back into bed. If only we didn't live on the other side of that bridge. For the first time, I hated Brooklyn. I couldn't for the life of me remember why it had ever seemed a good place to live.

At last I agreed to head to the hospital. The obstetricians' office was closing soon, and I could be examined by the doctor on call, Dr. Sherman, without getting admitted.

The receptionists in the triage room seemed thoroughly uninterested in my situation. Dr. Sherman was occupied with another birth. By the time I lay down to be examined, I was seven centimeters dilated. Once again, I asked if I could go home.

Dr. Sherman seemed perplexed by my insistence that birth was not imminent. After intense negotiations, we agreed that I would be admitted to labor and delivery, but that I would be left alone to rest for the night. As far as I was concerned, this was the easiest way for me to get a bed and a blanket.

My nurse was a sturdy, unflappable Korean woman who showed me the regular pattern of my contractions, like series of tall parabolas on graph paper, and gave me a quizzical look upon my lack of reaction. She assured me she'd meet my baby before her shift ended, at seven A.M. I smiled politely, pulled my blankets up to my chin, and tried to find a comfortable position.

When Dr. Sherman reappeared, hours had passed and I was no further along. She recommended "a tiny dose" of Pitocin to speed up the process.

I'd heard that induction was one of those unnecessary interventions performed for the doctor's convenience rather than the well-being of the mother and baby. I knew the Cub well enough to know that he was going to come when he wanted to come.

As I argued, I sensed that I was getting treated like a woman who might not be in total possession of her faculties. I recalled that one of the other obstetricians had mentioned an enema as a natural, safe option to ease the labor process when things seemed a little stuck. I offered this to Dr. Sherman to buy more time.

In truth, I didn't know exactly what an enema was, let alone what it might be like to experience one right at the cusp of full-blown labor. By the time I staggered back to bed from the bathroom, my weeks of stoicism were completely behind me. I was writhing and cursing and nearly blind from the pain.

Peter suggested trying the alternative labor positions we'd practiced, but nothing could have seemed more ludicrous to me at that point than getting on a ball or into a tub or onto all fours, let alone slow dancing with my goddamn husband. When he attempted a few of the massaging techniques we'd learned, I yelled at him not to touch me.

When I finally asked for the epidural, Peter asked me if I was sure. This was the procedure we'd agreed to follow when we read *The Birth Partner*. Yes, I was sure. I'd never been surer about anything in my life. I wanted it now. Actually, now was too late. I wanted it to have happened already. I wished I'd reserved it the day I was born.

Right then, the anesthesiologist was busy with an emergency cesarean. By the time he arrived, I was nine centimeters dilated and shaking so hard that I could hardly roll onto my side or hold still for the needle. That blessed needle.

I sucked ice chips and fell into a light sleep, waking only when Dr. Sherman entered the room. I felt strangely rested, a gentle calm. My nurse's shift was nearly over, and I felt sad for her that she'd been wrong about meeting my baby.

Airily, I told Dr. Sherman I felt fine. She sat down to examine me yet again.

"Well," she said, "I see a little head full of black hair, so I'd say it's time to push."

For months afterward, Peter would laugh every time he recalled my response: "Oh, really? Okay," as if I'd been told it was my turn at the checkout counter.

He held one leg, the nurse held the other, so that I could brace myself against them. I located the muscles I'd exercised in prenatal yoga and bore down and pushed. I had the weird feeling that I knew exactly what I was doing.

Dr. Sherman and the nurse and Peter were an excellent cheering squad.

"You're doing great!"

"He's almost here!"

"I see him!"

I thought they were just being supportive and overenthusiastic. I'd heard of pushing as the most difficult, most interminable part of the process. Still, I appreciated the praise. I pushed as hard as I could, then rested. Then pushed, then rested. Then pushed.

That was it.

My howling boy was laid against my heart. I put his mouth to my breast and he went quiet. I heard myself catch my breath and choke back tears.

His face was like none I'd ever seen before, and yet it was one I'd always known. His dark penetrating eyes, his golden cheeks, his perky little nose. His thick black hair, his rosebud lips.

There wasn't a blemish on him, not a dent. Even the numerals of his weight and height, his birth date and time seemed fortuitous.

Beyond being like me or unlike me, he was of me. Every expression, every gesture, the curves of his flesh, the gleam of his eyes. His scent, his breath, his spirit. Everything about him was an unforeseeable mystery and everything about him was like home.

My nurse, who'd stayed half an hour past her shift to meet my son, posed for a picture with him and asked his name.

Leo. Of course he was Leo. Who else could he be?

And then I was wheeled with my boy bundled in my arms to the postpartum wing like a queen on parade.

"Congratulations!"

"Thank you."

To me, both phrases sounded brand new and replete with meaning, as if they'd been coined for just this occasion.

When our families rapturously passed Leo around, his features seemed to precisely echo my sisters', then my mother's, then my father's. Then Peter's, then his mother's, then his father's. My son seemed made to be heralded, the baby we'd pick out of a lineup if our concern were an heir, the perpetuation of the finest of our bloodlines.

He was so quiet that day, the only quiet day of his life. He slept and blinked and calmly looked around. Every two hours, he howled and I put him to my breast, and we sank back into bliss.

There it is. My triumphant birth story that I don't think I'll ever tell again.

25

WHEN I ENTER THE NICU by myself for the first time, storing my frozen milk, washing and sanitizing my hands, standing on tiptoe to reach a clean gown—I tell myself, *I can do this*. Whatever it takes to be a good NICU mom, I can summon it. Or fake it.

I greet Dr. Kahn with a smile and ask how she's doing while I wait to hear whether today is a good day or a bad day.

Dr. Kahn knows that Peter has returned to work. She even remembers Leo's name.

"Mila's doing well," she says.

Well. Better than okay. I dial up my cheer.

Dr. Kahn almost never glances at her notes in my presence. Clearly, my daughter is her most critical case. It's a particular kind of privilege.

Mila is breathing well—with the help of the ventilator, but she initiates most breaths on her own. Her intake of breast milk continues to increase by the day—again, an "amazing" sign, says Dr. Kahn. Now she absorbs eight milliliters per feeding: eight drops, more or less.

And her weight is up by ten grams. It doesn't bring her above one pound six ounces, never mind her birth weight, which I never would have believed could be an aspirational number. Still, it's something gained.

Peter is the one who ventures to ask the questions about her brain. I remind myself that no news is good news.

I ask about those agitated movements my daughter sometimes makes, that I can't help seeing as a cry for help. Dr. Kahn says that the movements are a sign of my daughter's strength. That one alternative to the flailing, and to the reddish hue of her skin, is that she would be pale and listless.

I feel bolstered, much as I felt when, at some point in the last week, I learned about bilateral grade IV intraventricular hemorrhages. The bleeding could have happened in both ventricles of her brain. It could have invaded the brain tissue on both sides.

I thank Dr. Kahn and head toward the room where my daughter lies. Without Peter, I feel I could lose my footing or lurch in the wrong direction before I reach her isolette.

I whisper to my daughter that I'm there. I nudge her hand so that she can grip my finger. I hold as still as possible. I want my presence to be something she takes for granted, even if only for a brief spell of the day.

When all the trappings of early parenthood as I know them have been stripped away, I guess this is what's left: a mother holding her child however she can.

Now that I'm here alone, the nurses seem to move around me more easily. None of them ask where Daddy is today.

I can't help wondering how much they know about my daughter's brain. Whether they ever question their labor and devotion, the facilities and resources allocated for her care. I don't ask. A good day in the NICU is a fragile construct, much like my new persona.

Something looks different about my daughter today. It's not that she's any bigger, or less gaunt, or more formed. It's that I've been given a new way to see her. The jerky movements of her limbs and the strained cast of her face show not only her suffering, but her resilience. A new emotion emerges amid my pity and sorrow and fear. I'm awestruck by my daughter.

She's holding on to life with everything she's got. And if she can fight like this, then the least I can do is to be here with her. To have faith in the rightfulness of her existence. To love her with everything I've got and with no guarantees.

For the first time, a nurse asks if I want to take my daughter's temperature and change her diaper. I recall some upbeat lines in the books about how NICU parents often enjoy performing these tasks, to feel a sense of involvement in their babies' care— which seemed, at the time, like a sad farce to me.

I open both portholes. It's a strange sensation to watch my hands meet on the other side of the glass. I lift my daughter's right arm, light as a stem. I place the thermometer in her armpit and press her arm tightly to her side. I know from the beeping and the number that appears that I've performed this task correctly.

Changing her diaper, on the other hand, is a long and elaborate series of steps, each of which I fumble. Slip a pad beneath her bottom. Moisten paper towels to use as wipes. Fold the tape onto itself so that it doesn't abrade her skin. Hand the soiled diaper to the nurse for a weighing. Fold the clean diaper down, then down again. Most of all, don't recoil from her raw, bony flesh.

When Peter arrives, he still looks shaken from our night in the emergency room. I pump while he sits with our daughter. By the time I return, his lunch hour is over. When he leans in to kiss me, I flinch.

The nurses cheerfully bid him goodbye, as if he has more than fulfilled his duty.

Later, when I take my own leave, their expressions suggest that I haven't stayed long enough. I explain that I have a thirteen-month-old at home. They look startled, as I sensed they would. Is the startling fact that I was capable of giving birth to a sound baby? Or just the more mundane curiosity that I'm an apparently modern woman who had two babies thirteen months apart?

Here in the NICU, amid babies the size of Leo's calf, the fact of him startles me, too. Just as the fact of my daughter seems unreal outside the NICU—anywhere but here, but never more so than when I'm with my son.

Suddenly, there is only one book Leo wants to read: *Mama, What's In There?*

He plucks it off the shelf and plunks himself on my lap. I suggest some old favorites, but he smacks them away. Once again, he brandishes *Mama, What's In There?*

With a sick, shaky feeling at the hollowed, stitched-up center of me, I open the book and begin to read out loud:

Mama, what's in there?
Inside my tummy is our sweet baby bear . . .
Mama, what's in there?
Say hello to our littlest elephant, dear!

Leo opens and closes the flaps over each rounded belly, peers and points at the baby animals inside: the sleeping bear, the swimming dolphin, the litter of pups with a tab he can pull to make their tongues wag.

And then the final page, the page we've never read before: the human family.

"Mama, what's in there?"

Beneath the flap on the woman's belly is a round-cheeked, smiling baby, whose thumb lifts to its mouth with the pulling of another tab.

I rush through the last few lines and close the book.

"Mo," Leo says.

More. He wants me to read it again. *I can do this*, I tell myself.

I hold still as my baby boy opens those flaps, I modulate my voice to the chirpy tone of the dialogue, I force myself to breathe steadily as my body continues to cramp and bleed against his warm, wriggly rear end. And when he says "Mo" again, I read it again, then again, until he's satisfied.

26

FROM THE MOMENT I first laid eyes on my son, I would have died for him. But some days, I couldn't stop weeping. My station in life had become Leo's minion.

No matter how I tried to curry his favor, he seemed insanely pissed off. Not colicky, not crying—more like he couldn't believe his new station in life, either.

How dare you! Don't you know who I am?

One day, we ventured to a mother-baby group led by my prenatal yoga teacher. It felt like an act of sheer bravado to bring my son to a small, bare room where there was nothing to muffle his fury and no way for me to pretend he wasn't mine.

I had no idea how to make small talk with the other women. They all appeared to be thirtysomething first-time moms like me; unlike me, they appeared to be enraptured by their babies every single second. All the other babies behaved the way I'd always thought babies did: cooing, contentedly gazing around, occasionally mewling.

At the teacher's direction, we practiced rolling our babies from their backs to their bellies and back again, directing their gaze with our voices, soothing them with Brahmari breathing. Soon it became clear that making conversation here wasn't only easy—it was irresistible. We were all obsessed with our babies' waking times and feeding times, along with weight gain, burping positions, sleeping positions.

Leo was soon dubbed "the rock star," with his implausibly spiky hair, imperial demeanor, and ferocious yowl, not to mention his penchant for sussing out the best-looking women in the room and transfixing them with his bedroom eyes.

Week after week, my son was always the loudest, the fattest, the most melodramatic, the one who monopolized the grown-ups' attention. The one who acted as if he was starving even with milk dribbling down his chin. The one sure to have an explosive poop that shot all the way up to his neck.

I noticed other moms looking at me askance when I called Leo by the nicknames I habitually used at home: little monster, chunky monkey. Once, when another mom marveled at how much he'd grown since the previous session, I said, "Yeah, he's a fatty."

Looking scandalized, she said, "He's a *baby*," as if I'd announced I was auditioning him for *The Biggest Loser*.

In truth, I instinctively adhered to one form of Chinese superstition: to avoid singing the praises of your loved ones, particularly your children. It's social etiquette; it can take the form of false humility, but fundamentally it's rooted in a soil-grown practicality.

You might not worship the gods, but you don't want to draw their attention. Life is full of hazards: famine, poisonous mushrooms, a demon's whim. If you're the recipient of great good fortune, you keep your head low.

In this area, Peter and I had wildly divergent instincts. To the tune of "For he's a jolly good fellow," Peter would sing: "For he's the very best baby ... and if you deny it, you're wrong!" Every now and then, I'd whisper in general agreement, before saying loudly, "Hush. Don't gloat." As frustrated and incompetent as Leo often made me feel, I couldn't help taking pride in my boy. No one could say he lacked personality.

Peter and I joked about how, if Leo were one of a litter, the other babies wouldn't stand a chance. How, if he were ever abandoned in the wilderness, he would somehow manage to thrive: shrieking to direct the rescue teams, crowning himself the king of the jungle, getting adopted by some fabulously rich and childless widow.

More than once, Peter said, "Doesn't he make other babies look like they're barely alive?"

Now look at our baby girl.

It has occurred to me that this is as likely an explanation as any for what happened.

We were foolhardy. We drew the gods' attention to our good fortune. We invited them to smite our daughter.

27

AMID MY RESOLVE TO be that model NICU mom, I'm slow to notice that I'm sick. A cold, a flu, something I seem to have caught during my night in the emergency room.

It's just a cold or a flu. A fever, a runny nose, aches and chills, a throbbing headache. But it means I can't go to the NICU to see my daughter. Whatever I have is liable to kill her. Besides, I can hardly roll myself off our mattress on the floor of our dusty, tattered wreck of a home, where the late October winds increasingly bring portents of the bleak winter.

Now there is no hospital routine to follow, no stalwart performance to give, no gazing into my daughter's eyes or cupping her body with my hand, not even the waveforms on her screens to monitor. There is only the maze of my own mind.

When I try to read, I find myself staring at beautiful sentences and witty observations and thinking, *Who cares?* The only books that promise to hold my attention are two recent purchases that I haven't dared to touch: the premature baby books I spotted in the NICU during those first days in the hospital.

Both Peter and I are habitual information gatherers, but in our tortured, private attempts to make sense of our daughter's fate, we've resorted to paraphrasing an infamous statement that once seemed like comically evasive blather to most of the world as well as to us: there are known knowns, and known unknowns, and unknown unknowns.

A known known is that my daughter left my body far too early. A known unknown is why this happened or whether she'll be okay one day. The unknown unknown is too terrifying to contemplate.

Suddenly, these classifications make perfect sense. Maybe they're the only way to make sense of something so inexplicable.

After all, the alternative view can be summed up in the title of that modern-day bible: *What to Expect When You're Expecting.* Nowhere in the section for twenty-five weeks was there any mention of a scenario that ended like this.

These premature baby books were written to fill that void. Medical definitions and devices, illustrations of afflicted heart valves and intestinal tracts and retinal vessels. And numbers: statistics and probabilities, tables and pie charts and bar graphs.

I've deliberately avoided more numbers, above all. The numbers are, necessarily, incomplete and inconclusive. And they describe only the aggregate. A faceless average preemie, a nonexistent composite child.

The numbers can't account for the light in my daughter's eyes, the force of her kick, the way she stretches and yawns and blinks. The grip of her hand and the rise and fall of her breath.

There are no odds to foretell her individual destiny. After all, what were the odds of her arriving as she did?

Peter and I researched this one of our first nights back home. The rate of preterm births in the United States, we learned, is roughly 1 in 9, or 11.5 percent. The rate of babies born in our daughter's weight range—500 to 999 grams—is 1 in 200, or 0.5 percent. The rate of babies born at the edge of viability—below twenty-six weeks of gestation—is 1 in 750, or 0.00133 percent.

Factor in the total absence of risk factors and warning signs. The fact that none of the known causes of prematurity have yet to be identified in our case. The brain injury that made a veteran neonatologist cry.

"It was a lightning strike," Peter said finally. "We got hit by lightning."

The odds of getting struck by lightning over a lifetime, I now know, are 1 in 3,000, or 0.00033 percent.

Much like Dr. Kahn's use of the word *catastrophic*, these numbers, on that night, provided a degree of solace.

But when I contemplate the odds for my daughter's future, the numbers bend and bleed. They become ink blots, Rorschach tests, telling me less about my daughter and more about myself than I want to know.

I open the books, flipping from one to the other and back again. In the introductions, I read about why parents of preemies should read these books. To enable us to "advocate" for our babies. To be "empowered" in their care. "You need to get involved," one book scolds. "It's up to you to make it possible for your baby to thrive."

"Let's get started!"

Prematurity is the leading cause of death among newborns in the United States. It's also the number one cause of disability among children. For babies born extremely prematurely, four major variables play a role in their outcome: birth weight, gender, single or multiple pregnancy, and whether steroids were administered before delivery. If all four variables are advantageous, it's the equivalent of gaining an extra week in the womb. For instance, from twenty-five to twenty-six: a watershed moment when the odds improve exponentially.

In my daughter's case, only two of the variables are in her favor: being female and a single fetus. If I'd had any warning signs, there would have been a chance to administer steroids to speed up her lung development and minimize the overall danger—and, in all likelihood, prevent the intraventricular hemorrhage.

An IVH is one of the most devastating complications associated with prematurity. Among babies born at less than 1,500 grams, or 3 pounds 5 ounces—a weight that strikes me as a different stratosphere—the risk of an IVH is 20 percent. But only 4 percent of those unlucky babies develop a severe hemorrhage—meaning a grade III or grade IV. Among infants born after twenty-five weeks—officially, my daughter had those three additional days—the incidence of severe IVH is only 2 percent.

Which means that in addition to my daughter being the one extremely premature baby out of 750 babies, she was also the one out of 50 extremely premature babies who suffered a severe brain hemorrhage. That makes her one out of 37,500, or some percentage I can't figure out even with a calculator.

Setting aside all the other risks, a grade III bleed in itself indicates a 30 percent risk of serious intellectual disability plus a 20 percent risk of moderate to severe cerebral palsy. These numbers might be optimistic given that the initial assessment of my daughter's bleed was grade IV.

In my throbbing head, I wail: *Why her brain?* If she had to suffer an injury, why not a toe, an arm, an ear, or even a lung?

Compared to the fact of the injury to her brain, all the other sections on possible complications practically qualify as feel-good material. Heart murmurs, blindness, deafness, chronic lung disease. Even the statistic that she has a 75 percent chance of developing bronchopulmonary dysplasia: scar tissue that leads to long-term deterioration of her lung functions.

Apparently, the ventilator that helps her breathe can also cause that scar tissue, along with infection, rupture of her lungs, and permanent damage to her vocal cords and vision. The same dilemma applies to every aspect of her care.

Even as she struggles to recover, her nervous system is surrounded by what the books describe as a hostile environment: the pain and discomfort posed by the breathing tubes, the feeding tubes, the IVs, the heel sticks. The wires, the monitors, the alarms. Our NICU doctors and nurses do their best to minimize the disturbances—dim lights, soft shoes, hushed chatter, a blanket to cover her isolette—but it's an intensive care unit, after all.

The medications that might alleviate her pain or calm her nervous system can also interfere with her heart rate and breathing. In other words, the available methods of lessening her suffering could also negate those life-sustaining measures.

By the time I stagger to my pump, I'm dehydrated from weeping: dizzy, mouth and throat parched, eyes sunken. The books promise me that my milk will give my daughter a boost in every aspect of imperiled development: growth, immunity, relaxation, digestion, vision, breathing, blood, body temperature, and most of all, her brain.

I pump for twenty minutes, thirty minutes, until pain shoots through my breasts. Not a drop.

Peter brings me water and offers me a new insight: that the same factors that made her arrival so shocking could now work in her favor. The uncomplicated nature of the pregnancy until its end. My sound health and enviable prenatal care. The fact that there is nothing wrong with her even now other than the ramifications of her prematurity: no anatomical defects, no need for surgery.

"Right," I say. "It's only her brain."

He begs me to stop reading. I set aside the books until he's called away by Leo.

I understand that if my daughter turns out to have a serious disability, her life can still be well worth living. That her inner life might possess more richness and depth than I can fathom. That there might even be something very precious gained. But I can't pretend there is no great loss.

The thoughts in my head right now might appall other people. People who might inform me that *mentally retarded* is an outdated playground insult or that the term *disabled* should be renounced for a term like *differently abled*. People whose immediate worries about their own kids might involve bedtime battles, or playground bullies, or inadequate exercise, or excessive drinking, or a dead-end job, or a poor choice of mate. Never mind brain damage.

What I want is for my daughter to smile, run, sing, go to school, do fulfilling work, live on her own one day, be a contributing member of society. Am I supposed to pretend otherwise?

The only way to endure this limbo is to tell myself that someday it will end. Someday I'll bring my daughter home. Someday the rest of our lives will begin.

But what if her life turns out to be one that no parent would wish for their child?

I can't help thinking that if I had a child whose disability was the result of a genetic condition, an immutable aspect of her biology, it would be easier to accept. I wouldn't be able to imagine an alternate fate without imagining a wholly different child. But I don't know how to relinquish the daughter I held in my womb, the baby girl who would have been perfect if not for my inability to hold on to her.

I understand that my perspective at this moment is narrow and shortsighted. That if I ever have the chance to bring my daughter home, the person she turns out to be might be the only way I'll ever be able to imagine her. That any disabilities she might have might compel me to become a better mother: more selfless, more fearless, more heroic. That she might well teach me more than I ever thought I could learn about life and love.

But what about her? How would she be better off? Why should she have to bear such a burden?

Despair is not a useful emotion. It might also be unwarranted. There is a chance, however slight, that my daughter could turn out to have no disability. Or the kind of mild disability that might manifest in her walking late, wearing glasses as a toddler, needing extra time on tests. I'd consider any of those outcomes a miracle.

But I'm praying now to percentages and pie charts, odds that seem to have been stacked against her from the start, black numbers and lines on white pages that couldn't care less where her tiny, nearly weightless body may fall.

Later that night, around four A.M., we're startled awake by the ringing of a phone.

It's our home phone. It's the NICU. It's not a routine call.

It's a call that I told myself was bound to come. That I told myself would never come.

The neonatologist on duty is the same one who described my daughter's skin as "gelatinous" that first morning. This time, Dr. Mercado sounds shaken all over again.

Mila has exhibited signs of a possible infection. Another blood gas analysis was performed. It shows a steep drop in her hematocrit count, the volume of red blood cells in her blood. A drop so precipitous that this doctor can't help but suspect that the probable cause is another bleed in Mila's brain.

Dr. Mercado says that we might know more in a few hours. She does not discuss any options for treatment. But I know that another bleed in my daughter's brain might well lead us to the option of comfort care. Disconnecting her from the machines and holding her for the end of her brief, hard life. Holding her for the first and last time, for less than one hour.

No matter what I've told myself, I'm not prepared.

I don't know her yet.
She's not really a baby.
I love her, but not the way I love my son.
If she doesn't make it, it's for the best.

If there ever was a time when these terrible lies would have made it easier to let her go, that time is past. I know this now. My daughter has claimed her small, dark, turbulent corner of this world, and despite the wall I've tried to build between us, that's where I live, too.

28

WHEN LEO WAS FOUR months old, he decided to express the slightest discontent by letting loose with the loudest, longest, highest-pitched, most bloodcurdling shriek he could muster. Hour after hour, day after day, his shrieking shattered me.

I would have given him anything: my engagement ring, the deed to our house, every account password. I would have fed him my own pulsing heart if I knew it would pacify him once and for all.

I could see the shriek coming before the sound waves hit my ear. He would rear back to marshal all his force, engage every muscle, widen his jaws and throat to their maximum capacity. Whatever I did—nursing, singing, flying him around the apartment until my wrists gave out—only delayed the shrieking for a few minutes.

Often, the only remaining option was to strap him into the Bjorn and take aimless walks around the neighborhood in deep winter, which occasionally quieted him. Still, in a Brooklyn neighborhood infested with squalling tots, people would often stop and stare as we approached, sometimes from a full block away, scanning us for signs of criminal parenting.

One afternoon, I veered into Dr. Haber's office without an appointment and blurted, "I think he's lost his little mind." After a thorough examination, Dr. Haber could suggest only that I wear earplugs and wait for the phase to pass.

Had I done everything wrong from the moment I'd worried that his birth year might engender a timid nature? I already knew about being a "Chinese" mother. Now I read in desperation about being a French mother, a free-range mother, an authoritative mother. My own parenting style was probably best described as "instinctive," but every time my boy shrieked, he seemed to be saying that my instincts had led me to be a total failure of a mother.

Occasionally, a passerby would catch Leo in a quiet, regal moment and say something like, "I'd give anything to be a baby again." By now I saw babyhood through Leo's eyes: the helplessness, the emasculation. What could be more infuriating?

Peter usually couldn't leave work before Leo's bedtime, but every now and then, he scrambled home after receiving a text from me like this: *It's him or me. One of us is not going to make it.*

After weeks of interviews—which we could conduct only when Leo was asleep—we hired our first babysitter, a stout, kindly, middle-aged Chinese woman who appeared unflappable. On her first day, I escaped to a yoga class, after which I discovered a half dozen missed calls. Leo had so unnerved her that she couldn't manage to feed him.

Our second hire was a polished, professional nanny with a megawatt smile and reams of reference letters. We warned her about Leo's shrieking. She stayed to meet him when he woke and assured us she could handle him.

By her second day, her smile had vanished. She was shiny with sweat, lying down at every chance, complaining of splitting headaches. I shut myself in my office and opened the novel that I'd abandoned late in my third trimester, but as my boy's shrieks shook the house, all I could see were black squiggles on a white screen.

On her third day, the nanny begged to be fired. I tried to reassure her that she was doing fine and headed to my first lunch out since I became a mother. When I returned, Leo was shrieking on her lap while she sat on the stoop, looking ready to toss him into the street.

The moment Leo saw me, he gave me a smile that broke my heart: humbled, tremulous, quivering. I kissed him and carried him into the house. For a few minutes, we sat together quietly, contemplating each other and the lingering bleakness of the sidewalk outside. He was as sweet and subdued as he could be. But he could keep it up for only so long. He was who he was, the boy I'd somehow brought into being.

Neither of us could survive a day without the other. We knew each other in ways no one else could. But most of the time we were together, all either of us could do was complain.

29

*A*NOTHER BLEED IN HER BRAIN.

As Peter and I tread through our morning with Leo, I'm not aware of a coherent sentence passing between us, but I know that we're heading to the hospital together today. Every now and then, we exchange a look or a touch that attempts no reassurance other than this: we're together, and we'll somehow endure.

By the time we leave for the hospital, five hours have passed with no further update since the call at four A.M. In this situation, is no news still good news?

There is Dr. Kahn in her white lab coat, hunched over a monitor, twitching her nose to adjust her glasses, amiably greeting us as usual.

For the first time, we fail to respond in kind.

Dr. Kahn glances at her notes. Mila's last weighing, her oxygen settings, her intake of milk—

"No," we stammer. "Her brain. Has she suffered another bleed in her brain?"

"There is no news on her brain," Dr. Kahn says. "The status of the bleed is what we've already discussed. Mila is scheduled for her weekly follow-up head ultrasound tomorrow."

Bewildered, we hasten to explain the call at four A.M.

Dr. Kahn stiffens. She says that she is aware of the hematocrit count. She will monitor Mila's response to another course of antibiotics, phototherapy. Perhaps another blood transfusion—

But what caused that steep drop? If there was no reason to worry about another bleed in her brain, why would Dr. Mercado have called us at four in the morning?

Dr. Kahn's gaze radiates disapproval. The hematocrit count is one of many indicators that can fluctuate widely in a baby like ours. She can't speak to our interpretation of what we were told.

The three of us stare at one another as we stand outside the room where Mila lies in her isolette. The rare trust that we've built suddenly hangs in the balance.

I take a deep breath. "We seem to have a misunderstanding," I say. "Dr. Mercado called us at four A.M. sounding extremely worried. Ever since then, we've hardly been able to breathe—"

This only seems to confirm Dr. Kahn's grave disappointment. We're failing to observe the NICU rules. Rule number one: no news is good news. Rule number two: there will be bad news, but we have to focus on the big picture. And now, for the first time, Dr. Kahn tells us rule number three: never trust a preemie.

Later, I understand what she means. Premature babies defy expectations at every turn, sometimes for good, sometimes for ill. But right now Dr. Kahn sounds like she's accusing my daughter of being a troublemaker.

Dr. Kahn turns away, to other binders full of notes, other babies who need her ministrations. Haltingly, Peter and I stumble toward our daughter's isolette.

His jaw is clenched. My heart thuds dumbly; my blood feels chilled. We try to talk and sputter.

I suppose Dr. Mercado is guilty of nothing more than letting us in on her fear. Maybe her fear will turn out to be justified by the ultrasound tomorrow. Maybe it will recede amid all the other specters that have haunted us since our daughter's arrival.

Either way, our baby girl is here before us.

Today, as I cup her body and hold her hand, I don't hear the voices in my head that often hiss at moments like this.

From now on, each day that she survives will be a blessing. I will the life in my hand to seep through her skin.

Peter heads to the airport for a reporting trip he feels compelled not to cancel: meeting poor families in rural Louisiana who are being denied access to health care because of the governor's refusal to accept federal funds. His main character will be a mother who worked for decades caring for elderly people in nursing homes, for barely above minimum wage and no health benefits, and now subsists on nine thousand dollars a year: a figure deemed too high to qualify her for Medicaid, leaving her unable to afford treatment for life-threatening heart and blood ailments.

My friend Mika has offered to fly in from Eugene, Oregon, and I've overridden my lifelong instinct to refrain from seeming needy.

Two weeks ago, at the hospital, Mika was the only friend I managed to call. When I heard her melodious voice, with her husband and their beautiful kids, ages eight and five, in the background, I nearly hung up. I didn't want to ruin their family time.

"What happened?" she cried.

I stammered and wept, and soon she was weeping, too.

When she arrives, we curl up together in the drafty room Peter has cleared for her. But even this tiny pocket of happiness feels like some kind of betrayal of my daughter.

When Leo summons me at five thirty in the morning, I wake Mika to lift him out of his crib and pacify him while I pump. At the hospital, she sits with me by Mila's isolette

and says that she's beautiful: the first time anyone has compli-
mented my daughter in such an ordinary way. When we find
that the day's construction has filled Leo's bathtub with choking
dust, Mika kneels down to scrub every crevice with an old
toothbrush.

After some hesitation, I ask how she would cope with a
disabled child. In the past, Mika and I have mutually confessed
worries about our kids having outie belly buttons, flat butts, early
male pattern baldness. Now she simply says that she doesn't
think you can overestimate your love for your children or what
that love can overcome.

For the first time in his working life, Peter misses his flight
home, just sitting at a greasy chicken eatery in Monroe, Louisiana,
mistakenly thinking that he has hours to kill. He doesn't return
until the middle of the night, when I've already taken an Ambien.
I ask about his trip, but I can't listen.

I point out that since he's been away, he hasn't even asked
about her.

Her. Between Peter and me, she is still always *she*, always *her*.

In a literal sense, my accusation is true enough. He hasn't
asked out loud, mostly because I haven't given him a chance.

In Peter's absence, I've hardly allowed myself to contemplate
my daughter's condition. The head ultrasound has not shown an
additional bleed. But her weight has dropped yet again, to its
lowest mark ever, below six hundred grams for the first time.

Since her arrival, even as her intake of breast milk has steadily
increased, she has lost one-fifth of her birth weight. She now
weighs less than one pound five ounces. Her belly looks swollen
and rigid while her limbs continue to wither.

What Peter registers is the accusation that he doesn't care.
When he's no less worried and bone-tired than I am. When all
he's doing is trying to keep his job. When he would sacrifice
anything and everything for his family.

A glass gets thrown. A chair gets smashed onto the floor. All at once, on this bleak autumn night, amid the rustling of brittle leaves and occasional sirens, it seems easy to shove each other into the chasm.

Somehow we both pull back from the brink. We survey the damage, salvage what we can, stagger to our mattress together. After he falls asleep, I take another half of a sleeping pill.

In the morning, I wake to a calendar alert I set a few months ago: week twenty-eight of my pregnancy, or the start of the third trimester.

I tell Mika we're sorry if we woke her in the middle of the night. She cuts off my shamefaced explanation: both Peter and I are under a lot of strain, she says, and in any case, she slept with earplugs.

Sending her off to the airport, for the first time I notice widespread reports of a monster storm heading our way: Hurricane Sandy. One year after the anticlimax of Irene, the same warnings about tidal surges, high winds, mass evacuations, family emergency plans. I just want Mika to get home in time for her daughter's birthday party.

Her flight leaves without incident, but the forecasts are increasingly apocalyptic. A "Frankenstorm" gathering force, the impending collision of a tropical storm with a winter storm during a full moon.

Peter and I exchange wry, worn, fatalistic grins. We feel a strange invincibility, as if we couldn't possibly get struck by another disaster right now—even as we know that, of course, it happens to people all the time.

30

ONCE LEO MASTERED CRAWLING and cruising, every territory that had been off-limits became another parcel in his kingdom. His fury finally shifted into a general gusto for life, and he evolved from my ruthless tyrant to my domineering and irresistible lover.

Every time he spotted my hair in a topknot, he'd frown and protest until I let it down—and shook it out, like a shampoo commercial. Then he'd tackle me with a hug. His kisses were lavish, marked by a predatory virility that's probably adorable only in a male under the age of one.

As spring hit its peak, I couldn't get enough of frolicking with him in the neighborhood. But we'd just hired a part-time caregiver, Janine, who'd won him over with her fun-loving, take-charge manner—and, I suspected, because she was pretty.

When I opened the novel that I'd abandoned with Leo's impending arrival, I couldn't find my way back into the heart of the story. All I could think about was the timing of his nursing sessions, the consistency of his oatmeal and scrambled eggs, the sequence of his lullabies: all the daily minutiae that affected his moods and routines, which had come to measure my worth as a mother—my worth as a person.

Meanwhile, my son began to build a secret life away from me. Janine called him her boyfriend. The nannies in the playground nicknamed him "the rough lover."

Each hour that I sat at my desk, I missed him. Even when I heard him shriek, I wanted to rush to soothe him, no matter if I might fail.

My mother always called me a morbid child. Most of my earliest writings were about death: a rose dying, a broke father leaping from a fire escape. I remember standing in the surf at Jones Beach, pondering how this one wave, the one lapping my feet and leaving scalloped edges of foam on the sand, would never, ever come again.

But there's nothing like motherhood to make you aware of how each moment of your child's life carries you into the future, where all of those moments become the past. How, even as you yearn for any given day to end, you know that one day, you'll weep over how the years have flown. How even the most humbling moments will be precious memories that you'll one day share with your child, stories that he'll ask you to retell the way kids do, until the day he doesn't want to hear them anymore, when he thinks that he's grown and you're old.

Failure, I realized, is how you know that what you're doing is worthwhile.

In June, when Leo was nine months old, I was scheduled to give the commencement speech at a public high school where the students, mostly Chinese and Latino immigrants, had transferred after being pushed out by their previous schools. I'd been invited to appear as a "successful person" who shared a bit of common background with them.

When I tried to draft my speech, I felt like an impostor. I found myself clicking through my own website, reading old essays and blog posts, listening to my own interviews, in a futile attempt to piece together my identity.

On the day of the commencement, nothing in my closet looked right. In the mirror, all I could see was a little pooch: the belly I could have sworn had disappeared a couple of months after Leo's birth. I yanked on a pair of Spanx.

At the podium, I shared my own shaky start in education: how my nursery school teachers had asked my mother to find another program for me because I was so shy—and scared of speaking English—that they thought I was retarded (the only term in use at the time). How my mother taped me reading *The Cat in the Hat* to prove that I wasn't. How my teachers conceded that I could stay in the school, but that my parents needed to stop speaking Chinese to me; otherwise, they said, I would never succeed in English. How this launched the dual currents that shaped much of my early years: I found my voice in the written word as I lost my native tongue.

I described the first story I wrote, about a timid mouse who has no friends, until one day she gets on a roller coaster, screams, and finally finds her voice. I talked about rejections from editors and agents, crises of faith in my stories and myself. How I've come to understand that success doesn't mean being over failure, or above it. Not only because the work of a writer involves constantly chipping away at the reality that the sentence never completely captures the thought and the manuscript never completely fulfills the vision—but because failure is an essential part of any meaningful work.

I ended with a quote by Rainer Maria Rilke: "Try to love the questions themselves, like locked rooms and like books written in a foreign language . . . It is a question of experiencing every-thing. At present you need to live the question."

Then I told them that at present, the *immediate* present, they needed to party.

The students were beautiful and glowing and extremely gracious about getting lectured on the inevitability of failure on the day of their high school graduation.

Afterward, I went home with the plaque and the flowers they'd given me and sat down at my desk. Was I a mother or a writer? It didn't have to be a choice, but that's how it often felt. Motherhood had taken me far away from writing, so far that I had no idea how to begin again. But it had also expanded and deepened me as a person, and the time had come to see what this person would write.

After a few days of scrabbling around those long-neglected pages, I found myself riding an exhilarating wave of momentum. In the evenings, Peter and I ventured out on a few dates. We finally seemed to be settling into a new equilibrium as a family.

Then Janine suffered a host of mysterious ailments and repeatedly called in sick. Once again, I set aside my novel. I found myself strangely winded as I pushed Leo in the stroller and chased him in the playground. I hadn't been so exhausted since the frenzy of his first weeks.

One day, when I started to nurse him, he yanked away and clambered off my lap. I tried again and again, until I found myself putting him in a headlock while he screamed and thrashed.

I called a lactation consultant who'd been written up in the *Times* as the breast-feeding guru of Brooklyn. I tried drinking special teas and nursing only in dark, quiet rooms and corralling Leo into every conceivable position.

At last the consultant asked, "Could you be pregnant?"

"Ha," I said.

31

As hurricane sandy approaches, I wait for the Frankenstorm to fizzle into hype. Instead, New York declares a state of emergency and orders mass evacuations of low-lying areas. The forecasts mention storm surges of six to eleven feet, once-in-a-century flooding.

And, for only the second time in history, the entire transit system will be shut down, with a strong likelihood of all bridges and tunnels being closed, too. Which means we'll be completely cut off from our daughter.

Peter is the one who could battle his way home through any disaster, but he still can't leave me to take care of Leo on my own. I ride the train over the bridge, feeling sick to my stomach at being separated from both of my babies as the storm draws near.

I sit by my daughter's isolette in my usual position, one arm through a porthole, holding as still as I can while cramps shoot through my back and shoulders.

"Mommy, do you want to hold her?" The nurse's tone is chirpy and casual, as if she's pointing out a regular option on the menu that I've somehow overlooked.

"What?" I stammer. "Yes, of course. But not if—only if—"

"I need to change her bedding," she says. "You can hold her. It's okay, Mommy. Don't worry."

She raises the lid of the isolette. There is my daughter before me, with no barrier between us. In quick, abrupt motions, the nurse disconnects the tubes and the wires, peels the sensors off my daughter's skin. On the monitors, the numbers go blank, the waveforms go dead. A red light flashes, an alarm beeps. The nurse silences it.

She wraps my daughter in a blanket, lifts her out, and places her in my arms. She reattaches the tubes and wires and sensors, slips the newborn cap over Mila's head.

I can hardly feel my daughter. Five hundred ninety grams, barely more than one pound.

In terms of a household object, one pound is something. A bag of coffee, a package of butter. My own baby feels like nothing in my arms. An implausible vessel for all the organs and functions necessary for human life. Something that could slip out of my embrace in an instant.

Yet here is her face, inches from mine. Her skin is peachy pink. Her eyes are open.

We're sharing the same air, occupying the same space. I gaze into her eyes. I whisper into her ear. Her hand reaches toward mine through a peephole in her swaddle. I see the delicacy of her skin. The softness of her earlobes. The feathery lashes peeking out from her eyelids, which are luminous like seashells.

The nurse takes my phone and snaps a few pictures. I'm afraid to smile, as if such a movement could dislodge all the connections keeping my daughter alive. Once the nurse finishes making her bed, I relinquish her back to her isolette.

Before I leave, I ask the nurse where she lives and how the NICU will fare through the storm. I learn that some of the nurses and doctors will stay overnight in the hospital so that, whatever happens, none of the babies will lack for care. I stammer to explain that I won't be able to visit through the brunt of the hurricane. I check and recheck our storage bin of breast milk in the freezer, even though I know that, at the current rate of my daughter's feeding, the bottles in there could last at least a month.

The truth is, compared to any ordinary infant, my daughter couldn't be better equipped to survive in my absence.

In the city, the storm damage is unprecedented. People are killed in their own homes by falling trees and electrocution. Subway tunnels are flooded to the ceilings. Highways are covered in mud and debris. All airports are closed, as well as every MTA road and bridge.

Yet we are fine in our house, as are our families and everyone around us. We call the NICU, where Dr. Kahn is on duty. She says that the hospital is built like a fortress on a hill. Storm or no storm, Mila is just as I left her.

At some point, Peter and I realize that today is an anniversary we've never before failed to celebrate: eight years since our first date in Shanghai. This year, there's some comfort in simply sitting at home with Leo, as if we're once again one intact family.

That night, we watch live footage of an emergency evacuation of the premier downtown hospital where I rushed to the emergency room last week, where I wished I'd gone the morning my daughter arrived. Now its backup systems have failed, stranding its intensive care units without power. NICU babies are carried down pitch-black staircases in battery-operated incubators and loaded into waiting ambulances.

The next day, with Janine on duty, the *HuffPost* offices and all of lower Manhattan still blacked out, and no way for us to visit the hospital, Peter and I take sunny walks through the neighborhood, idling and eating at whim. As if we're ourselves before our daughter's arrival, or even before we had babies at all.

We're back in the world, but the world around us is in shock. People are still wide-eyed, surveying the damage, stepping around downed trees and power lines. Strangers ask one another if they're okay, if their house got hit, if they lost anything.

Everyone is eager to share where they were, how close it came. To feel united in a collective trauma. To trade in words like *calamity* and *tragedy* and *catastrophe*.

For us, the strangest thing about wandering through the aftermath of the storm is that the constant peril surrounding us has suddenly become a ubiquitous theme in public conversation.

The devastation is undeniable, but the truth is, for most people, it's primarily a story. A story rife with startling images and sweeping metaphors—the surging waves, blocked crossings, massive floods, blazing fires, shattered homes. A story shot through with a sense of proximity to danger that lends a frisson and a profundity to every mundane detail. And the aftermath is a chance for most people to count their blessings: life, health, loved ones safe and sound.

I overhear anxious conversations and catch myself grimacing when I realize that the topic of discussion is a child's college application or a cracked car windshield, a canceled vacation or waterlogged files. I hear a new callousness in my voice. I realize that this quality could mold and harden until it becomes inextricable from the rest of me. Yet I can only contemplate such concerns during this odd interlude when I'm unable to visit my daughter.

One evening, despite our fear of getting stranded away from Leo, Peter and I manage to rent a car with barely enough fuel for the return trip. Most gas stations are still blacked out or running dry. Flashing police cars guard the ramps to the bridge. Traffic is halting but unremarkable. It's only when we reach the other side of the river that we're stunned by what the storm has wrought.

Lower Manhattan looks like a ghost town, bombed out, plunged into darkness. All the apartments and office towers and restaurants of Chinatown, Tribeca, Chelsea: abandoned carapaces. No traffic lights, no street lamps. Every sidewalk and street barren and desolate.

I know that the destruction is infinitely bigger than me and my problems, and yet, for a moment, I'm dumbstruck by how precisely the scene before me resembles what I've imagined the inside of my body to be like since my daughter slipped away from me.

As we cross into midtown, we're suddenly awash in light and movement and noise. People leaning over dinner tables, clinking glasses at bars, picking up sundries at Korean delis. Another mile uptown, the hulking edifice of the hospital looms like a lighthouse, its walls high and thick enough to protect my daughter from any weather, if not from the ravages of her arrival on this earth.

32

"WELL," PETER SAID, "it's positive."

I demanded to see the test stick. There wasn't much to argue with: YES, it said, with a + for good measure.

"This is all your fault," I said.

He had no idea what I meant. I reminded him of what happened back when Dr. Sherman raised the question of birth control at my postpartum checkup six weeks after Leo's birth. "No birth control!" he'd exclaimed in a burst of new-dad exuberance, while I groggily nursed Leo and sopped his spit-up. Dr. Sherman acknowledged that since I was exclusively breast-feeding, we had six months to think about it.

Six months later, my period still hadn't resumed, I was still breast-feeding, and the frequency of our bedroom activities still reflected our status as exhausted new parents. We'd assumed that when the time came to deal with birth control, we'd know, and we'd deal with it.

Now we were dealing with it.

Peter reasoned that having two babies so close together meant that I'd get back to my writing, and we'd get back to each other, and the chaos of these first years would be over once and for all, sooner. That seemed plausible only if I could survive these years, and I wasn't sure I could.

Gingerly, he broached the question of whether I wanted to have this baby. Given my emotional state, this was a legitimate, even necessary, question. But it shook me. What had covertly sprouted inside me was our baby. I'd never doubted any woman's right to choose until my own, at this moment.

Ever since I'd gazed upon Leo's face for the first time, I couldn't help believing in some version of fate—or, more accurately, the Chinese concept of *yuanfen*: the mysterious ways that the threads of our lives intertwine. My mother once defined the term as "somewhere between opportunity and destiny." Right now, that's where our second child seemed to be waiting.

Peter summoned a celebratory spirit. I tried to match it, but what I felt was disbelief and worry.

This creature was far evolved from the tiny pip of Leo when we first spotted him. It was already baby-shaped, nestled upside down in that cave, heart pulsating, hands and feet paddling.

"Wow," Dr. Sherman said. "It's very active already."

Peter and I looked at each other: Another baby like Leo?

Dr. Sherman guessed that I was about eleven weeks along. She would refer me to a radiology clinic for a more detailed scan and more precise dating.

She told us that a burst pipe had recently flooded the office, and while they'd managed to salvage nearly all of their files, mine was thought to be stuck under a cabinet, still irretrievable. She scribbled notes on a blank sheet of paper and I hastily filled out a prenatal patient history. Then Dr. Sherman asked for some routine information that should have been in my missing file and that I didn't know offhand.

"Oh, well," she said. "You're one of the patients we never have to worry about."

The radiologist estimated the baby's gestational age at exactly twelve weeks, with a due date of January 23. I diligently entered this date into my calendar, with a few milestones along the way: the halfway mark at week twenty, the start of the third trimester at week twenty-eight, the pregnancy reaching full term at week thirty-seven.

On the handwritten file the radiologist sent to the obstetricians' office, a few days had been added to the gestational age, nudging my due date to January 19. To me, the distinction mattered. My babies would be sixteen and a half months apart. I wanted those four days.

Dr. Sherman was, understandably, inclined to favor the official document. I revised all the dates in my calendar.

Peter and I marveled at how determined this baby must have been to join our family—and how undemanding. No holy water, no prayer, no red strings on our wrists.

We wondered if maybe we'd done it the right way after all. We hadn't expended time or energy strategizing how to achieve our vision of an ideal family. We hadn't given ourselves the chance to agonize over what another baby right now would mean for our marriage, our careers, our sanity.

We told each other that this baby was destined to approach infancy with the same unobtrusive ease with which it had approached conception. That this baby was bound to be mellow, patient, the polar opposite of Leo.

We couldn't help laughing about how we'd skipped the entire first trimester. All the symptoms that had seemed so overwhelming last time, all the developments I'd followed from week to week. A blueberry, a raspberry, an olive. The face, arm and leg buds, mouth and tongue, eyelids. A plum, a peach. Bones and

cartilage, knees and ankles, fingers and toes. All of that had tran-
spired without a moment's attention from us.

Wasn't that efficient of us? Wasn't it kind of a neat trick?

At one point, I said, "This will be the shortest pregnancy
ever."

33

BY THE END OF the week of Hurricane Sandy's aftermath, Leo has resolved that our estrangement is over. At the just-reopened park, he insists that I chase him, then turns and tackles me, immobilizing my face in his jaws.

Even as I laugh, my heart twinges. I'm not sure I can ever separate love from fear again. Still, my baby boy believes we can be new lovers, and because he believes this, and because he is a baby, maybe we can.

Among the tree branches littering the asphalt, Peter finds a twig shaped like a wishbone. He and I take hold of opposite ends, close our eyes, and pull. I'm left holding a short, splintered stub.

I ask him what he wished for. Peter sweeps me into his arms.

"The same thing you wished for, dummy," he says.

For her to be okay. That's all, and that's the world.

Power is restored to nearly all of Manhattan. Subway service will resume for the Monday morning commute. We scramble for some kind of routine.

After Leo goes down for his morning nap and the crush of commuters has subsided enough that I can usually get a seat on the subway, I head to the hospital. Dr. Kahn has rotated out of the NICU, a disorienting development I've dreaded. But Dr. Alston, an unadorned, lanky, warm African American woman, seems no less devoted, and our interactions feel a little less fraught.

The NICU is newly crowded with an influx of the babies who were evacuated from hospitals that lost power during Hurricane Sandy. I struggle to claim a chair and a few inches of space to sit by my daughter's isolette.

Cupping her body, holding her hand, all I can think is *Grow. Please grow.*

Her progress is so slow and halting that I don't allow myself to believe it's real until, one day, she's back to her birth weight: one pound nine ounces. This time, the number is a reason to celebrate.

Her limbs look faintly plumper, their motions a little calmer and more deliberate. Her cheeks a little rounder, her eyes a little brighter. For the first time, I notice she doesn't have nipples on her chest, or creases on the soles of her feet: developments still to come.

Dr. Alston tells me that Mila's weight gain is still far below her optimal rate of twenty to thirty grams per day. She wants to replace four of Mila's eight daily feedings with high-calorie formula instead of my breast milk.

I can't help stammering my incomprehension. In his first months, my son gained a pound a week on nothing but my milk. Ninetieth-plus percentiles in height and weight. How can I fail, even now, to give my daughter the barest minimum that she needs?

"This is a different situation," Dr. Alston says. "Who can say why?"

She also tells me that Mila has a condition called patent ductus arteriosus, or PDA: a heart murmur caused by an open blood vessel between her heart and lungs. I've probably been told this before, but it hasn't come to the forefront of our worries until now.

Like nearly all of my daughter's diagnoses, the PDA would be normal if she were still in the womb. Since she would receive all the oxygen she needed from the placenta, the opening would allow her blood to flow from the heart through the pulmonary artery into the aorta, bypassing the lungs. In fact, all healthy babies are born with this opening, which closes and eventually disappears after they take their first breaths—a development that often gets disrupted among extremely premature babies, for whom the lingering PDA allows some blood to flow backward from the aorta into the pulmonary artery. Still, this is often considered a benign condition that will eventually resolve on its own.

In Mila's case, Dr. Alston is concerned that the PDA is taxing her already overworked heart and lungs. She wants to administer medication to help close the vessel. If the medication doesn't work, the next step would be surgery.

Dr. Alston assures me that the medication is safe and likely to work. And the surgery is a relatively simple procedure. All these complications are fairly routine with a baby like mine.

Then Dr. Alston smiles and shares an observation about Mila's tendency to curl her own hand under her chin in her sleep, as if in leisurely contemplation: *Hmm, where do I feel like going today?* Dr. Alston shows me a photo, which she couldn't resist taking on her own phone. The pose is distinct and adorable, and we laugh a little together, even as I can't help feeling uneasy at the incongruity of such a pose on a baby so bound by medical devices that she can't even turn her head.

Still, it's a moment to see my daughter through a new lens, as not only a medical case, but also a source of wonder and joy, like any ordinary baby.

* * *

When the hands of the clock on the wall of the NICU approach five P.M., I take leave of my daughter, guilty with relief. I'm already anticipating rushing into the arms of my baby boy, bewildered at how I've lasted all these hours without him.

There is the hospital, and there is home. Everything else is a blurry in-between, the glare of wintry sun and stainless steel, elevators and escalators and revolving doors, staircases and plat-forms and subway tracks, the train hurtling through dark tunnels and rattling over the bridge.

I often break into a run on the three blocks from the subway station to our house, careening toward Leo's grin, his noise and mischief, all his overabundant life that now sustains my own.

Suddenly he walks everywhere. I already miss the way his butt wagged when he crawled, the bear gallop that he deployed over the roughest terrain.

Peter does his best to rush home in time for Leo's bath. After we've put him to bed, I pump and reheat the postpartum soups and stews my mother has cooked. Over e-mail and phone, Peter copes with the latest work crisis. Finally, we watch our show.

Then I pump again, label and store the milk, wash the equip-ment for the last time that day. We brush our teeth side by side. I swallow half of one of my few remaining sleeping pills. I hang the clothes that I might wear again on one of the two hangers that hold every item of clothing I ever wear these days.

In the dusty, drafty room where the air now feels icy enough to freeze our noses and toes, we pull on wool socks and fleece sweatshirts and crawl onto our mattress on the floor.

Anything can become a way of life, I realize. Even keeping vigil over a baby on life support can become a daily routine. Weeks, even months will pass before I become aware that I've developed the habit of keeping my fists clenched at all times, even in my sleep.

34

IT WAS JULY IN THE CITY, and I was pregnant for the second summer in a row. The demands of my body were quieter this time around, more receptive to being deferred. My food didn't have to be the fattiest, gooiest food available; it just had to be food that I could shovel down with one hand while tending to my boy with the other.

I'd given up on getting him back on the breast. Instead, I pumped and poured the milk into his sippy cup, but he was losing interest in that, too, and with each passing day, I had to pump longer and harder for decreasing amounts.

I resolved not to worry. I wanted to savor this first summer with my baby boy, who seemed to be barreling through his life stages at warp speed. In truth, I wasn't sure how my heart would make room for another baby. How could I deprive Leo of my full attention? How could I have allowed this sneaky interloper in my belly to infringe upon our hard-won romance?

Gradually, the news dribbled out in the manner of a sheepish confession. Our parents rejoiced, the way people of a certain age can't seem to help rejoicing over additional progeny. The reactions of friends were stunned gasps and awkward silences.

By mid-August, I quit pumping. Five months of liberation from lactating stretched before me. Now I couldn't understand what had taken me so long to claim it. If I kept writing at my current pace, I'd have a complete draft before my second baby arrived. Nothing publishable, but a solid anchor through the all-consuming toil of life with a newborn.

When I returned to my prenatal yoga class, my teacher's jaw dropped. She asked if I was mixed up over the schedule. This time, I felt even more profoundly out of place among the earnest first-time mothers-to-be. When the teacher asked fondly about Leo and I mentioned his galloping, there were stifled gasps in the room: I had a crawler at home and I was having another baby? In spite of the calm I tried to project, my hands started shaking.

One evening, labor positions were discussed, with the traditional position of reclining in the hospital bed assumed to be retrograde, even oppressive. When the teacher asked how I'd delivered my son, I felt flustered and defiant as I explained that that position was the only one I'd actually used. There was an awkward pause.

I nonchalantly skipped the next class, then another, and spent the found time playing with Leo or writing my novel instead. When someone asked me whether I found prenatal yoga useful, this is what I said: "The baby will come out one way or another."

35

THE NICU RECEPTIONISTS make a point of enunciating
each letter when they answer the phone: "N-I-C-U, how
can I help you?" But everyone else I've encountered here
pronounces it the way Peter and I learned to on our first day:
"Nic-u." It rolls off the tongue easily, casually: Nick U., like the
nickname of a classmate or an old school.

Peter and I observe the happenings here—a malfunctioning
pump, an annoying visitor—the way other people discuss work,
news, sports. But he still has an office, colleagues, another arena
where he exists.

Ever since the post-Sandy influx, I often enter the lactation
room to pump, having left my daughter in her isolette and
contaminated my hands, only to back out in frustration upon
finding the room fully occupied. I perform contortions to squeeze
around the other moms and try not to note how much milk they
pump. When they make a bit of small talk, I respond politely.
When they seem eager to commiserate, I turn away.

I'm an introvert by nature, but here in the NICU, my reserve
stems from this: I know in a glance that none of these women's
babies is worse off than mine.

Sometime on our second day here, I spotted a printout taped to the door of the visitors' lounge: a NICU parents support group meeting every Thursday afternoon. The next day was Thursday. I'd never envisioned myself in any kind of support group, but I'd never envisioned myself as a NICU parent, either.

I told Peter we should go. If we were ever in our lives in need of support, wasn't that time now?

But with each passing hour, it became more obvious that we wouldn't want to hear about the travails of parents of a twenty-seven-week preemie, or a twenty-nine-week preemie, or a thirty-two-week preemie. Our travails would make other parents feel better. Theirs would not do the same for us.

"We're the universal donors of commiseration," Peter observed.

By now I know most of the nurses, though I occasionally mismatch the names and faces. Many of them are middle-aged women who were recruited from the Philippines or the Caribbean decades ago. Most seem to have only one child, if any. I've found myself wanting to explain how I ended up burdening them with the care of my baby, but I keep quiet.

One day, when a warm, chatty nurse hears about my son, she asks the question that I've imagined the others have all wondered: "Was he early?"

The answer strikes my own ear as implausible.

She asks to see a picture of him—something I've learned not to flourish around here. Once, when Peter and I jabbered about Leo's earliest days to Dr. Kahn, she simply said, "It won't be the same with Mila."

We knew that, of course. We were struggling to comprehend that our two babies were brother and sister. Laboring to hope that the flourishing of one might improve the prospects of the other.

After the nurse admires the picture of Leo, she asks if my second pregnancy was complicated.

"No," I say. "Not at all."

"No eclampsia?" she asks.

"No."

"Nothing?"

"Nothing."

She envelops me in a sudden, strong hug.

"The only thing worse than visiting her," Peter says, "is not visiting her."

We're hungry, thirsty, spent. Our heads throb, our backs and shoulders ache. While other parents hold and nurse their babies, we strain to reach through the portholes of our daughter's isolette. Our arms fall asleep, our legs, our feet.

Sometimes visiting our daughter is like prayer for two unbelievers. We have no choice but to treat this as our daily ritual of devotion. Even when we believe in nothing else, we have to believe that the act itself is what matters. Sometimes the mere presence of our bodies has to suffice.

At the end of the day, I click the portholes shut. I trade my hospital gown for my coat, retrieve my handbag, and return the key. Once I step into the elevator, I could be any other visitor here: a new aunt, a walk-in, one of the many pregnant women arriving for genetic screenings or maternity tours, as I did just weeks or months ago.

Now, when I spot women in the last stages of pregnancy, I'm struck by a simple wonder: How did they manage to hold on?

In the hospital corridors, I sometimes glimpse familiar faces. Dr. Flores carrying a cup of coffee. Nurse Mila arriving for a night shift. More often than not, I duck my head.

By the time I join the evening rush-hour commuters, I'm completely anonymous. All those seats people offered me when I was pregnant seem like such wasted luxuries in retrospect. Why would anyone offer me a seat now? Everyone around me might well be just as troubled, just as weary.

36

IN SEPTEMBER, ON THE day of Leo's first birthday, Peter and
I headed to the hospital for my anatomy scan. The receptionist
asked if we'd been here before. "Um, yes," we said. "One year ago
today, in fact."

She expressed disbelief, as did I.

Then I saw the baby. While the technician focused on the critical issues—the fingers and toes, the heart and kidneys—I
couldn't help noting a certain lacuna. I closed my eyes.

It was too perfect. A baby boy, a baby girl. Two of us, two of
them. I felt as if my baby and I were sharing a secret. The same
way that, one day, we'd paint our nails, braid our hair, roll our eyes
at the boys. Us girls.

Then the doctor confirmed it, and Peter leaped with joy.

It wasn't an *it* anymore. Our baby girl.

Cheerfully, the doctor said that she was measuring slightly
small, but all parts of her anatomy were growing in tandem and
developing normally. Given the uncertainty about the timing of
her conception, he recommended pushing her due date back by
a week.

An extra week: More reason to celebrate. Once again, I

changed all the dates in my calendar: week twenty-eight, week thirty-seven, and then our new due date: January 26. Somehow the numerals seemed fortuitous.

Leo's first birthday party was a simple picnic in the park with family. Peter and I hadn't managed to prepare a single decoration or give a thought to Leo's outfit. We bought stacks of extravagantly priced prepared foods—none of which we remembered to unpack. We brought out a big chocolate cake and tried to take a few pictures, but no one looked in focus. Strangely, Leo rejected his slice. I tried to stuff a few bites into his mouth, then gave up and ate my own slice, at which point I realized that the frosting was dotted with chocolate-covered espresso beans.

My mother noted that I didn't have the glow of my first pregnancy. My skin was patchy and prone to breakouts; my hair seemed flat and dull. Maybe there was truth to that old wives' tale that a daughter steals her mother's beauty. Or maybe it was just that when I had my son in utero, I wasn't also taking care of a one-year-old version of him.

My usual fall hay fever was merciless, my sneezing and nose blowing so constant that Leo took to making a loud honking noise every time he saw a box of tissues.

Peter and I signed off on the renovation plans, ordered the tub and tiles and faucets. We reassured ourselves that the disruption was necessary, a temporary inconvenience for the sake of our burgeoning family. Once we finished this project, we'd be set for life in our house.

I dreamed that my baby had some kind of sharp protrusion: a claw, a beak. A part that could not be fully human. My belly was translucent but foggy, like an ice floe on a lake or the glass of a fish tank in a Cantonese restaurant. Something hard-shelled tapped against the surface, something that could puncture me. She was freezing and remote and weakening.

When I tried to describe the dream to Peter—"The baby had, like, a lobster claw"—he laughed.

A few nights later, I was jolted from deep sleep by a sharp jab. I gasped and sat up in bed, pressing a hand to my belly. I shook Peter awake.

"Something's wrong," I whispered. The jab was unlike her usual tumbling and kicking. Sharper than anything I'd felt before. Like a distress signal.

Peter reminded me of the dream of my frozen belly, which I'd already forgotten, and we went back to sleep.

After all, I already knew that strange, vivid dreams are a common symptom of pregnancy. It's only when you have a baby on life support that you recall dreams like these as missed chances to save your child.

Dr. Flores reviewed the file the hospital had sent over and asserted that there was no reason to revise our due date. The earliest ultrasound was considered the most accurate, she said, and all the other milestones had matched our original estimate. Now she measured my belly. As with my first pregnancy, the size of my belly matched the projected week of my pregnancy exactly: twenty-four centimeters, twenty-four weeks. I changed all the dates in my calendar one last time.

It was a quick visit, no ultrasound or pelvic exam, as was routine for this stage of an uncomplicated pregnancy. Just my vitals and my weight and the baby's heartbeat. Everything textbook.

That was my last prenatal checkup.

On the last day of September, which was also the Mid-Autumn Moon Festival, my family gathered to take my father to a birthday movie. Michelle and I couldn't help laughing at how single-minded we were about finding the theater bathroom. My father had picked a cop drama, which turned out to be so violent that I found myself shutting my eyes and shielding my belly. Afterward, at a Chinese restaurant, we shared my favorite kind of moon cake, lotus paste with salted duck egg yolks, the rich, crumbly yellow orbs symbolizing family and togetherness.

The first week of October still felt like summer when Leo and I picnicked in Prospect Park. I'd forgotten to pack a bib, so I rummaged in the bottom of the diaper bag until I found a newborn-sized drool-catcher. As soon as I snapped it onto his neck, Leo yanked it off in disgust.

He galloped to the stroller and dug up a ziplock bag that Janine apparently kept there, with clean utensils and a properly sized bib folded inside. He handed this bag to me with a forbearing expression; he wasn't going to rub it in. Then he fed himself with a fork with utter poise and nonchalance, even smirking when I rushed to take a picture.

He befriended—well, tried to steal food and toys from—another family on a blanket near ours. The other boy was solicitous of his little sister in a sweetly casual way, and for the first time, I couldn't wait to see my own baby boy as a big brother.

Monday, October 8—I finished writing an unwieldy chapter. The next day, the work would get easier, because I knew exactly what was going to happen: the miscarriage.

That evening, Peter and I emptied our closet in preparation for the renovation. He lugged up the dusty old suitcases and wardrobes that had sat in the basement through the boiler explosion, the sewage flood, and every other house disaster over the last seven years and cleaned them as thoroughly as he could.

When he wasn't paying attention, I moved a few small boxes. Nothing heavy, nothing that felt like a strain. I kept having to stop to blow my nose anyway, to cope with fits of sneezing.

For dinner, Peter made a salad and ordered a sausage pizza. When we went to bed, he set an alarm for his early flight to

Chicago. Eventually, my sneezing subsided and we made love. Sometime before four thirty A.M., we got woken by an automated alert on his phone. I was annoyed, he was apologetic. In an effort not to disturb me again, Peter kissed me goodbye and went to wait out the rest of the morning on the couch. I managed to fall back asleep, but the pain was gathering.

At four thirty A.M., I gasped and looked at the clock. I heard my husband walk out the door, the rattling of the wheels of his suitcase. I thought to call out to him, but somehow I couldn't. The door slammed shut behind him. I took a handful of antacids. I tried to go back to sleep.

Then I heard myself utter a prayer in earnest for the first time in my life: *God help me.*

37

FOUR WEEKS IN, my daughter has grown to two pounds. Over nine hundred grams: two whole pounds.

Today, the rest is details: the first round of medication did not work to close the PDA. A second round is being given. Mila is also getting caffeine to stimulate her breathing. Even her weight gain is still so slow that six of her eight feedings now consist of the high-calorie formula instead of my breast milk. In the lactation room's freezer, the tiny bottles labeled FEI GIRL are stacked so high that I've been told not to bring in any more. Now my output simply goes into our crammed freezer at home, or to my parents' freezer, or to a shelf at my in-laws', among lentil soups and pasta sauces.

Still, I float into my daughter's room and say brightly, "So, she's over two pounds!"

The nurse on duty is a self-assured, talkative woman. Today she does not smile. "I measured her head circumference and length. She's not really growing," she says. "We're giving her steroids because she's not really getting anywhere with her breathing."

Possible side effects of the steroids, I have read, are cerebral palsy and mental retardation.

Then the nurse says, "The IVH was grade III," as if I might have forgotten.

"The hope is that it might not be as bad as we think," she says.

Hearing these words, I feel like I can't breathe. But of course I can. No matter how I might feel, my body works to keep me alive. That's the difference between me, along with every other person who walks the earth, and my daughter.

It might not be as bad as we think.

Later, I repeat these words to Peter. His brow furrows. Together, we seek out Dr. Kahn. At first, she seems annoyed, as if we're being troublesome NICU parents again.

"Is there something we don't know?" Peter asks.

His directness slices through Dr. Kahn's defensiveness.

"No," she says. "We had that conversation."

She tells us that the head circumference and body length are not reliable measures and that she would let us know if she was worried.

But for a NICU doctor, what truly counts as a worry at this point? Is basic survival the only baseline?

Now the nurse tells me not to worry. With pride, she assures me that my daughter is receiving the best care possible here in this NICU.

I venture to ask how often it happens here that a baby doesn't make it. I have yet to hear whispers of this, to see anything that might correspond to such an outcome. To correspond more closely, that is, than our own situation.

"Oh, very rarely," the nurse says. "I've been here almost twenty years. That is very, very rare. Almost never."

Only then do I realize that I would rather hear that other babies die all the time, despite the best care. Because then I would have a sign that my daughter is the one destined to defy the odds.

38

WHEN I WAS A CHILD, one of my favorite books was a compilation of children's stories that included a brief, unsettling tale about a quiet girl who always wears a yellow ribbon around her neck.

No one knows why. Every time the boy who loves her asks about the ribbon, she says that she can't explain now, but someday she will. Years pass. They grow up, they marry, they grow old. He asks, he pleads. One day, she finally gives in. Slowly, she unties the yellow ribbon from her neck. You probably know how it ends.

Every time I'm asked about my daughter in the wide, bright world outside the NICU, I feel like that girl, holding myself together—just barely—at the seams.

In the immediate aftermath of my daughter's arrival, the sympathy and support from people around me sustained me in ways that I can no more single out than I can thank my bodily organs for continuing to function. No matter if people couldn't understand what had happened, they understood the state of emergency for our family.

The most comforting exchanges were the simplest. The friends who kept calling until they reached me, and then just listened. The notes of plain acknowledgment of our anguish. The unobtrusive arrival of care packages and homemade soups. The offers to babysit Leo during our hospital vigils.

When the receptionist at Dr. Haber's office told me that everyone there was praying for my daughter, I was moved to tears. In my previous life, I might have bristled at the presumption.

But by now, most people assume the emergency has passed, and they seem to expect a happy ending. I can't blame them. What I find impossible to explain to anyone is the unending limbo in which my daughter exists.

Everyone knows someone who had a preemie. So they're eager to tell me about a sister's kid, a cousin's twins, a colleague's triplets—all of whom were born early, all of whom turned out "totally fine." Every one of these kids—every single one—is now attending Princeton, or getting a Ph.D., or teaching in Japan, or somehow or other being *totally fine*.

Generally, when I'm presented with these stories, I nod and smile. "That's nice to hear," I might say. Every now and then, I might venture, "Well, it could be years before we know."

But then people stare at me in incomprehension—or with a hint of disapproval. Or they simply proceed to tell me another happy ending.

I remind myself that, in their place, I wouldn't know what to say, either. I understand that they think they're offering encouragement. But what they're implying is that my problem is not my reality, but my attitude. My deficit of hope, my lack of faith. That if I would only refuse to believe in anything but these happy endings, my daughter would turn out *totally fine*, too.

What I can't help hearing is that people don't want to know the truth about my daughter or the odds against her. They don't want to contemplate the ultimate uncertainty of her future. They're saying that unless she turns out *totally fine*, hers will be a story that no one wants to know.

And if she somehow turns out to be fine? Let them say I was hysterical, faithless, silly. But, I vow, I will never tell her story as if she has to be unscathed to justify her existence. I will never gloss over the heartbreak, the setbacks, the journey.

Whatever happens, I will never call her a miracle child.

The truth is, for anyone inclined to dismiss the obstacles still ahead for my daughter, all it would take is a picture. Then they would see nothing about my daughter but her damage.

Jola is the Polish woman who comes to clean our house. Because she speaks little English and I speak no Polish, our interactions tend to be warm but brief. When I first returned home from the hospital, one worry that occurred to me was how to tell her what had happened. It was only a few weeks earlier that she and I acknowledged my belly.

It turned out that our language barrier made the explanation easier.

"The baby came too early," I said. "She's in the hospital. It's very dangerous."

Jola cried "Oh, Deon"—the way she always pronounced my name—and hugged me. With a combination of phrases and gestures, she conveyed that her sister had a premature baby, too, though she wasn't sure how many weeks early. She didn't assure me that my child would be fine. Only when I asked how her nephew was doing did she tell me that he was a grown young man, in good health and "very tall."

Now, four weeks in, when Jola asks about my daughter, I decide to show her the photo of the first time I held my daughter outside her isolette. It occurs to me that Jola might recognize how far my daughter has already come.

Eagerly, Jola takes my phone, smiling. Then her smile fades. She hands the phone back, looking stricken.

"Oh, Deon," she says. "I'm so sorry."

"What's going on?" my internist asks.

There's constant static in my ears, twinges of sharp pain at my temples. My head is foggy and throbbing. I'm worried about some kind of infection. Also, I'm down to my last Ambien.

In the same way that it's easier to explain what happened to someone who isn't fluent in English, it's easier to explain what happened in a doctor's blunt shorthand. Even so, I don't mention the injury to my daughter's brain, which still seems unspeakable.

My internist tells me that his own son, now kindergarten age, was also born extremely prematurely and stayed in the same NICU. Somehow I'm startled by the fact that this situation could befall someone professionally tasked with looking after people's health.

After the exam, he tells me there's nothing wrong with me other than exhaustion. But he is reluctant to prescribe Ambien. I manage not to fall down on my knees. I tell him that the neonatologists have approved it. He says that he'd prefer I take Benadryl, which he considers a safer alternative.

I'm doubtful whether the drowsy effect of Benadryl will provide the knockout punch that I need. Then again, I can buy an unlimited supply over the counter.

On my way out, I ask him—abruptly, urgently—how his son is doing now.

"He's good," my doctor says.

I'm as guilty as anyone. I want to hear the happy ending, too.

Leo is the only person who never asks questions Peter and I can't answer. He's the one with all the important ideas: it's time to dance, to eat, to sing.

He still insists on reading *Mama, What's In There?* a few times each day. The flaps over those animals' bellies have begun to fray and rip, leaving their babies exposed.

Lately, he seems to have a heightened sense of responsibility, an eerie awareness of everyday perils. One morning, I'm immobilized, pumping, when he pauses at the kitchen counter. "No!" he shouts, with a particular sharpness. I turn to see him stretching his hand toward the handle of the knife left on the cutting board that he's suddenly grown tall enough to reach.

My scream is stuck in my throat; I can't grab him fast enough. In one swift motion, he shoves the cutting board and knife back toward the wall, out of his own grasp.

Another time, with cold rain pouring down outside, I let him play in the kitchen sink for the first time while I sit down, once again, to pump. I wait for him to dump a bowl on his head, stomp his feet in the suds, spray water on the walls. Instead, with a grim, dogged expression, he sets to wiping the countertop. Then he grabs a brush and scrubs the flanges and bottles from my last pumping session.

One evening, I tell Peter that I hope that one day Leo will look back on this time and realize that we somehow maintained a stable, happy home for him. Not because I want his gratitude, but because someday I want to take pride in this achievement, the only one that matters to me anymore.

Peter says, "I hope he'll also know that he saved us."

And, as if on cue, Leo starts pumping his right fist: it's time to dance.

39

O N NOVEMBER 7—two days short of one month after my
daughter's arrival—Dr. Alston tells us that Mila will be
extubated today. The breathing tubes will be removed from her
windpipe. She will graduate to the noninvasive support of CPAP:
continuous positive airway pressure, pronounced *see-pap*. She
will have to take every breath on her own.

How can she be ready?

Dr. Alston's manner is sympathetic but unwavering. The
second round of medication to close the PDA has been successful. The steroids have done their work to reduce inflammation in
her airways. The longer she stays on the ventilator, the harder it
will be to wean her off, and the higher the risk of permanent
damage to her lungs.

Dr. Alston asks me and Peter to wait in the lounge until the
procedure is over. A discharge is under way; I don't recognize
the parents—a rangy, attractive, French-speaking pair—which
means their baby needed just a few days in the NICU. While the
mother signs paperwork, the father readies their bags and flashes
us charming smiles.

I smile back and say congratulations. They seem so clearly headed for a lovely future outside these halls.

Suddenly, a woman's scream rings out, and out, and out. The sound is coming not from the NICU rooms, but from the other direction, through the walls behind us.

Inside the NICU, to the right of the front desk, is a set of swinging doors marked with signs that only authorized medical personnel are allowed and surgical garb must be worn. Past those swinging doors is the woman who is screaming.

These screams can't be the sound of a woman in labor. They must be the sound of a woman faced with her dead or dying child.

The receptionists continue their chatting. The everyday bustle of the NICU goes on.

The screams tear through the walls, shake the ceiling, shatter the air.

Then they stop.

Dr. Alston tells us the extubation went smoothly. We stumble and rush to our daughter's isolette.

When we see our daughter's face, we recall what Nurse Kerry told us about the CPAP: that it would look even worse than the ventilator. The nasal prongs, which seem too big for Mila's nose, are attached to a thick, hard tube that completely obscures her mouth. The adhesive material that shields the area beneath her nose is even larger than the tape that masked her before. Two hoses are strapped to the sides of her head, held in place with a gray Velcro band that stretches across her newborn cap. She looks as if she has been trussed up for a NICU costume party as a Viking warrior or a baby bull.

Still, this is a graduation. We thank Dr. Alston and express our excitement to the nurses. We whisper words of encouragement and pride through the portholes in her isolette. We take pictures.

On our way out to get lunch, I glance at those swinging doors.

Once we're past the steel door of the NICU, I look down the hall in the same direction, where an arrow on a sign points to LABOR & DELIVERY.

A moment comes back to me from that first morning.

When I staggered out of the elevator on the twelfth floor, I saw two signs in front of me, pointing in opposite directions. LABOR & DELIVERY to the right. PATIENT CARE to the left.

I went left. Just as I turned, I caught sight of Peter rushing out of another elevator and heading right.

"No, this way," I gasped.

Now, for the first time, I ask Peter what happened next.

We're sitting on the same side of a booth at one of the depressing, greasy eateries within a block of the hospital. Cautiously, he studies me. I'm calm, even curious.

He walked me into the triage area, the same room we'd entered thirteen months earlier. Now I remember the dusty pink of the decor. This time, the front desk staff seemed even less interested. They were looking at photos of beach resorts. They told us to fill out forms.

By the time I was laid out on a triage bed, surrounded by nurses, technicians, medical equipment, all the instruments of crisis, I wanted to cede all control. I was desperate for pain relief. I wanted never to feel anything again.

I don't know this baby yet. This isn't the worst thing in the world.

Peter mentions how they listened for her heartbeat. Now I remember how confounded I was when they attached the Doppler monitor to my belly.

It's over, I wanted to shout. *She's gone.*

But there was her heartbeat. Even to my ears, it sounded fainter and slower than a fetal heartbeat ought to sound. They told me it was growing fainter and slowing down.

A fresh-faced, brown-haired doctor bent over me and introduced herself, looking me straight in the eye. "How far along are you?"

Twenty-five weeks.

She told me I was fully dilated, and that Dr. Bryant was in the middle of another delivery. "If she wasn't breech, I would let you try to deliver naturally. But we don't have time for that."

Breech? The doctor reporting that the baby was coming out feetfirst sounded as bizarre to me as if she had called the baby slow to crawl. I was twenty-five weeks pregnant. Why would this baby assume the proper position to be born?

"We're going to try to give you a spinal block if there's time," the doctor said. "If there isn't time, we'll have to do general anesthesia."

The pain was merciless. Not the pain of labor, but the death throes of my baby girl.

"I'd rather be knocked out," I rasped.

The doctor couldn't hear me. I summoned my strength to say it louder.

"Okay," she said: meaning she'd heard me, not that she was promising to heed me.

At that point, Peter tells me, he pulled the doctor aside.

"Are we delivering a baby here?" he asked. Until then, he'd thought that somehow they'd stop the contractions and eventually send us home, shaken and confused but still pregnant.

And then I was wheeled through the long white corridors. The blur of fluorescent ceiling lights, impassive faces, swinging doors.

"How far was it?" I ask Peter now. To me, the distance could have been miles.

"Not far," he says. On the other side of the swinging doors from the area where my daughter now lies in her isolette.

The probing of gloved hands. The yanking of curtains. A crowd of masked faces introducing themselves, more doctors and nurses, a team of anesthesiologists. Everyone was so nice, as if I might truly care to learn their names.

I had no idea, until now, that Peter was asked to step outside while they administered the spinal block. The next thing I knew, I felt a long, horizontal slice through the center of me. I must have screamed.

A voice from the crowd said, "You might feel pressure, but you shouldn't feel sharpness."

"I feel it, I feel it," I cried.

A gas mask was clamped over my face. I was told to inhale.

And I entered that dimly glowing cave. Only then did Peter return to my side, gripping my hand. Amiably, I tried to discuss the cave formations with him, such a beautiful shade of orange.

If I think hard, I can recall the briefest snatches of the sober voices on the other side of the curtain. Dr. Bryant joining the crowd. The official time of birth: "eight on the dot." The first Apgar score: 1. One on a scale of 1 to 10.

But all of that activity seemed to be taking place so far away from me. Only now do I understand that the curtain was drawn at my waist.

The ticking of a clock in a quiet room. The hand of my husband still in mine. I kept my eyes closed as long as I could.

"Is she alive?" I asked at last.

"I don't know," Peter said.

Scraps of toast sit before us, puddles of congealing yolk. My body settles against his. Something has finally been unearthed between us.

There are still gaps. There will always be gaps. At least one is an abyss, wide enough for a human being to fall through.

The next time we see Dr. Kahn, we chat about Mila's graduation to CPAP. We ask about Dr. Kahn's rotation. Then, after a pause, I ask her what happened to my daughter after the delivery.

One moment, she was still inside my body. By the time I entered the NICU for the first time, she was encased in her isolette, entangled in wires and tape and tubing.

Dr. Kahn seems to have expected my question. She tells us that she was in the operating room, ready to receive her latest patient as the cesarean was performed.

"You were there?" Peter asks, just as I say, "It was you?"

Dr. Kahn nods. "I resuscitated her," she says.

Neither Peter nor I hear much of what she says next. One word rings in our ears: *resuscitated*.

Before we leave Dr. Kahn to her work, I blurt out another question. "Shouldn't I have taken an ambulance that morning?"

"Actually, emergency response times in New York City are less than optimal," Dr. Kahn says. "The car service was probably the right choice."

There was no way for my daughter to have been rescued any faster. There was no window of time—not then—when, if Peter or I had done anything differently, we could have saved her.

40

WHEN YOUR CHILD'S LIFE hangs in the balance every minute of the day, the air you breathe is thin and pure. Everything and everyone else falls away. Peter breathes the same air as he walks this cliff with me, but it's impossible for us to walk in lockstep.

One month in, he wants to go to a Nets game at the new basketball arena a few blocks from our house. He wants to show his colors as a Brooklyn fan, after a lifetime of rooting for the Knicks. To distract himself from the stress of his job. Most of all, to escape our lives as NICU parents for one night.

Months ago, when he bought these tickets, they symbolized community and home, for which he sacrificed a career that had been core to his identity. Now they also symbolize, to him, that whatever happens with our daughter, our lives will go on somehow.

So one evening, while our babies sleep in their separate corners of the city, we walk to the arena. Following his lead, I admire the architecture, the lighting, the concessions. We stand for the national anthem, sit down for the tip-off, and suddenly my tears drip into my barbecue-topped mac-and-cheese while the crowd cheers and my husband sits helpless beside me.

He is so blameless, so reasonable, so strong. He can separate himself from what happened to our daughter. He is physically separate, whereas I'm still recovering from surgery. I spend a quarter of each day strapped to the pump. My body is still held responsible for her survival.

The thing about being married and having a child is that there is always occasion for blame. Even under the best of circumstances. The bathwater was too hot. An outlet cover went missing. The safety gate was open.

I don't blame my husband for what he said on the second day about letting her go. But I can't shake the sense that, ultimately, I am alone. If I'm alone, nothing is safe.

The catastrophe happened to both of us, but it happened inside me. I'm the only one who knew our daughter in that unseeing, cellular way. She was part of me. He'll never be haunted the way I am. This is a good thing, isn't it? If we were both in my state of mind, how could we cope?

One evening, I flinch as usual from his kiss, but he persists.

"Kiss me," he pleads. "Kiss me as if we'll be lovers again someday."

41

ONE DAY AFTER my daughter's graduation to the CPAP, Peter and I are huddled on the couch, watching our show, when the phone rings. It's ten at night. It's the NICU.

"Her right lung completely collapsed," Dr. Alston says.

Since Mila's extubation, her desats have been frequent and steep. A few hours earlier, I watched that number on her monitor plummet again and again, to the lowest levels I'd ever seen: below 80 percent, then 70, then 50, then lower. The red light flashing, the beeping of the alarm sounding faster and louder. The nurses told me she might be overstimulated by my touch. Or trying to poop. They turned up her oxygen to 23 percent, 25, 30, then higher.

In the hours since I left her side, the desats became so worrisome that an X-ray was performed. That's when Dr. Alston discovered my daughter's lung had collapsed.

Since her first days on the ventilator, Mila has been given surfactant, the foamy substance that lines the alveoli of the lungs of a normal baby, preventing the air sacs from collapsing between each breath. But this isn't the same as being born with lungs mature enough to produce the substance on their own.

Every breath she takes still requires tremendous exertion, like the first breath she ever took.

Now air has leaked out of her right lung into the space between her lung and her chest wall. There might be a tear in her air sacs. The mechanical ventilation might have caused her lung to overstretch, even rupture. After the X-ray, she was given medication to open her lung. The upper lobe has since opened, but not the lower. A second dose is being administered now.

The tone of Dr. Alston's voice is sober but confident, laboring to reassure. She tells us to go to bed. Rushing to the hospital now would only make it more difficult for us to face the morning.

There's a sharp, twisting pain in my heart. Still, no matter what I think I suffer, it's the barest glimmer of what my daughter has no choice but to endure.

The next day is her one-month birthday.

One day is good, Dr. Kahn once told us. *One week. One month.*

But what kind of life has it been for my daughter?

"We'll make it up to her," Peter vows.

I slash away at his stance until he breaks down.

"I just want to bring her home," he finally says. "I want to worry about getting up at night to give her a bottle. I want all the normal overwhelming stress of having a newborn."

This seems too much to hope.

The next day, when I sit down by my daughter's isolette, I castigate myself for all that wailing about the injury to her brain. Even the way I've shifted to willing her to somehow be okay seems so stupid, so entitled, so naive.

She still hovers at just over two pounds. After one month, she still looks as though she could fade away.

Breathe, I whisper to her now. *Please breathe.*

The nurses attempt to seem reassuring, but they've turned up the oxygen setting on her ventilator to 45 percent, the highest it's ever been. Even so, she desats again and again. Each time, I tell myself that there must be something I can whisper, some lullaby I can sing, some way to position my hand on her skin to keep that number from plummeting.

When I enter the foyer of our house, where our mail has spilled out of the mailbox and piled up in drifts on the floor, I spot two envelopes addressed to my daughter. With these envelopes in hand, I climb the stairs and walk through the renovation site, through the doorway of our old bedroom, and into my office, for the first time since my daughter's arrival.

The plants are dry and dying. Dust outlines each letter of the keyboard. A book about grief—research for my novel—is splayed open. My computer is asleep but still running.

The translation widget in one corner of the screen displays a Chinese word that I looked up the day before my daughter's arrival. *Huo*, fourth tone, as in *Huo bu dan xing*, a simple and elegant proverb that often gets awkwardly translated as "Misfortunes don't come singly." My main character was about to recall this saying.

I had grappled for a better translation. "Trouble never walks alone." This was more literal and more graceful but less precise. "When it rains, it pours." This captured more of the brevity and the colloquialism of the original, but sacrificed the image of a procession and the gravity of the meaning.

Since the day before my daughter's arrival, the translator has displayed the same pair of words. *Huo*: calamity.

Inside the first envelope is my daughter's social security card. Her full name and ten-digit number, identifications other than the tags that mark her in the hospital. The smooth blue rectangle feels unreasonably optimistic.

The second envelope holds her birth certificate. I never paid attention to the wording before.

I certify that this child was born alive at the place, date, and time given.

The document doesn't certify that this child will survive. It certifies only that as a matter of public record, a baby was born alive, however narrowly she edged by.

That night, the phone rings again. It's the NICU. It's close to midnight, still the day that marks one month since her arrival.

"She's having a rough night," Dr. Mercado says.

I'm glad that Dr. Mercado is the one calling. Her manner is less considered than the other doctors', and right now, that feels bracing, even vital.

Dr. Mercado says, "Mila stopped breathing tonight."

42

JOAN DIDION WRITES, "Survivors look back and see omens, messages they missed. They remember the tree that died, the gull that splattered onto the hood of the car. They live by symbols." I underlined this quote when I was researching grief for my novel.

Now, looking back, all I see are omens. Absent any medical elucidation, omens are all I have.

I complained about my baby boy. *One of us is not going to make it,* I typed.

I yanked a pair of Spanx over my belly and made a speech about the meaning of failure.

Could you be pregnant? asked the lactation consultant. *Ha,* I said.

My file vanishing in a freak flood at the obstetricians' office. My exemplary but suddenly erased patient history. The hastily scribbled prenatal chart. The missing information that Dr. Sherman wanted that I couldn't remember then and can't remember now.

You're one of the patients we never have to worry about.

I fretted that my babies would be less than a year and a half apart. I never considered a separation of thirteen months.

This will be the shortest pregnancy ever, I said.

I vowed that my second baby would be the opposite of my first. Peter used to gloat, *Doesn't he make other babies look like they're barely alive?*

The murky, shifting due date. As if it was already ordained that the only date that would matter would be completely unmarked on my calendar.

It'll come out one way or another, I said.

My dream about a distant tapping against the foggy glass.

The sharp jab in the middle of the night.

The chapter I was about to write. *Huo*: calamity.

The alert on Peter's phone sometime before four thirty that morning.

Tonight, I know what happened.

I didn't want her enough.

This seems the only plausible explanation. Maybe it was a smiting by the gods. Maybe she heard every worry, every complaint.

The baby initiates the birth.

Maybe she senses, even now, our equivocating, our fear, our instinct to guard our family against her.

Mila stopped breathing tonight.

Hearing these words seems so unbearable, even as I know that I have no choice but to bear it, to bear it and to pray for her to take each breath, and the next, and the next, and the next—that, even tonight, I can't help but think that if she were to finally stop breathing once and for all, at least my sorrow would bring some measure of relief.

43

MILA'S OXYGEN WAS TURNED up to 100 percent. Chest compressions were performed; her heartbeat had drastically slowed. She responded immediately. Dr. Mercado reintubated her and placed her on the ventilator again. A chest tube has been inserted between her ribs to drain the leaked air and allow her lung to expand.

"Since then, she looks great," Dr. Mercado says: pink and peaceful and kicking.

This is, more or less, how my daughter looks when I see her. Even her cheeks look the tiniest bit plumper. It turns out she has gained forty grams—more than an ounce—since she was reintubated.

The other nurses direct my attention to the nurse who was on duty last night, a fine-boned, solemn woman I've noted only because she has asked both me and Peter, on separate occasions, to show our ID bands before she would allow us by our daughter's isolette. The print on those bands had already faded so completely that they were blank white strips by the time they frayed and fell off. I had memorized the ID number without trying. Peter was indignant to have to plead his case. After all, who would stake a false claim such as this?

Now it strikes me that if my daughter had to stop breathing on anyone's watch, this nurse was probably a good pick.

As if to leaven the gravity, she exclaims, "Oh my God, Mommy, your baby gave me such a scare!"

The other nurses chuckle. In fact, the nurse still looks rattled. She describes what happened when my daughter stopped breathing, but I can't hear a word.

The next time I see Dr. Alston, she refers to the cessation of breathing and the collapsed lung as relatively routine setbacks when a baby like mine is extubated. "It's the kind of thing you can't know until you try," she says.

In a week or two, the extubation will be attempted again. In the meantime, the latest X-ray indicates that Mila's lung has expanded, but the chest tube was initially inserted too far, necessitating a procedure to adjust its position. Another kind of thing that happens to a baby like mine.

On a positive note, Dr. Alston notes, Mila has continued to gain weight since the reintubation: thirty, even fifty grams a day. These are huge leaps, as if she is making up for lost time.

I stammer to ask whether she has simply been working too hard to breathe. Even after everything else we've discussed, this prospect seems nearly too sad to formulate.

Dr. Alston hesitates, then acknowledges that this is a reasonable explanation.

At home, I find myself rushing to look up that week-to-week pregnancy calendar. All the developments I once savored with such complacency. If my daughter were still in the womb, what would have happened over the last month? What was she meant to be doing inside my body?

By week twenty-nine, I read, the baby should be over three pounds. My daughter is now at thirty weeks and, despite her recent gains, still just slightly over two.

Her skin has become nearly opaque. I haven't seen her blink or turn yet, though I've been told she favors resting on her right side. I think she has fingernails but I can't be sure. She has started to retain warmth in her own body. She has grown a morsel of fat.

She has struggled to simply survive each day, each hour, each breath. Will she ever have the chance to catch up?

44

THE CONSTRUCTION IS AT A STANDSTILL. A plumbing inspection must be performed before the new bathroom fixtures can be installed. Jovially, the contractor tells us that we can move back into our bedroom. To me, everything touched by the renovation feels cursed.

During the weekend, while Leo naps, Peter lugs our mattress back upstairs, through the new doorway of our bedroom, and onto our old bed. The shades haven't been raised since the day before my daughter's arrival. Bluish dusk descends outside, much like the light before dawn that morning. The freshly painted, newly close walls press in.

And then it's happening all over again, as I knew it would. The pain, the calls, the prayer. My baby boy's cries. The red lights, the driver's sidelong glances, the blood.

Another moment comes back to me.

When I staggered into the sunlit lobby. The morning was fresh, everyone calm and cheerful. I paused in front of the security guard. I needed to get the words out in a rush.

"I'm having a miscarriage," I said. "Which floor?"

* * *

What happened? Now I understand why I can't stop asking this question. It's not only to locate the moments when I still could have saved her. If her arrival had been preceded by a fall, a car crash, some terrible event outside my body, then I would know that *something* happened to her. I would know that all the interventions to save her life have been appropriate measures to allay the repercussions of that event, not hubristic attempts to alter her destiny.

"Something did happen," Peter says. "We'll just never know what it was. Something like a fall or a car crash. Something happened."

Tonight, when we climb into our bed instead of crawling onto our mattress on the floor, I know Benadryl won't do the job. I take one half, then another half of my last Ambien to ensure I'm unconscious until morning.

45

THE FOG IN MY HEAD has subsided just enough that I can read books again, but the travails of fictional characters now seem like cruel contrivances. Memoir seems like the only form that might sustain me, yet I've become an impatient, barbaric reader.

When I first start to flip through tales of the widowed, the heartbroken, the bereaved, I can't help thinking that at least they have the certitude of grief. Of course, I still have access to hope. Hope is perilous, but so is pregnancy, I guess. So is life.

When I encounter the words *unbearable* and *unthinkable* and *unimaginable*, I feel the urge to hurl the book across the room. I think of how many infant tombstones can be found in any old cemetery. How women in ancient times often birthed ten children to have four survive. How such numbers are not unusual even now, in places like Sierra Leone or rural India. How did those women—how do they—make sense of these events? How much does the everydayness of the tragedy mitigate the grief?

Something happened, I tell myself. This becomes a kind of mantra, every time I slip into self-pity. I must have used up my fair share by now.

Another mantra: *It is what it is.* Her brain, for instance. Nothing can reverse the damage. No one knows the extent of the damage, or the nature of it, or when it will manifest. *It is what it is.*

All I can do is walk a humble path of acceptance, faintly lit by hope. Hope for her to breathe, to feed, to make her way home. To crawl, to walk, to sing. To go to school and make friends and live on her own one day.

But whether or not that happens, it is what it is. She is who she is. Whatever damage she sustained will be part of who she is. I will love her for whoever she is.

Also: *Day by day.* Each day she survives is another day she has survived. Each day I hold her is another day that I'm learning how to be her mother.

Nearly six weeks after my daughter's arrival, I finally raise the shades in our bedroom. Daylight streams in.

On this dazzling November weekend, we take Leo to a newer, bigger playground, where he zooms down the slide in his Superman position, then swaggers away while older kids start to emulate him. Sunlight sparkles through the tree branches over-head. Against the blue sky, the leaves of two trees, one still green, the other ruby red, mingle together, translucent and aglow. We pause under this canopy and take a picture.

At the hospital, my daughter is breathing well, and she has just surpassed one kilo, or two pounds three ounces. There is roundness in her cheeks, her calves, her toes.

During the evening shift change, Peter and I eat hot bowls of ramen. The trees at Columbus Circle have been decorated with Christmas lights, my favorite kind, tiny and silvery blue, like stars.

"This was a good day," I tell Peter. I fall asleep with just one Benadryl.

* * *

At the obstetrician's office for my postpartum checkup, I happen to see my birth history form for the first time since my daughter's arrival. Leo's Apgar scores: 9/9/9. Then Mila's: 1/6/6.

Until now, I recalled hearing only the first number.

Dr. Bryant says that I'm cleared for all normal activity—which, to me, means finally picking up my son. The bleeding has subsided to a little spotting. The cramping has given way to a thick, itchy numbness across my skin. The incision is a raised reddish purple scar.

Birth control is mentioned. After a pause, Peter and I ask for a referral for a vasectomy, which we discussed before we came.

This is a declaration of faith in our daughter. That she has completed our family.

It's also a statement of fear. How could we ever risk bringing another life into the world?

We'd assumed that any doctor, let alone an obstetrician, would endorse our responsible decision. But Dr. Bryant seems troubled.

"I don't know if you're done," she says. "I don't think you want to do anything so final."

We leave with a list of phone numbers, which we promptly misplace.

A few days later, my bleeding stops completely. The next week, for the first time since I conceived my son, I get my period.

I can't help wondering if this is some cruel cosmic joke—or just the way life happens.

46

THE WEEK OF THANKSGIVING, Peter and I enter our daughter's room to find it empty. We stand paralyzed until a nurse tells us that Mila is across the hall. Her former room is being cleaned now that most of the Hurricane Sandy transplants have been discharged.

In her new room, I careen from isolette to isolette. "Here she is!" I call out.

Tactfully, Peter beckons me across the room. I look again. The name tag on this isolette is blue. This baby is a Latino boy.

For days afterward, every time I enter the NICU, my legs carry me to her original corner.

When Dr. Perry, the lumbering, bearlike man in charge for the next month, says it's time to attempt the extubation again, I tell myself it's not an event at all.

Over the next days, Mila's breathing rate and oxygen levels hold more or less steady. She continues to gain weight, anywhere from five to forty grams per day. Even her nostrils appear to have grown into the CPAP prongs this time around.

On Thanksgiving Day at the hospital, I overhear Dr. Mercado

chatting with a nurse about buying an expensive pumpkin pie that turned out to be moldy. There is talk of a potluck among the nurses and parents. We leave guiltily, but it's Leo's first Thanksgiving at my parents' house.

Throughout dinner, Peter copes with the latest work crises— these days, rumors swirl of an ugly split brewing between Arianna and the CEO of AOL, Tim Armstrong—and Leo won't sit still for a moment, and my stomach blanches every time I think of my daughter alone on this holiday.

We call my ninety-four-year-old grandmother in California to wish her a happy Thanksgiving. When it's my turn to talk, I take the phone into another room. I know that no one has told her what happened. In my family, especially when it comes to bad news, we tell only what we have to tell.

I ask about her health. She can still outwalk me, but her voice sounds weaker and vaguer. Lately, she has lost her appetite. She is struggling to recover from a minor surgery. She tells me that she can't sleep at night without taking Ambien, but my aunt and uncle admonish her about the dangers of addiction.

I tell her that at her age, she has earned the right to take any drugs she likes. As far as I'm concerned, I say, she can smoke crack.

She hoots and cackles. Then she asks about my pregnancy. She says I will soon have the perfect family, with my baby boy and my baby girl. She reminds me that the year of the dragon is the most fortuitous of all. She says my daughter is destined to be strong, fierce, indomitable. I tell her that I hope she's right.

47

A CCORDING TO DR. PERRY, Mila's rate of growth is still less than optimal, averaging below twenty to thirty grams per day, and I should bring in only my "hind milk": the higher-fat, thicker milk that flows toward the end of each session. When I stammer that I'm not sure how to do that, he tells me to simply time my flow and collect the milk that starts at the halfway mark.

What if most of my milk—the drops wrung from my body that can't quite be said to flow—comes at the beginning?

"Whatever your halfway mark seems to be," he says. "Just collect the second half."

"What about the rest?" I ask.

Well, he would never want to tell a mom to discard any of her breast milk—but, well.

"What if what's left isn't enough?" I ask.

"The more you pump, the more you produce," Dr. Perry says.

Over the next days, I learn to set a timer on my phone, position the bottles for the speediest switch, and set aside only the first, wateriest drops, which I add to Leo's sippy cups. Still, on good days, I harvest barely enough for my daughter's daily intake.

During bad sessions on bad days, I might pump for thirty minutes and not get a drop.

While I pump, I gaze at photos of my daughter. Of my son. I close my eyes. I hold my breath. I gulp cold water, hot water, lactation supplements, and special teas. I chastise myself to relax.

Peter becomes so concerned that he buttonholes Dr. Mercado when she's on duty and asks her opinion of the feasibility of such a regimen.

"Dr. Perry," she says, "does not have breasts!" Yet it's clear that she won't override him.

In Mila's new room, her neighbor is a baby in an open-air crib who often screams and bawls no matter what the nurses do. With this squalling added to the usual sound track of gurgling and beeping, along with my dull dread of each impending pumping session, finding a moment to simply be here with my daughter feels more difficult than ever.

There is also a new worry. Since last week, when Mila reached thirty-one weeks' gestational age, she has been scheduled for a weekly screening by an ophthalmologist for retinopathy of prematurity, or ROP: an eye disorder that affects premature babies as a result of the disruption to their eye development upon birth.

In a normal pregnancy, the intricate web of blood vessels that supply oxygen to the retinas continues to grow until the baby reaches full term, extending outward from the optic nerve to eventually cover the retinal surface. A preterm birth can halt the formation of those blood vessels and cause them to develop abnormally.

For some babies affected with ROP, the blood vessels will resume normal growth on their own. For others, surgery can successfully treat the condition. For the less fortunate, ROP will lead to visual impairment, even blindness. Stevie Wonder was a preemie, I've been told.

This week, my daughter's ROP has "progressed," according to

Dr. Perry, to stage 1: mildly abnormal. The eye doctor has seen a white border where the normal growth of the blood vessels was halted.

On the last Tuesday of November, exactly seven weeks after my daughter's arrival, a nurse named Liberty asks if I want to practice "kangaroo care": holding Mila against my chest, skin to skin. This has seemed to be a privilege reserved for every parent and baby in the NICU except me and my daughter.

I fumble to position my chair, to undo my shirt and bra, to sit down without getting my own limbs tangled among the tubes and wires.

With a succession of quick clicks, Liberty lowers the entire side panel of the isolette, portholes and all, and removes the CPAP contraption.

My daughter's eyes look sleepy and surprised. Her tendrils of hair have thickened to a dark fuzz.

Liberty lifts her out of the isolette, naked except for her diaper, and settles her against my chest. My daughter still feels as if she could slip out of my embrace in an instant.

Liberty reconnects the CPAP, adjusts the tubes and wires. I cradle my daughter with one arm underneath her bottom and one hand supporting her head while my fingers stretch to hold the tubes and wires in place. Almost immediately, she desats.

Liberty turns up the oxygen. The experience might be overstimulating, she says, or Mila might be too comfortable against my skin, forgetting to breathe.

At last the oxygen level steadies. My daughter's eyes close. She sleeps in my arms, her mouth open, one hand curled beneath her chin. She breathes against me. I breathe against her. Her heart beats against my ribs. Mine beats against her cheek.

The world goes still. Whoever my daughter will be, she's perfect. However long this moment lasts, it's enough.

48

THE BILLS I'VE DREADED finally arrive, as if there might have been some kind of grace period built into the webs of bureaucracy, whether out of basic decency or data showing a correlation between efficiency of bill collection and the ability of a debtor's baby to breathe.

From the hospital, for services rendered to me on the day my daughter arrived, a coinsurance fee of $1,436.34. Prior to insurance payments and adjustments, the original total was nearly $24,000. This is actually nearly the same amount that the hospital charged for my son's uncomplicated delivery.

When I stare at the huge discrepancies between the original charges and the insurance payments, the only thing that seems clear is that this system has a method and logic all its own, a way of profiting both partners to the negotiation that is intended to remain obscure to me.

The first bill from the NICU shows a balance due of $406.26 for these procedures: "Deliv/Birth RM Resusc" and "Init Inpt Neonatal Crit Care." The lines of type blur. I want to pay whatever it takes so that I never have to look at these bills again.

The original amount charged for each subsequent day of care, prior to insurance payments and adjustments, is $2,624.00. But, from bill to bill, there is no consistency that I can see in terms of what was covered, what was reimbursed, what was adjusted. The balances due range from $243.00 to $3,688.00. I don't need my faculties completely intact to realize that at this rate, we could soon find ourselves mired neck deep in debt again.

When I call the insurance company, I remind myself to act like someone I imagine they would particularly like to help: eager to pay my share as soon as I'm assured of the correct amounts.

The insurance company representative refers to each bill by a claim number that doesn't correspond to anything on the papers in front of me. The bill for the first day of my daughter's NICU stay, for instance, is claim 15. The last bill is claim 6. Still, I manage to glean that all of these bills appear to have been incorrectly processed. The rep tells me not to pay anything until I hear directly from her that the discrepancies have been resolved.

She never calls back. According to another representative, the first bill still needs readjustment, the second and fourth are still being reconsidered, and the third was processed as out of network. I'm told that some of the neonatologists are in network and some are out.

As calmly as I can, I explain that in the NICU, I have no say over the providers or the shift changes. I don't mention that I never had a say in my daughter's admittance to the NICU at all. I'm told that the bills will be notated for reprocessing. In the meantime, I shove them out of sight.

49

O N THE FIRST OF DECEMBER, Dr. Perry removes the CPAP. Mila has graduated to the nasal cannula: a thin, clear tube that fits under her nose and loops over her ears. This stage of breathing support is designed for mild respiratory problems, delivering extra oxygen through a smaller set of nasal prongs. Aside from the patches of clear adhesive fastening the cannula against her cheeks and a narrow strip of white tape under her chin to secure the feeding tube, I can see all of her head and face.

But her respiratory problems don't seem so mild when I'm holding her and she desats again and again. Within a couple of days, Dr. Perry puts her back on the CPAP.

This time, she protests. Looking furious, she writhes and kicks in a markedly different manner from the flailing of her earliest days. At thirty-two weeks of gestation, her personality appears evident in a way that seemed far-fetched seven weeks ago. But the more she protests, the more she desats.

Yet the next time I enter the NICU, she's on the cannula again, looking rosy and satisfied. Nurse Kerry explains that she and a few other nurses petitioned Dr. Perry to give Mila another chance on the cannula—"high flow" this time, delivering oxygen with nearly as much pressure as the CPAP. While Kerry talks, she carefully cuts new pieces of gauze to adhere the cannula to my daughter's cheeks. They're in the shape of hearts.

Meanwhile, Mila's retinopathy continues to "progress," as they say, now from stage 1 to stage 2: mild to moderate abnormality. A dangerous ridge of tissue has formed at the white border of the retinal surface where the normal growth of the blood vessels was halted.

The more she grows, the more there is to fear.

One day, I hold my daughter against my chest for hours and her vitals remain steady. I don't move a limb until I have barely enough time to pump and rush home. At that moment, the nurses are busy with other babies. For the first time, I decide that I can place her in the isolette myself.

I stand up, struggling to support her neck while I fumble with the door of her isolette. The wires tangle and pull, catching against the armrests of my chair, and I lose my balance. I hear a soft thud. I've banged my daughter's head against the lid of her isolette.

Once I've made sure that she is unharmed, I let out a small, sheepish laugh. I suppose this is another version of progress.

50

THESE DAYS, WHEN I ENTER THE NICU, I no longer linger at the doctors' workstation. When I see Dr. Perry, the conversation has started to feel like a formality. When my daughter is doing well, there isn't much to say.

The rate of oxygen being delivered through her cannula gets turned to low-flow. Her breathing and her oxygen rates hold steady. She usually gains twenty to forty grams a day. At this rate, she passes two and a half pounds, then three pounds.

Her ears look perfectly formed. The rounded pouches of her cheeks give a slight downward pout to her pink lips, forming sweet little parentheses where her cheeks meet her chin. There are silken folds at her neck, her thighs, her wrists. She has grown into her isolette. She takes up space.

She has a downy coating of peach fuzz on her upper arms and her back. Her eyelashes dramatically lengthen and curl. Her fingernails need trimming. Her hair comes in more slowly above her forehead, giving her the appearance of a receding hairline. Her head is still slightly indented at the temples. Her nether regions have a little cushioning. She has developed nipples on her fragile chest and a few creases in the new plumpness in her palms and feet.

One day, I find her sleeping in what strikes me as an odd position: on her belly, which is a standard position in the NICU, but with her mouth and chin pressed into her mattress, pushing the cannula up against her nose, smushing the bridge. I assume that she must have been positioned like this for a reason, but when the nurse glances over, she exclaims, "Mila, what are you doing?"

The nurse turns my daughter's head sideways, readjusting the cannula and the prongs. Just as she walks away, my daughter lifts her head and neck—a slow, forceful motion that stuns me, as if I'm watching a dragon hatchling stretch its wings for the first time. She pauses, gazing forward, flexed in midair.

There is a coiled strength to her movement; a sense of purpose that guides the gathering of her muscles, the lift of each vertebra of her spine. She plants her mouth and chin into her mattress again. She seems to dig in a little, daring us to defy her preference.

The next time I enter the NICU, Dr. Perry grins at me. At noon that day, my daughter was given a bottle for the first time, and she drank it straight down. He says that if she continues to progress at this rate, we might be able to take her home before the end of the year.

As winter grips the city, Leo gets whacked with a new virus every other week. My boy crying inconsolably, unable to rest, his nose stuffed, his skin burning my palms. Given what I witness at the hospital, I should know that these bouts of illness are nothing this child of mine can't endure.

After a particularly miserable night, I bring him to Dr. Haber's office. Once she establishes that he's not in danger, she contemplates him perched on the exam table, chubby legs dangling high above the floor, wide-eyed and clinging to me.

"You forget how little he is," she says.

I'm perplexed. No one describes Leo as little.

"I mean young," she says. "Maybe not you, but me. I forget how young he is."

Yes, at fifteen months, Leo has no longer been allowed to make us worry. When Dr. Haber begins the exam, he sobs and flails, then struggles to recover his dignity. He sees the stethoscope and bravely lifts his own shirt to bare his belly.

My heart refuses to learn perspective. Again and again, it breaks.

"Do you want to sit down?" Dr. Perry asks.

Greeting Dr. Perry as we entered the NICU, Peter and I expected a mention of Mila's intake or weight, maybe some small talk about holiday plans. We didn't expect him to lead us into the conference room where we once sat down with Dr. Kahn to study that billowing cloud of blood in her brain.

I paste a smile on my face. My fists are clenched, as usual.

Dr. Perry tells us that Mila's weekly head ultrasound has come back. Slowly, he says, "The fact that it's nine weeks later, and there's no further sign of bleeding, no swelling, no fluid buildup, is about as good as we could've hoped."

He's telling us good news.

My smile widens. I thank him.

Then he mentions, as if this has been clearly understood between us, that a brain injury like Mila's indicated a forty percent chance of serious disability. He says that the most likely scenario now is a mild to moderate disability: difficulty learning to walk, for instance, or some kind of learning disability. There is also a chance that she won't have any disability at all. He doesn't offer odds.

I just want to ask one question. A question I've never asked aloud until now.

How did the intraventricular hemorrhage happen?

I realize that I've always assumed that it happened while she was still inside my body.

Dr. Perry hems and haws a bit. With the caveat that there's no way of knowing exactly what caused the hemorrhage, he explains that it could have resulted from the trauma of the delivery itself, or the intubation and mechanical ventilation, or any of the myriad medical interventions that sustained her vital functions during those first hours in the NICU.

It was a side effect of the efforts to save her. It was the price my daughter paid for her life.

51

SHE'S GOING TO BE OKAY," Peter says with increasing conviction.

Unprompted, my mother delivers an array of delicately patterned footies and bundlers in preemie sizes. "I can see it in her eyes," she says. "She's going to be okay."

When I look at my daughter now, I can't help believing this, too. But I don't think I'll ever say it out loud.

Already, I can't help discerning a new set of worries looming in the distance.

I'm worried about how I'll ever tell the story of my daughter's arrival in the world. I can imagine celebrating the day that she comes home, or even her due date, but not the day she nearly died.

I still can't bring myself to say the words: *Her birthday. The day she was born.* The best I can do is say *When she arrived. She was delivered.*

What if I finally allow myself to celebrate her arrival, to hold her every day and night the way I hold my son—and then, when she reaches six months, or one year, or two, or later still, I discover that the future I think might finally be promised to her has been swept away?

I don't know, even now, how to live with such uncertainty.

How to let her stumble, bump her head, be an ordinary baby. How to leave her side and know that she's safe. How to ever know that she's safe again.

I'm worried, most of all, that I'll never love her the way she deserves to be loved. That these months of separation and agony and limbo will always hinder our bond somehow. That I'll never be able to forget how I wished for the chance to let her go.

52

B Y MID-DECEMBER, THE cannula is removed. After a day or two of too many desats, it reappears. A few days later, it's gone again—this time, for good.

All that obscures my daughter's face now is the feeding tube, which is threaded through one nostril instead of her mouth, so that she can nurse unobstructed. Only when I see her face in a photo do I realize this tube would still mark her as a sickly infant to an outsider. To me, in the flesh, she looks glorious.

She weighs four pounds.

The first time I attempt to breast-feed her, she lolls indolently. I tickle her cheek, nudge her lips, tap her chin: all the tips I studied before I ever nursed Leo and never once used. At last her lips part. I seize my chance.

My daughter is on my breast. She sleeps. She doesn't suckle. Every now and then, her lips pucker briefly; no milk passes from my body to hers. Yet sitting cramped beside her isolette, I feel like this could be the most luxurious sensation I've ever known.

Eventually, I notice a new couple standing beside the next isolette. The woman is tall and fine-featured, with a sleek bob. She doesn't look as if she could have been pregnant days or weeks ago. Her clean-cut husband seems to be a doctor, comfortable with the vocabulary and roles in this room. He chats with the nurses about medications; he chats with the doctors about medical schools.

Their baby's condition looks similar to my daughter's when she arrived. Although his skin appears intact, his limbs are reptilian and withered, his head large and fetal. His face is obscured by tape and tubing, his body webbed with IVs and wires.

Yet the mother smiles graciously at me. When she sees my daughter out of her isolette, with her skin against my skin and her rosy face unobstructed and her mouth at my breast, this woman has no idea that we've been here for nearly three months, and yet she smiles. Both she and her husband seem so composed that I think I must be misreading their situation.

They look so conspicuously like the kind of people uniformly admired by their peers and bragged about by their families that I can't help wondering: What could they have done wrong to lead them here? How could their baby have ended up next to mine?

Most days, when my daughter is due for her feeding, she just wants to sleep. Every few days, I manage to feed her a bottle of milk. Depending on her drowsiness, this takes anywhere from five minutes to an hour, with frequent breaks to burp her, tickle her, tease her mouth with the nipple until she wakes up enough to suck a little bit before she falls asleep again.

The longer she depends on tube feedings, the longer she'll stay in the hospital. Sometimes I worry that I'm force-feeding her according to hospital protocol rather than respecting the dictates of her own body, but I suppose that's a privilege she forfeited when she exited my womb, where she could have received all the nutrients she needed with no effort at all.

The first time I burp her, sitting her up on my lap with my hand supporting her chin, I notice a bright pink splotch across the nape of her neck. Has she had this mark all along? The nurse on duty hasn't noticed it before, either.

Dr. Kahn tells me it's a kind of birthmark caused by dilated capillaries just beneath the skin, commonly known as a stork bite, since it often appears where the stork might have held the baby in its beak, by the scruff of the neck.

What baby could be a less plausible candidate for having been magically delivered to our doorstep in a white cloth bundle by a stork? And what else don't I know about her?

Dr. Kahn tells me the birthmark will probably disappear by the time my daughter turns two. She also reports that the retinopathy has progressed a little more, to moderate abnormality. I ask how worried I should be.

With a slight smile, Dr. Kahn tells me the retinopathy is likely to resolve on its own or be successfully treated with laser surgery, with probable outcomes ranging from unimpaired vision to the need for glasses as a baby.

She also tells me that Mila will be fed only fortified breast milk from now on; no more formula. This is more good news, but what it means to me is that my daughter will depend on my body alone, and I can't understand how I can possibly be entrusted with this charge again.

"What if I run out of milk?" I ask.

"We'll cross that bridge if and when we come to it," Dr. Kahn says.

I know we're about to come to it. I've stopped discarding my foremilk, but my supply keeps dwindling.

Dr. Kahn tells me it's highly unlikely that Mila will ever breast-feed exclusively. Which means that unless I absolve myself to some degree, I will condemn myself to endless months of pumping even after I bring my daughter home.

Dr. Kahn says that she has watched NICU mothers drive themselves out of their minds over their milk supply. In situations like mine, she says, it's common for milk production to cease around the three-month mark.

"Your milk has already seen Mila through the most critical time," she says. "It's as if your body knew what it needed to do. In a sense, you've already pushed it to go against nature."

In the nearly three months since my daughter's arrival, every time I've attached those hard plastic flanges and switched on that dry, mechanical suctioning, I've never once felt that tingling, unstoppable rush of milk that my son used to effortlessly call forth.

These days, my mind seems finally to have wrapped itself around the fact of my daughter's existence, but my body still doesn't believe it.

One weekend in late December, on my way to meet my family for a holiday dinner and a Broadway play, I find myself engulfed in a drunken horde of frat boys dressed as Santa Claus and sorority girls dressed as slutty elves. Until my sisters tell me about SantaCon over bites of food that I can't taste and sips of wine that burn my stomach, I'm not sure if I hallucinated. During the first scene of the play, I fall asleep on my father's shoulder. For this rest alone, my first unmedicated hours of sleep since my daughter's arrival, I'm thankful for the outing.

Just before Christmas, my daughter is moved into the room for "feeders and growers": the babies who need minimal care before they go home. Now we sit among babies who were born at thirty-two weeks, thirty-four, thirty-six. This room is quiet and peaceful. Alarms rarely flash or beep.

On Christmas Day, I forgo visiting my daughter to take Leo to my parents' house. All I can see clearly is a photo of Mila that Peter sends from the hospital, with the update that she has reached 1,985 grams, or 4 pounds 6 ounces.

The next day, I enter the NICU ready to celebrate my daughter's passing two kilograms. A nurse sets upon me, looking panicked. The bins of breast milk labeled for my daughter, which used to spill over, are completely empty.

In a frenzy, I call Peter and my parents to deliver all the stacks of bottles that I've stored up over nearly three months. At the rate of Mila's current consumption—an ounce and a half at each feeding, twelve ounces per twenty-four hours—the supply will be gone in a matter of days.

All my worries narrow to this single, immediate worry: how to provide my daughter with the sustenance she needs.

My sister Michelle sets to pumping for Mila, every morning and every night, in addition to nursing Mateo and storing milk for him for her return to work.

Meanwhile, I pump every ninety minutes throughout the day, even though this means frequently curtailing my time holding my daughter. I pump before and after and during each meal. I pump instead of playing with Leo. These days, he imitates the sound of the pump before I turn it on, heaving and hissing perfectly in rhythm.

At night, I set an alarm to go off every two hours. Going to bed suddenly becomes easy. I lie down knowing that if I can't fall asleep, those two hours will pass, and then the next two, then the next. The entire night will pass.

Knowing this, I sleep for half an hour, one hour, two. I wake to my alarm, stagger to my pump, stagger back to bed, set the next alarm, drift off again. The sleep feels effortless and sustaining. The rhythm feels simple, even natural. As if, for the first time since my daughter's arrival, a connection has been restored between my body and my reality.

The last days of December, I can't help asking Dr. Mercado if she has a date in mind for my daughter to go home. In a cheerful tone, she says that it will probably happen in a week or two. Mila needs to show that she can maintain her own body temperature outside the isolette, pass the car seat test, avoid episodes of apnea or bradycardia, and maintain her daily growth with only bottle-feedings.

"You know what, let's take away that feeding tube," Dr. Mercado says. "It's not so aesthetically pleasing. Let's see her pretty face."

Just like that, my daughter's face is free: no tubes or hoses, no gauze or tape. Only her soft, chubby, pink face.

On December 29, I wake to a calendar alert that my pregnancy would have been considered full term at thirty-seven weeks today. At the NICU, my daughter's isolette is empty. She's asleep in an ordinary bassinet, the newborn cap snug on her head.

On New Year's Eve, I'm not aware of any countdown other than the countdown to the next pumping session. By the time I enter the NICU in the new year for the first time, my daughter is over five pounds. We bring in a huge chocolate cake for the nurses.

One day, we run into a thin, older nurse who somberly tended my daughter on her first day while I wept in my bloodstained gown. Now she bursts into a smile.

"Mila is a champ," she says. "I knew she was a fighter. From the first day, I knew."

We bring in a car seat so that Mila's vitals can be monitored while she sits in it for an hour and a half—the same car seat that carried Leo home from the hospital. Nestled in its center, padded on all sides, she barely looks life-sized. But she sails through the test.

Any day now, I will bring her home.

53

O<small>N</small> M<small>ONDAY</small>, J<small>ANUARY</small> 7, when I ask Dr. Mercado if she has any clearer idea of the date of Mila's discharge, she hesitates.

"I guess it could happen tomorrow, or the next day," she says. "I guess it could happen today."

My daughter has reached thirty-eight weeks of gestation. She can maintain her temperature outside her isolette. Weeks have passed without episodes of apnea or bradycardia. She weighs five pounds six ounces today: nearly quadruple her birth weight.

How can I trust myself to take care of her without the numbers and waveforms on her monitors? How will I spot danger without the flashing lights and beeping alarms? How can we be ready? After three months in the NICU, how can we be anything but ready?

When I mention the possibility of going home today, Nurse Liberty seems taken aback. She says that she has just noticed Mila exhibiting a condition called stridor, a kind of high-pitched, noisy breathing, which she flagged for Dr. Mercado that morning.

Still, Liberty sets up the hearing test, which Mila passes. I thank Liberty fervently and quietly. My daughter can hear. At this point, I want to snatch each piece of good news as I run all the way home with my daughter, my head kept low.

Dr. Mercado's manner is still breezy as she explains that, ideally, Mila would be seen again by the ophthalmologist before discharge. Then again, we'll need to bring her to his office for weekly follow-ups in any case. There is also the question of the MRI, which probably can't be scheduled on such short notice, but whatever the result, it won't give us any clearer predictions for her future.

The only outstanding issue is the stridor. Dr. Mercado is not particularly worried, since it hasn't affected my daughter's oxygen levels and it seems to manifest only when she is working hard to extract milk from the bottle. Still, she would like to reach an otolaryngologist for a second opinion before Mila leaves the hospital.

While Dr. Mercado talks, my eyes stray to the notes on her monitor. There is the name of the baby of that new couple, the fine-featured woman and her doctor husband, along with a number that stills my heart: twenty-three weeks.

Two fewer weeks in the womb than my daughter was granted. Two weeks that place their baby and mine on opposite sides of the edge of viability.

God, have I been self-pitying, thoughtless, blind. Maybe my daughter was the direst case here until their baby arrived. Maybe there were more critical cases all along.

Peter has canceled meeting after meeting. At six P.M. Dr. Mercado says that the otolaryngologist is busy with a surgery and gives us his contact information.

"So, if you want, you can take her today," Dr. Mercado says.

We stare at her in disbelief.

She smiles. "I mean, unless you've changed your minds."

We manage to smile back and thank her before we scramble to our daughter's side. My hands shaking, I change her diaper for the last time in the NICU. For the first time, I dress her in one of the outfits from my mother: a cream-colored footie with pale pink and green flowers and a little ruffle at the neck, plus a matching cap.

Liberty is having problems with the printer, ferrying half-blank sheets back and forth. Word spreads among the nurses. They poke their heads in and out, exclaiming and marveling.

When Liberty finally compiles a complete set of discharge papers, there are no special instructions. Just a daily dose of vitamins and an ounce and a half of breast milk or formula every three hours. When the last paper is signed, she finally smiles.

"For so long, Mila was our smallest baby. Now look at her." Liberty shakes her head.

The ID band that was taped to her isolette is handed to me. I clutch it in my fist.

We thank and hug Liberty—*Liberty!* In the corridor, more nurses gather. We happen to catch Dr. Kahn, who looks a little startled; if she were on duty, the discharge would have been more methodical. What does it matter? She smiles and poses for a few pictures with Mila.

The nurses laugh: all this time, Mila has been asleep in the car seat, her cap dipping insouciantly over one eye, with one hand raised in a wave: *I'm out. See ya!*

Together, we exit the steel door. We step into the elevator and descend to the ground floor. At the revolving glass doors, we pause to tuck a blanket beneath her chin. We carry her into the cold, crisp air of the city on this January evening and tightly secure her into the waiting car.

The river streams past and the bridge sprawls ahead while my daughter sleeps beside me. By the time we reach home, night has fallen thick and black and quiet, Leo is asleep, and Mila is due for her feeding. My heart thumping, I carry her into our bedroom and close the door.

She stirs and stretches. She opens her eyes. She opens her lips. For the first time, she suckles. And then, for the first time since I last nursed my son, I feel that strange, tingling rush: the letdown of milk. The flow of life from my body to hers.

She drinks it in.

PART III

My darling, the wind falls in like stones
from the whitehearted water and when we touch
we enter touch entirely. No one's alone.
—ANNE SEXTON, "THE TRUTH THE DEAD KNOW"

54

S HE SETTLES INTO OUR home as if she knew she was headed
here all along. Day and night, she sleeps, her cheeks rosy and
her breath soft. She sleeps in my arms, at my breast, in my bed.
She sleeps as if we have all the time in the world now to spend
together.

She blinks at the morning sun streaming into her bassinet.
She slips her arms out of the swaddle and stretches luxuriously. She
grunts and releases a trickle of undigested milk out the side of her
mouth. She gazes at me and rests her cheek against my heart.

Within a few days of bringing her home, my milk brims the
pumping bottles, then overflows, as if she and I have been saving
up for this moment.

I breathe deeply against her skin, but I still can't detect her
scent. My mother says that this is because she smells just like me.

Sometimes her face looks so much like a feminine version of
Leo's—eyes set a little wider and more upturned, every feature
softened and refined—that the resemblance feels strangely fore-
told, as if the two of them were always meant to reflect each other.

At first, Leo swaggers past her with hardly a glance. When we
direct his attention to her, he looks incredulous, as if we've asked

him to kiss a chair leg. Obligingly, he leans his head against hers for a moment. Then he moves on to business as usual: littering the house with granola, hiding in the cabinet amid pots and pans, demanding to dance to James Brown.

Her eyes widen, her brow lifts. She registers a little alarm, a little wariness. Then she falls asleep again, either to the tune of "People Get Up and Drive Your Funky Soul" punctuated by Leo's laughter and commands, or back in the hushed shadows of our bedroom upstairs.

"How old is she?" my mother ventures to ask.

Her "actual age," counting from her delivery, is three months. Her "adjusted age" is still under forty weeks of gestation: less than zero.

"Now is when her life begins," Peter says.

Here are all the loveliest aspects of having a new baby, suddenly restored and granted to us. Every moment we hold her or watch her sleep, we know what it means to feel blessed.

Only the relentless feedings threaten to undo me. Despite the odds, she nursed her first night at home. So how can I fail to keep up my end?

The lactation consultant assures me that she has helped plenty of preemies successfully transition to breast-feeding. When she hears a few details of my daughter's history, her warm, bullish manner falters. She says that Mila will be the smallest baby she has ever tended. Yet once she tests Mila's suck, she buoyantly predicts that we'll be exclusively breast-feeding within a few weeks, as long as we follow an exacting regimen.

I arouse Mila for each nursing session with a series of careful exercises. Each session is followed by pumping and bottle-feeding. The process takes sixty to ninety minutes, and then it begins again in less than an hour.

During these first days, Mila loses one ounce after another.

When she passes a week without pooping, Dr. Haber directs us to call the NICU.

"N-I-C-U, how can I help you?"

None of the neonatologists we know are on hand. A pediatrician expresses concern until she learns that Mila is being fed only unfortified breast milk. She says that Mila's body is likely adjusting to the transition.

Just when Peter returns to work and I'm starting to despair of my ability to keep up the feeding regimen on my own, Mila's weight gain becomes steady enough—half an ounce to an ounce each day—that the consultant gives the go-ahead to taper off the pumping and the bottle-feeding. Soon, I gather all of my pumping paraphernalia and shove it out of sight.

By the end of January, when Mila has passed six pounds and her due date, she no longer needs to be woken for each feeding. Every two hours, day and night, she sounds the alarm. The two of us tumble into a quiet, foggy, trancelike cycle, our bodies syncing until there is little differentiation between her rhythms and mine. Because she is mine, and I am her mother.

Except that every day or two, I interrupt her sleeping to bundle her up and rush her through the frigid wind to a doctor's office.

The otolaryngologist is a gentle, charming man who also has a toddler son and a newborn daughter—a regular newborn. He inserts a tiny camera and light through Mila's nostril down to her larynx, causing her to scream and cry while we watch her vocal cords work at maximum capacity on a high-definition monitor.

He confirms the stridor and adds a few more diagnoses: laryngomalacia, an abnormal softening or lack of muscle tone in the tissues of the larynx above the vocal cords; unilateral vocal cord paralysis, a condition in which one side of her right vocal cord fails to vibrate to produce sound; and gastroesophageal reflux disease, a more severe form of the common infant tendency to spit up, in which the reflux irritates her esophagus.

All these conditions might affect her breathing, her voice, her feeding, and her growth. But they all might still be outgrown, and for now, the doctor wants only to monitor her progress with monthly follow-ups.

Every week, she gets reexamined by the ophthalmologist, a handsome, gray-haired man who greets Mila with tender familiarity. He has known her for months in the hospital.

He reclassifies her retinopathy from stage 2 to stage 1. The blood vessels of her retinas are starting to resume normal growth on their own. He also explains that since she is at elevated risk for other eye disorders—nearsightedness, strabismus (crossed eyes), and lazy eye—he will continue to monitor her through childhood.

The first time Dr. Haber examines her, she says, "She looks a thousand times better than I expected."

Dr. Haber notes a few mild abnormalities, likely inevitable side effects of so many weeks in an isolette. Stiffness and weakness in her upper body—though Dr. Haber asserts that she appears unlikely to have cerebral palsy. The long, narrow shape of her head, though my and Peter's heads are oval, too, as is Leo's. Asymmetry in her head and neck, a tendency to favor one side, which could be a sign of torticollis—a word that sounds terrifying to me, though the condition, literally "twisted neck," is a common one that often resolves with careful stretching and positioning.

Every few days, I bring her in for a weight check. Every time I panic, Dr. Haber shows me how steadily Mila maintains her own growth curve.

"So let's find something else to worry about," she says.

During every visit, Dr. Haber is so unhurried and attentive that, amid my gratitude, sometimes I long for the casual, brisk manner in which Leo's checkups used to take place.

At home, my daughter simply looks like what she is: my baby girl. But when I take her into taxis and foyers and waiting rooms where people stare and murmur as if they have never seen such a tiny creature, a harsh lens clicks over my vision. Once again, she looks more like a medical case than a baby.

My NICU vocabulary gives way to a new set of deceptively ordinary words: *intervention, development, delay, assessment, evaluation.* These words sit alongside terms that need no context to signal their weight: *Handicap. Disability.*

We've been referred to Early Intervention, a government-funded program that provides free developmental therapy to special-needs babies through local nonprofit agencies. The bureaucratic roadblocks are remarkably seamless, as if they were actually designed to help people who need help.

When three specialists arrive at my door to interview me and evaluate Mila, I find myself stammering and trembling. They shake a rattle in her face. They clap and sing. They roll her back and forth, sit her up, stand her up. They scribble notes on her cries. They want to watch her feed, but she keeps her eyes and mouth stubbornly shut.

They reassure me that Mila has little chance of being turned away from the program—"a shoo-in," one calls her—even in the unlikely scenario that they fail to assess significant developmental delays at this stage. The severity of her prematurity, along with the complications she suffered, place her at such high risk that it is, in itself, a qualifying condition.

Soon, the evaluation arrives in the mail: *Severely delayed feeding skills . . . severe weakness of her oral peripheral area . . . overall motor weakness . . . below the first percentile . . . prognosis for spontaneous improvement is poor . . . did not appear alert . . . did not maintain eye contact . . . did not watch objects . . . weak cry, more like a whimper . . . unable to bring her hands to midline, to her mouth or perform purposeful arm movements . . . mixed receptive-expressive language disorder . . .*

How can the case described here be the baby stirring in my arms now? Is the girl I think I'm getting to know only a wishful projection?

By the time I meet with a woman referred to as "the City"— an Early Intervention official endowed with the power to approve or deny services—I've coached myself to act like what I imagine a good mom of a special-needs baby to be: above all, grateful.

The physical therapist is a gaunt, gravelly-voiced woman who wears chunky jewelry, harem pants, and billowing scarves and robes. She describes herself, unnecessarily, as a former hippie. She notes Mila's mild asymmetry, performs a series of gentle exercises and massages, designs a sleeping position to minimize her tendency to turn to one side. Then she calls it a day. From her perspective, for now, there's nothing really wrong with my daughter.

By contrast, the feeding therapist is a sturdy, brassy, no-nonsense woman who, upon meeting my daughter, wrinkles her nose. "Boy, she's really acting like a preemie," she says.

I restrain myself from throwing her out of my house.

My daughter is floppy and disorganized and excessively drowsy. Her suck is all wrong—she smacks at the nipple, ingesting too much air. I'm feeding her wrong, burping her wrong, holding her wrong.

The next time, the feeding therapist notes that Mila is "doing much better." She says, "That first time, she was just a disaster."

Eventually, I learn to appreciate her bluntness and vigilance. I will also learn that all of the therapists, including the specialists who evaluated my daughter, are the mothers of children who had or have special needs: a teenage boy with severe cerebral palsy due to a virus his mother caught during pregnancy, a baby born with a harelip who is now the father of three.

The assessments that I can't help hearing as damning judgments are everyday realities to them that call for action. No amount of tact or praise will make them disappear. Shame and guilt won't do a thing to help my daughter.

Still, sometimes the therapists' pronouncements blur into a fog of worry.

A few weeks after my daughter's discharge, at an adjusted age of zero months, she rolls over. Unfortunately, the first time she chooses to demonstrate this skill is an occasion when I've placed her on her belly on the couch, a position meant to ease her digestion, and then walked a few steps away—an admittedly inadvisable action that generally has no consequences during a newborn's first months.

A sudden, strange sound stops my heart: my baby girl bawling. Her little body is helpless on the carpet, like an upturned ladybug. She is unhurt, quieting as soon as I pick her up. I cradle her until we calm down together.

I tell myself that it's only a fluke, but soon she repeats the feat, safely on her play mat. Rolling from front to back is a milestone that Leo achieved at two months, after weeks of melodramatic struggling, at more than twice my daughter's current size.

When I mention Mila's rolling to the therapists, they point out that any milestone achieved early could also be a sign of abnormal development.

One month after her due date, she smiles: lopsided and shy at first, then slow and suddenly full like a sunrise. Six weeks after her due date, right on cue, she becomes fussy in the evening just as she starts to sleep longer at night.

She coos and gurgles. She focuses on people's faces, often with her brow furrowed. She slurps her fingers. She protests and swims during tummy time.

If Leo's cry was royally furious, hers is indignant yet prim. She lifts her neck, widens her eyes, and sputters a bit, ladylike. Finally, she squawks: *I'm sorry, I don't mean to make a fuss—but this is not right!*

She seems to work out each area of concern on her own, in her own time, so consistently that I sometimes wonder if she studiously takes note of every one of my worries.

My desk gets buried under hospital bills that arrive in completely arbitrary order, with no more consistency to the charges than the first batch. Which days of her NICU stay were processed as in network or out. Which days require no patient responsibility or 10 percent coinsurance. Which days have not been reimbursed at all. Some bills that were fully paid arrive again and again. Other bills arrive in multiple copies with differing amounts.

Though I'm not much of a conspiracy theorist, the only consistent logic I can discern is the prevailing motive of wearing a person down. More than once, after I've tried and failed to elicit a coherent explanation for a balance, I pay it just so I won't have to look at the bill again. Sometimes a duplicate turns up in the mail anyway.

Leo continues to catch a new illness every other week, while Mila seems wondrously immune. The latest virus gives him diarrhea—an entertaining phenomenon to him, at first. "Whoa," he says, wide-eyed. "Uh-oh." Then he sidles into the bathroom, struggling to maintain a modicum of dignity. "Bye," he says urgently, when I follow him. "Bye!"

Soon, he becomes inconsolable and I take his temperature.

The receptionist at Dr. Haber's office repeats, "One hundred point five?"

"No," I say, just as my legs buckle. "One hundred and five, and still climbing."

I can't, I think. *I can't, I can't.*

The blur of hospital elevators and corridors, masked faces and gloved hands, flashing red lights and beeping alarms.

A syringe of acetaminophen and a three-hour nap later, Leo's fever drops. Still, my fists won't unclench.

His interest in reading *Mama, What's In There?* has finally waned. Most of the flaps have fallen off. I slip the book off his shelf, but I can't quite bring myself to throw it out.

55

WHEN SPRING ARRIVES AND the neighborhood bursts forth with shoots and blossoms, I feel like the world is throwing a coming-out party for us. As we blow bubbles in the park and scarf down Sunday brunches, first-time parents engage us in pleasant commiseration about one baby, then gape when they notice the other. Peter and I play along as if the age gap between our children is the most staggering feature of the life of our family.

Mila continues to achieve milestones without much fuss: holding her head upright, pushing up on straight arms, sleeping through the night. The retinopathy has resolved completely. The reflux and stridor, laryngomalacia and vocal cord paralysis, all continue to improve. The results of a follow-up hearing test are normal. Her weight gain is still slow but steady. Even her checkups with Dr. Haber now follow a routine pediatric schedule.

Her habitual expression is contemplative, reserved, even slightly worried. My sisters say her expression looks like mine.

Leo often runs to hug her with loud, frank enthusiasm while she tolerates his embrace with such a subtle smirk—*Oh, you again*—that I'm reminded there are many different ways to wield power, even between a baby and a toddler. At the same time, his way of playing with her often falls somewhere between harmless roughhousing and attempted murder: a sly jab with his foot, a kiss that leaves teeth marks on her forehead. Any time I turn my back, I'm liable to find him laying his full weight on top of her little body, grinning, while she quietly waits for rescue, alarmed yet stoic and trusting.

He calls her "Baby," so that's what Peter and I call her. I still almost never say her name out loud.

These days, I can't get enough of the way Leo is learning to voice his enduring demands: "Hair down, Mama. Hair down!" Just as I start to reclaim more time with him, the daycare center we've coveted finally offers us a spot. Within days, Leo reinvents himself as the teacher's pet. I'm always the first parent at pickup, but I still feel guilty.

I hold my tongue when our new babysitter, Lily, deposits Mila in the stroller, then gets herself ready in an unhurried manner. My daughter bawls as if she thinks that she has been forgotten. I rush to pick her up.

I tell Lily that Mila can't be left to cry like this. "She's not a normal baby," I hear myself say.

Her height and weight still don't register on the growth charts. At the playground, on the street, Peter and I have taken to shrinking even her adjusted age—*three months, two months, six weeks*—yet people's reactions still suggest that she doesn't look the way she should.

The doctors and therapists often express wonder and relief at her progress, but their questions inevitably tend toward the basic. Does she have head control? Can she put a little weight on her feet?

Why does she sometimes still feel like a stranger to me? Who would she be if she'd had nine months in the womb and a normal delivery?

One night, Peter and I are huddled on the couch when the main character in our latest show suddenly wakes up in a hospital. The stark walls, the flickering monitors. Involuntarily, we both shudder.

In bed, he says, "The word I can never forget, the word Dr. Kahn said—"

"I know," I say. *"Catastrophic."*

"No," he says. "I'd forgotten that one. She was saying that to make us feel better."

"Right," I say. "So what was the word?"

"Resuscitate," he says.

We kiss good night.

"I'm sorry I didn't take better care of you," he mumbles, just as he drifts to sleep.

At the onset of summer, I can't make sense of the lush sunshine or the span of a year. I can't understand time anymore.

When I sleep, I dream terrible dreams. My baby boy is drowning in front of me. My baby girl is in the hospital again. The unbearable, the unthinkable, the unimaginable: still these words seem to apply. When I wake to realize that both of my babies are safe in their cribs, I remind myself to never complain again.

Ordinary misfortunes send me reeling. My phone shatters. The front door of the house fails to shut securely. People steal our packages, making off with baby books and goldfish crackers, leaving the boxes torn on the floor. The dishwasher breaks down, the new shower sputters, the washing machine floods the basement.

She sucks her toes now. She kisses her reflection in the mirror. She becomes a beast to diaper and dress. As fast as I can lay her on the changing table, she flips over.

The therapists say that this resistance, which I've taken as a sign of a strong-willed personality, might be a sign of sensory processing disorder.

In late June, we take our first vacation as a foursome to a laid-back part of the Jersey Shore. The day we head out, Mila refuses to nurse. The more she fusses and yanks off, the more I tense up and the more impossible it seems to ever sync our bodies again. At a gas station, at the hotel, I manage a few nursing sessions, but most of the time, I'm strapped to the pump again, wringing out every drop.

"Look," Dr. Haber says, "the longer she breast-feeds, the better. But don't you think it's time you made things a little easier for yourself?"

Outside, the beach beckons. Leo howls for me to jump with him in the tide. I hand Mila to Peter with a bottle of formula.

Back home, the breast-feeding resumes, sputters, and tapers off for good. Michelle delivers the bottles of breast milk she has stored for my daughter all these months. I parcel them out, one or two per day, and buy cartons of formula, feeling ashamed every time.

Over the next weeks, my daughter finally grows teeth and holds her head steady. She eats her first meals of pear puree and baby oatmeal. She scoots from one end of a room to another, rocks herself back and forth in preparation for crawling. She develops a passion for tearing sheets of paper into shreds and chewing them into wads I find hidden inside her cheeks.

She still looks tiny. She can still fit in most of the outfits she wore when she first came home from the hospital. Even her hair grows almost imperceptibly.

Leo's jealousy scales new heights. Only I am allowed to get him out of bed in the morning, though he sends me back to my room if my hair is wrapped in a towel. In the evening, he pilfers my hairband and slips it over his own arm to go to sleep.

He refuses to be left with Lily for a single moment. Even when Peter manages to get home by his bedtime, Leo looks at him coldly. "Dada, go away. Night-night, Dada." If Peter lingers, he might give him a dismissive wave: *Honey, go cook!*

Gradually, I hand off Mila for longer stretches. She rarely seems to mind. I tell myself it's better this way. Leo needs me more right now. With my daughter, I think too much, I remember too much. I can't stop worrying.

56

WHEN LEO'S SECOND BIRTHDAY dawns on a glorious Saturday in September, Peter and I feel as if we've been granted a do-over. We spend hours cleaning the house, sweeping the backyard, preparing burgers and mushrooms and corn for the grill.

Leo's requests are surprisingly modest: balloons and bubbles. My dad brings a helium tank and fills the house, the front stoop, and the backyard with buoyant bouquets. My mother and sisters bring a half dozen bubble-blowing toys.

It's a wonderful party, with our families, a few close friends, babies underfoot and cousins running around, a riot of laughter and crumbs and ribbons and spills, smoke from the grill and runaway balloons.

When I bring out the cake—chocolate, without espresso beans—Leo beams as if he's waited for this moment all year. After he blows out the candles, he starts the applause himself. Between each bite, he hugs me, smearing my face with frosting. Mila accepts his embrace with a slightly disdainful manner. Peter has barbecued throughout the party, and his head and neck smell lightly toasted. I've never felt prouder of anything than I do of my family that day.

The lawn sprinklers mysteriously switch on toward the end of the party, spraying everyone sprawled on our little patch of grass, and somehow this only adds to the festivity.

Mila crawls everywhere. She claps her hands and rolls a ball and bangs toys together and pulls herself to standing. She loves to play peekaboo, ducking behind doors and around corners. "Where's Mila?" I call, until she pops out, discreetly chuckling.

She snatches Leo's toys directly under his gaze. She finds moments when he sits unguarded on my lap to yank him by his hair and quietly lodge herself between us while he screams.

At the playground, when she swings in the baby swing with the sun kissing her face and the wind dancing through her wisps of hair, I have to glance away, as if she might be a mirage. Peter suddenly buries his face against my shoulder.

"She escaped," he says. "She really escaped."

Most days, she inhabits her life so naturally that I can almost forget her time in the NICU. It's only when she puts up a ferocious fight—against her brother's incursions, against my attempts to trim her nails or fasten a row of buttons—that the grim set of her face and the furious flailing of her limbs still my heart.

That was you.

With the arrival of autumn, my annual hay fever sets in. Each family outing feels as if it could be the last of the year. The winds gather, the leaves fall.

Peter is cautiously optimistic about this new phase of his *HuffPost* career. The corporate drama surrounding the merger seems to have abated. Peter has largely extricated himself from personnel intrigue to focus on journalism: overseeing the launch of a new international news section and hiring the site's first foreign correspondents.

For me, the management of Mila's sessions and appointments

and bills has finally settled into a part-time job. Any day now, I'll get back to my writing.

But I have shooting aches in my hands and wrists and sharp, twisting pains in my stomach. A molar where I had a root canal throbs beneath its shiny crown. My insomnia rears up. The incision is still a raised purplish scar, the surrounding skin faintly numb.

Each time my husband and I make love requires a concerted effort to forget.

At my daughter's one-year checkup, she weighs fourteen pounds: what Leo weighed at two months. By Dr. Haber's reckoning, Mila is doing great—for a baby who suffered what she did. Her movements are still a little stiff, her voice a little weak. On the checklists in the therapists' progress reports, all the things she can do are still vastly outnumbered by all the things she can't.

When my family gathers for a combined birthday party for Mila and Mateo, I'm overwhelmed with fatigue.

Every time she takes a tumble, I see that billowing cloud. Even when we play peekaboo and I pretend not to know where she is, my skin sometimes prickles with fear.

The more I love her, the more there is to lose.

Another heap of hospital bills arrives in the foyer, jamming the mailbox and spilling onto the floor. Some I've already paid, some had previously showed a zero balance, others I'm receiving for the first time though the dates of service are over a year ago. The representatives are as pleasant and powerless as ever.

I have more than a year's worth of my own checkups to make up. Every time I lie back for an exam, my legs quake. I can't shake the sense that the slightest medical problem, if properly traced, would lead to some deep ruin within my body that nearly killed my daughter.

The internist interrogates me about my stomach pains, which are most acute at night. Especially when—I realize but don't say out loud—I'm alone in the dark. He prescribes a pill to calm the gastrointestinal tract and a low-dose antianxiety medication.

The dentist can't figure out why I feel pain where everything looks intact. The endodontist suspects a microfracture, an invisible crack that allowed bacteria to fester. A periodontist extracts the tooth with a few vicious tugs. By the time I enter the subway, the anesthesia has worn off. I stumble at the top of the slush-covered staircase and fall halfway down to the platform.

People stare but don't offer a hand. Blood is seeping through the cotton balls wadded at my gums. The pain throbs against the rattling of the train.

I can't trust myself to endure pain anymore. I tried to ignore the pain that woke me at four thirty that morning, when my daughter's life was already seeping from me.

The winter is the most brutal that anyone in the city can remember. The sidewalk cracks, the pipes freeze. Peter heads to Davos for the World Economic Forum, where the *World Post* is launched. Already, the resources devoted to his reporters are dwarfed by the marketing and PR. In the photo that runs in the *Times*, his expression looks skeptical, though maybe only to me.

I push Leo's stroller home from school in a blizzard; it takes us an hour to travel two blocks. The flu strikes him, then Lily, then me. Mice pop out from the kitchen cabinets. Mila wakes up dry-heaving and vomits every mouthful of liquid I manage to get her to drink.

Leo pees in every corner of the living room, though he recently completed potty training largely on his own. "I don't like this house. I want different house!" he screams.

My throat is so swollen I haven't eaten for three days. By the time Peter returns, I've literally collapsed.

When I finally stumble out of bed, January is nearly over. My clothes hang loosely. My kids are healthy, busy with a new toy kitchen. Leo has added his collection of farm animals to the wooden fruits and vegetables on the stove.

"Cook chicken, cook pig, cook cow." He picks up the farmer, then wags a righteous finger. "No cook people," he says.

"Mama," Mila says. She says *Mama* now. *Baobao* when she wants to be picked up. *Dada, hi, bye.*

She guzzles whole milk. She loves pancakes. She climbs up the entire staircase by herself. She flips through books page by page. She pretends to talk on the phone.

She develops a favorite trick of climbing to the top of the couch and glancing back at me with a daredevil grin as she lets go, launching herself onto the cushions while my heart stops.

And then, one morning, she takes two steps, two tiny, wobbly, earthshaking steps, before she plops down and lifts her arms toward me, wanting a hug.

When I pick her up, something inside me has shifted. I hug her more tightly, more roughly. Who am I to handle her as if she might vanish? My daughter has staked her claim to this earth more than most of us ever do.

I twirl her, I toss her, I swing her upside down. Her eyes light up. Her laughter rings out. Her hair floats in midair. There's no way I won't catch her, no chance of her slipping out of my arms.

PART IV

Whose distressed baby is it?
—*NEW YORKER* HEADLINE, FEBRUARY 11, 2014

57

ON THE AFTERNOON OF Thursday, February 6, the house is quiet—Mila napping, Leo in daycare—when a series of e-mails from Peter appears in my in-box. They contain phrases I can't comprehend, somehow connecting our daughter with his corporate boss, along with links to articles with some variation of this headline:

AOL CEO TIM ARMSTRONG BLAMES BENEFIT CUTS ON
"DISTRESSED BABIES."

I click on one of the links: *New York* magazine's Daily Intelligencer. The tone of the article is incredulous and derisive, but also ironic and knowing, in the way of most digital media.

"Tim Armstrong should probably stop doing conference calls. The AOL CEO, who fired a guy during one for taking his picture, was perhaps too brash once again today, baldly telling his entire company that their benefits were being rolled back because two women went and got themselves pregnant."

I can't make sense of Armstrong's quote. The words float off the page in disjointed fragments. "Two things that happened in 2012 ... distressed babies that were born ... a million dollars each ..."

At the bottom of the page, there's a sampling of tweets on the subject:

"I swear I didn't have any babies in 2012. Don't hate me for messing up your 401K."

This is from a *HuffPost* reporter who works for Peter.

I close the link. I close my computer.

I tell myself that these walls are solid. That my daughter is safe, and I'm not going under.

Peter and I have plans to go to a reading that evening, then to a Nets game: our first date night in months. For the rest of the day, I don't look at my e-mail. I don't open any news sites.

When I head to the bookstore, I'm lipsticked, buoyant, impermeable. The reading is bound to be lighthearted and diverting, on the subject of romantic love, by the "Modern Love" editor who published my essay about our float down the Mekong, our struggle and triumph as a couple.

I kiss Peter hello. He asks if I've seen his e-mails. Yes, I say, but I don't understand.

Peter explains that one of his deputy editors knocked on his door that morning to ask for guidance on a breaking story. Tim Armstrong had just been interviewed on CNBC about the company's latest earnings, which he called "Olympian . . . the best results we've put in in the last decade"—and about his recent cuts to the employee retirement savings plan, which he blamed on Obamacare.

Peter's team had recently skewered a number of ultrarich CEOs who claimed that Obamacare was forcing them to offset increased costs onto the backs of their employees. Now his own CEO, one widely known to have a personal fortune of nearly half a billion dollars, had just aligned himself with that pantheon.

Peter's personal reaction was disgust as an employee of a company that incessantly trumpeted itself as a happy, enlightened place to work, with "Go AOL!" chants, free coconut water and granola bars, and Friday-afternoon beer kegs. Not to mention its self-proclaimed mission, like every other tech company, to improve the world with its innovations. Not to mention the *HuffPost*'s brand, specifically, as a progressive, anti-elitist forum.

But his instincts were journalistic. He told his editor to cover the story straight up, without snark and without pulling any punches, either.

Half an hour later, the editor knocked on his door again. "You won't believe this," she said.

Tim Armstrong had just held a town hall meeting to further explain the benefit cuts, during which he offered up this clarification:

"Two things that happened in 2012," he said. "We had two AOLers that had distressed babies that were born that we paid a million dollars each to make sure those babies were okay in general. And those are the things that add up into our benefits cost. So when we had the final decision about what benefits to cut because of the increased health care costs, we made the decision, and I made the decision, to basically change the 401(k) plan."

Peter's jaw dropped. In order to justify corporate cost cutting, Tim Armstrong was shifting the blame from Obamacare to employees' babies?

Again, he emphasized the need to tune out the fact that the CEO in question was their boss. He and the editor discussed angles of analysis and whom to call at AOL for comment.

Then the editor said, "He's talking about your baby, isn't he?"

Until that moment, this hadn't occurred to Peter. Ever since we brought Mila home, he'd been so enraptured that he couldn't wrap his mind around anyone slapping such a label on her. Never mind his own CEO, before an audience of more than five thousand of his co-workers.

"Yeah," he said. "I guess he is."

On his own computer screen, Peter watched the headlines

DEANNA FEI

proliferate, from *Capital New York* (ARMSTRONG: "DISTRESSED BABIES" FIGURED IN 401(K) ROLL-BACK) to *Fortune* (ADD TIM ARMSTRONG'S "DISTRESSED BABIES" TO THE PILE OF GAFFES) to *Daily Kos* (BREAKING: THERE'S STILL AN AOL, AND ITS CEO IS STILL AN A-HOLE) to *Gawker* (graphic: Tim Armstrong's salary in distressed babies).

On Twitter, "distressed babies" was becoming a meme:

"How many distressed babies does AOL pay this guy?"

"I hope these 'distressed babies' are happy."

On the overhead TV screens throughout the newsroom, Peter watched close-ups of Armstrong rotate among playbacks of the CEO's previous blunders. On cable news shows, talking heads debated health care costs, privacy laws, the Affordable Care Act, corporate responsibility, crisis management, potential legal and civil liabilities, AOL stock prices—all in the context of "distressed babies."

His own newsroom gawked and tittered at the spectacle. A number of Peter's colleagues—editors, writers, PR flacks—knocked on his door to gossip: *Can you believe this? What an idiot.*

One of the first reports—by *Re/code*'s Kara Swisher, a prominent tech journalist famously close to Armstrong—summarized Armstrong's town hall comments as referring to "the difficult and costly pregnancies of two employees," as if "distressed babies" could only be the result of such circumstances. All the subsequent speculation had focused on "AOL moms." None of the experts challenged these assumptions. None of the commentators seemed to consider the possibility that one of the employees in question could be a father.

Except for those of Peter's co-workers who knew the barest outlines of our daughter's arrival and immediately identified her as one of those "distressed babies." The sympathetic ones came by Peter's office to express recognition of his uncomfortable position. *Hey, he's talking about your kid, right? How's she doing? How are you?*

236

He was just trying to do his job. He assigned more pieces, brainstormed more angles. But he didn't edit the copy. In that capacity, he realized, he was conflicted out. Somewhere in the middle of this frenzy, he felt the need to reach out to me.

Now he touches me tenderly, expresses concern for my emotional state. I brush him off. Whatever happened, it still seems dissociated from me.

I manage to tell Peter that I found his e-mails off-putting. The tone, the brevity, the presentation of "distressed babies" as a media spectacle. As if the story was about someone else, even as he was telling me that it involved our family.

He apologizes. I accept this and assure him that everything is fine.

Throughout the reading, I smile and hold his hand. We accept a red heart-shaped bracelet from the editor with a laugh and chat about life in New York with small children.

On our way to the basketball arena, my head starts to pound. Through the game, my stomach churns. I can't separate the roaring of the crowd from the roaring in my own ears.

Walking home, I can't bring myself to hold my husband's hand. Inside my pockets, my fists are clenched. I'm not angry, not yet. I'm trying to hold myself together.

In bed, Peter asks me what's wrong.

To me, Tim Armstrong might as well be a titan, an oligarch, the archvillain of a comic book franchise. Likewise, the blogosphere and Twitterverse might as well exist in another galaxy. Peter is my husband, the father of my babies, the man in bed beside me.

"I don't understand," I say again. "Why did you send me those links?"

Peter says that he felt the need to loop me in.

Loop me in. This strikes me as a canned bit of corporate-speak, the kind that's permanently infiltrated our everyday vocabulary, like *circle back* or *touch base*. Phrases that come from the same realm in which the head of a large American corporation publicly called my child a "distressed baby" and attached a price tag to her life.

Did Peter think I'd be titillated, like a jaded member of the media? Fired up, like a finger-wagging professional commentator? Appalled, like an ordinary informed citizen before she heads home to her own family?

My walls are collapsing. Why didn't my husband shelter me from this storm?

It's only when Peter watches me break down that the distance he has maintained between himself and the story finally crumbles. Once the impact hits him, it hits hard.

Yet now that he sees my perspective, I see his. How was he supposed to pull off the feat of juggling his roles as my husband, our children's father, a principled journalist, and a good employee—one whose family depends on his salary as well as his company health benefits—today of all days?

While I finally drift to sleep, spent and medicated, Peter finds himself unable to lie down. He pounds out a note to Tim Armstrong, writing directly as the father of one of those babies. He explains Mila's arrival and what our family endured and how he gave his best at work throughout the ordeal. He explains how easily colleagues identified our daughter, our sense of violation, his anger at being scapegoated.

Through the rest of the night, we both toss and turn. At five thirty in the morning, Mila wakes. Peter gets up to take care of her. There is a reply from Tim Armstrong in his in-box, an offer to discuss the matter in more detail. The sky is still dark when the phone rings.

Tim Armstrong apologizes, emphasizing his ability to relate as a father of three. He says that he meant to explain his pride in how the company takes care of its employees. He says that he was pointing to the saving of those babies as a worthy expenditure, the kind he chose to safeguard over the previous structure of the 401(k) plan.

Holding Mila on his lap, Peter speaks not as an employee to his boss, but man to man. He is somewhat appeased by Armstrong's responsiveness, his regret, even his explanation.

Peter starts to say that one unfortunate aspect of this firestorm is that AOL actually provides relatively generous employee benefits, for which our family has been particularly grateful, and that he doesn't understand—

At this point, Armstrong becomes energized. He seems to think that Peter is offering his insights as a loyal employee, one who has been called upon numerous times in the past to huddle with him and Arianna to strategize extricating the company from the latest PR disaster. Armstrong pivots to suggesting Peter talk with AOL's head of HR, to share his thoughts on their benefits package and the best ways to communicate with employees about changes.

Still groggy in bed, I can hear the shift in Peter's voice as he acquiesces.

Then Tim Armstrong asks if there is anything he can do to make this up to our family.

"Anything," he repeats. *"Anything."*

For my husband, this has become both personal and political. Wronged as we may be, our family is one of the privileged families in America today. What about that critically ill mother in rural Louisiana whose lifetime of labor hasn't earned her the ability to afford medical care? What about the next corporation, the next round of cuts, the next vulnerable employees?

However readily Armstrong has expressed his personal regret to him this morning, Peter knows this phone call cost him nothing.

He asks for a public apology.

Armstrong replies that some further statement will be forthcoming.

By then, Leo is up, Mila hungry, the chaos of the morning in full swing. We rush through breakfast and showers, tooth brushing and face wiping. I pack Leo's lunch and snacks and a toy for show-and-tell. I bundle up my boy and kiss him and Peter goodbye.

Then I turn to my daughter. I can't see her clearly anymore through the black water rising around me.

A million dollars. Is that how much her life cost? Can she justify such a number?

For the rest of the day, I feed, I entertain, I bathe, I soothe, I don't allow myself a moment's pause. When both kids are asleep and Peter and I collapse onto the couch, all I want to do is watch our show.

But Peter can hardly sit. His shoulders are stiff, his fists clenched.

The media uproar over "distressed babies" has continued at a fever pitch. More talking heads, more commentary, more analysis, more tweets. Instead of a public apology, Tim Armstrong issued an internal memo, which was leaked to the media almost immediately:

"As we discussed at the town hall, we care about you and the company—a lot . . . In that context, I mentioned high-risk pregnancy as just one of many examples of how our company supports families when they are in need . . . As I have said over and over again, our employees are our greatest asset. Let's move forward together as a team."

With each clarification that Tim Armstrong issues, our family seems more and more at fault somehow, and our daughter's humanity seems less and less evident.

"All day, I've wanted to post a photo of her," Peter says. "You want to blame her for your cost cutting? You want to send out your wiseass tweets? At least take a moment to acknowledge this child. At least take a good, hard look at her face."

I nod. My chest feels so tight that I don't trust myself to speak.

"But I can't," Peter says helplessly. "I can't."

My husband has already tried to confront his boss in a private, honorable manner. He can't defend our daughter in public. But I don't have to cower like a damsel in distress. My daughter sure as hell never did.

"I can," I say.

Peter stares at me. We both know that I can't simply post a photo. For the first time since my daughter's arrival, I know what I need to write.

But I'm paralyzed with fear. For starters, Tim Armstrong could fire my husband. He could wipe out our income and our health insurance. Maybe he could blacklist us in the universe somehow. Right now, I feel as if he could obliterate my family with a one-word voice command and a jab of his fingertip.

I'm aware of how small I am in the world. After all, I was a preemie, too, with a birth weight below five pounds—a weight that once seemed shockingly small. At five foot two, I've never really wished to be bigger. My mother and grandmother stand below five feet. My older sister is a half inch taller than me, my younger sister a half inch shorter. I never associated being small with being weak or insignificant.

When my daughter arrived at one pound nine ounces, her size was the measure of her existence. She was about as small as a person can be.

Everything about Tim Armstrong is big. His name, his rank, his titles. His six-foot-four build, still that of the boarding school star athlete. The long strides he takes onto a stage, his mighty handshake, his deep, booming monotone. His visage on business front pages and company rollout campaigns, with his cinematic hair and cheekbones and jaw.

His net worth of four hundred million dollars. His mansion in Greenwich, Connecticut, his multi-million-dollar salary. His world of mergers and acquisitions, market capitalization and cash flow, shareholders and stock options.

I shake my head as if I'm shaking off a bad dream. What if our daughter was a drag on the company's bottom line? What right do I have to complain?

"It just doesn't make sense," Peter says. "That one baby's hospital bills could affect their finances. Either Armstrong is lying or the company was reckless."

I tell Peter to turn on our show. We both pretend to watch.

Ever since my daughter's arrival, my shame and guilt seem to have taken up permanent residence in my body along with my organs and bones, as fixed and familiar as they are unseen and unexamined. Likewise, my sense of being a burden, of encumbering others because of my failure to hold on to my own baby, has become the hidden pulse of my daily existence.

Somehow Tim Armstrong managed to broadcast those innermost feelings at a companywide meeting before they became fodder for the twenty-four-hour news cycle. And now that those feelings are out there for the world to digest, I can finally take a closer look at them myself.

What did I do wrong other than experience a medical emergency?

What resources did my daughter use other than the health insurance that my husband and I purchased?

How did Tim Armstrong and his corporation extend themselves for my family other than by complying with the basic terms of our benefits?

Distressed babies. I know about "distressed jeans" and "distressed leather." I've heard the terms *distressed securities* and *distressed properties.* Or *distressed merchandise*: damaged goods.

"Distressed babies" sounds like another bit of corporate-speak, except that I doubt it shows up on any MBA vocabulary list. The term is both a dehumanizing insult and a strange euphemism that seems intended to demonstrate extra sensitivity on the part of the speaker—as opposed to, say, *premature babies* or *sickly babies* or *goddamn pain-in-the-ass babies.*

It aims for a show of sympathy while positioning the speaker as the hero of this scenario. It brings to mind a fussy infant wailing to be picked up rather than a child fighting for every minute of her life.

Distressed babies that were born that we paid a million dollars each to make sure those babies were okay in general.

After all these months of struggling to say those words myself—*she was born*—now Tim Armstrong has said them for me, in a context that suggests that she probably shouldn't have been. *Babies that were born.* "That," not "who."

We paid a million dollars. Did he personally pay her bills? After all my dealings with the insurance company, this is news to me.

To make sure those babies were okay in general. Did he demand some guarantee from the doctors that I never received? Does Mila count as "okay in general" now? If not, should she be written off as a bad investment?

I tell myself that people make mistakes. But I can't pretend that these off-the-cuff remarks don't reveal a damning, perhaps unconscious judgment of me and my daughter.

Even if I accept that Armstrong's intention was not to scapegoat *those babies* but to point out his pride in having paid for their care—an apparently exorbitant expense that somehow drained AOL's coffers to the point that he was forced to recoup it from another component of employee benefits—that judgment just became explicit in his assumption that "distressed babies" must be the result of "high-risk pregnancies." Which no one in the media has questioned, either.

The implication is that our baby was a risky proposition from the start, and therefore her care was optional. We selfishly claimed more than our fair share of health benefits, and Tim Armstrong and AOL bailed us out. The medical treatment that saved our daughter's life was not a basic right or even a contractual obligation, but an act of corporate charity and proof of Tim Armstrong's personal generosity. And Peter's co-workers have only us to blame for those cuts to their retirement savings.

I reach for Peter's hand. I tell him that if he can move on as if this never happened, I can, too. Peter says that if that's what I want, he can. We go back and forth, around and around.

At last, Peter says, "I guess I can't." His anguish is plain on his face.

Ever since our daughter's arrival, my rawer emotions and overt trauma have often taken precedence over his. Sometimes, I remind myself, my husband needs rescuing, too.

When I sit down at my desk, it's past midnight. My hands are trembling and my heart is pounding, but my head feels very clear.

Thirteen months ago, my daughter left the hospital and never looked back. I'm the one living as if I'm trapped behind walls of glass.

If I don't come forward as the mother of my baby, I might as well forsake her. If I don't reclaim her story, I might as well label her a burden, a tragedy, a creature who shouldn't exist.

So I write. All the details that have seemed unspeakable, I write.

I'm the mother of one of those "distressed babies." I'm the reason the CEO of a large corporation felt the need to cut benefits.

A million dollars. At this point, I have no way of knowing if Tim Armstrong and AOL actually paid that amount, though this accounting certainly doesn't square with my rudimentary grasp of how insurance works. I understand that a CEO might have a different approach to valuation of a human life than, say, a mother. But I'm not sure, in the final accounting, how many of us could survive such a calculus.

Would it have occurred to Armstrong to single out the medical expenses of an employee who survived a car crash, or needed heart surgery, or got breast cancer?

For the first time, it occurs to me that when Dr. Kahn described Mila's birth as *catastrophic*, she meant the word in the medical sense. A catastrophic medical event is, almost by definition, unforeseeable and unpreventable.

Yes, our daughter needed costly intensive care. Yes, my husband and I are grateful—indelibly grateful—that our employer-subsidized plan covered most of those expenses.

But isn't that the whole point of health insurance?

At last, I describe Mila's first steps, those two tiny steps that she took in the days leading to Tim Armstrong's town hall meeting. And I finally use the word that, for me, might be the most dangerous word of all.

Miracle.

I don't mean that my daughter emerged from her birth completely unscathed. I don't mean that she is an act of divine intervention more than a person. I don't mean that she has to be a miracle—or even "okay in general"—in order to justify her existence.

She is a miracle in the way that any child taking her first steps is a miracle. And yes, she deserves a little extra credit. Some recognition of her strength, not only her suffering; of her resilience, not only her damage.

58

AMID THE CHAOS OF the morning—we're heading to the birthday party of a classmate of Leo's, we're out of clean clothes, we haven't prepared a gift—the question becomes where to publish. Ever since Arianna invited me to blog for her site nearly four years ago, the *HuffPost* has been my default platform: no pay but a potentially massive, if often reflexively knowing readership. Clearly, this essay would present an awkward conundrum for the editors. But even if I could set that aside, I don't want the *HuffPost* flash this time, no matter how many clicks it might attract. I want a rarer currency in the media landscape these days: simple, unvarnished, old-fashioned sincerity.

An editor at *Slate* expresses eagerness to run the piece. Just as we're about to publish, I learn from the editor that, hours earlier, Tim Armstrong announced a reversal in an e-mail to employees: "We have decided to change the policy back to a per-pay-period matching contribution . . . On a personal note, I made a mistake and I apologize for my comments last week at the town hall when I mentioned specific health care examples in trying to explain our decision making process around our employee benefit programs."

This strikes me as a belated attempt to follow the script of apology theater so that business can resume as usual. The first outlet to report Armstrong's statement, *Business Insider*, recounts the developments as if the reporter fancies himself Tim Armstrong's mind reader. The "distressed babies" comment was simply a "gaffe," an instance of "misspeaking," he writes. Without attribution, he states that Armstrong's true intention was "to illustrate that despite the fact that AOL was changing its 401(k) policy, it still cared about employees." Purely to prove that point, "Armstrong told a story about two women at AOL who had complicated pregnancies."

Still, in the interest of fairness, I insert a mention of Armstrong's statement, with a link to the *Business Insider* report, and post my final draft.

Meanwhile, Peter notifies Arianna Huffington about my decision to speak out. She is Peter's direct boss, after all, and among boldfaced names, she has become ubiquitous, counting virtually every influential person in the world as a personal friend. If anyone can blacklist us in the universe, she can.

When young women visit her office, Arianna habitually hands out copies of one of her many books: *On Becoming Fearless*. Now, in the midst of promoting her latest title, she has reinvented herself as an evangelist for well-being and mindfulness, for redefining success beyond money and power. Even if she won't publicly malign the man who holds her corporate purse strings, both Peter and I can't help hoping for her private support at this moment.

Instead, she e-mails Peter that my decision is "very disappointing." She asks to talk to me directly to dissuade me from speaking out. When Peter declines, she prods him further. He responds that, as she well knows, I'm a writer, with my own voice and my own story to tell. He says that it's not his place to muzzle me. She asks how he can possibly refuse to intervene.

Much later, I will see her inspirational tweet and status update for that day, likely automated, a quote from the Roman emperor and philosopher Marcus Aurelius: "The first rule is to keep an untroubled spirit. The second is to look things in the face and know them for what they are."

When Mila wakes from her morning nap and I lift her out of her crib, I'm still light-headed with fear, but my heart feels free. There is no barrier at all between us.

At our favorite home-style Italian restaurant, I'm shoveling food into my babies' mouths and mine while peeling stray noodles off their clothes and my hair when my phone rings. Producers at CNN want an exclusive sit-down. By the time Peter and I put the kids down for their afternoon naps, the national networks are calling— the evening news, the morning shows. I have no idea how they got my phone number, but there doesn't seem to be much point in asking. Privacy is not my foremost concern at this juncture.

Yes, you can zoom in on my daughter's face. Yes, you can film her crawling around, dancing to "The Wheels on the Bus," laughing when I swing her up in the air.

Yes, I will sit down and tell you everything that happened. Everything you want to know about her and me, and maybe some details you never wanted to hear. You want to see the hospital bills, too? Take the whole stack.

You want some photos? Even in her earliest days? Are you sure?

This is her, too. I won't be ashamed any longer. I'm proud of her, goddammit.

Our only stipulation is that Peter won't be interviewed or filmed. After all, he still has to show up to work in the morning.

The first TV crew is already ringing the doorbell when I change into an unstained sweater and clear a path in the living room through the toys. On camera, Mila simply performs her role as the lovely baby that she is. Even Leo sits and sings and plays on cue—at least in part because the TV reporters, in addition to being thoughtful and sensitive and personable, are all attractive females. Each time they take their leave, he asks them when they'll come back.

By nightfall, I've agreed to a handful of interviews the next day—basically, the most reputable outlets that managed to reach me first. I've gleaned that my in-box contains a slew of media requests, from Al Jazeera to the Fox Business Network, CNBC to *Inside Edition*, the *New York Post* to NPR. I don't have a strategy here: no lawyer, no PR adviser, no media handler. All day, Peter and I have also been struggling through the ordinary frenzy of a Sunday in deep winter with a two-year-old and a baby.

After we've put them to bed and Peter has insisted that I eat a few bites of dinner, he shows me an e-mail addressed to me from Tim Armstrong.

Tim Armstrong writes that he read my piece. He offers a gracious, unreserved apology for the hurt he caused. He says that this has nothing to do with the company or the press or the public damage, but is simply to express his regret and emphasize that he never intended to inflict any harm on me and my family. He asks if we can talk as soon as I feel ready.

I take his call. Even through my phone, Tim Armstrong sounds big, an implausibly sonorous voice booming down from a mountaintop. But he also sounds like a man who might be having one of the worst days of his life.

I accept his apology. I'm calm but dazed. "Okay," I say. "I hear you. I appreciate it."

In truth, I feel bad for him. A CEO is human, too.

After a pause, he repeats a certain question. Is there anything he can do for me and my family? Anything. If I can think of anything—*anything at all*—please don't hesitate to ask.

Over the years, I've heard various rumors about employees with grievances who accepted payouts from the company and quietly went away. I don't know how such negotiations take place. I don't know how Tim Armstrong might signal his willingness to cut a check. But the more he draws out the question, the more difficult it becomes to escape the sense that I'm being invited to name a price.

"Okay," I say again. "Thank you. Have a good night."

I understand that there are situations where money might be an appropriate form of atonement. Who knows what I might have said if we were less fortunate? I might wonder, but I'll never second-guess my response. I simply can't attach a price tag to my daughter's humanity or my silence.

I'm collapsing into bed and setting my alarm—at 5:45 A.M., a car will ferry me to the NBC studios—when a producer from the *Today* show calls to ask a few follow-up questions. Have I heard from Tim Armstrong? Did I accept his apology?

Simple enough: yes and yes. I'm not well versed enough in crisis management to understand that this third act of apology theater will begin to take precedence over the story of my daughter in the headlines and sound bites tomorrow, though I will soon learn that Tim Armstrong and AOL have just hired an outside PR firm that specializes in such matters to bail out their own flailing team of flacks, reportedly at an estimated cost of $100,000.

Then the producer inquires about a *Business Insider* report that contains the anonymous claim that "as a result of the extended care for the women, AOL paid $2 million 'above and beyond' what was necessary." She directs me to the link and waits for my rejoinder.

How do I defend my daughter against such numbers? The numbers seem to carry such solid, objective, inarguable weight, while she is still just a baby.

Then another e-mail catches my attention. I don't recognize the sender's name, but in the next moment, I feel I already know her.

"I can't thank you enough," she writes. "I am the mom of the other 'distressed baby' . . . I don't feel like I can speak out without jeopardizing my job . . . I am so glad you did." She tells me that her co-workers immediately identified her daughter as one of those "distressed babies," too. She shares a simple, brief version of her own story. And then she writes, "You captured perfectly how I've been feeling, and said it better than I probably ever could. Thank you. All I've wanted to do since Thursday is hold my daughter close, and upon reading your article, I wanted to give you and your daughter a hug too."

I read and reread her words. I can't back down now.

I pull up the *Business Insider* report again. *The extended care for the women.* Do they mean my fourth morning in the hospital following the cesarean? The anesthesia, the gas mask, the stitches?

"Above and beyond" what was necessary. How would Tim Armstrong and AOL know which charges might have been "necessary" versus "above and beyond"? Where do they think a less generous employer might have drawn the line?

I manage to explain to the producer that I've seen all the bills from my and my daughter's hospital stays, most of them more than once, and I've never seen any bills that appear to have been paid simply as an act of corporate largesse.

It doesn't occur to me, though I wish it had, to call back Tim Armstrong and say, *Here's what you can do for me and my family. Explain this.*

The morning is a blur of car services and temporary ID badges, professionally wielded hair dryers and powder puffs, microphones and studio lights. At the *Today* show, I'm alone in the cavernous glass-walled studio. Savannah Guthrie will talk to me via satellite from the Sochi Winter Olympics. For all the harried producers and technicians in the shadows behind me, it's just another start to the workweek.

In this blinding glare, outside my own home and away from my babies, I feel raw and exposed. But I can't retie that yellow ribbon now.

Throughout the day's interviews, I fudge the truth once: when

I'm asked if I know the identity of the other "AOL mom." I say only that I don't want to infringe on another family's privacy. Later, she will tell me that she knew from the way that I paused and looked into the camera that I'd read her note. That she felt I gave her a voice, too, and she couldn't help feeling proud of me. I will tell her that hearing this from her in itself made my speaking out worthwhile.

I still have no idea how my piece has been picked up, syndicated, Facebooked, tweeted: all the metrics said to measure impact. What I know I'll never forget is the outpouring of feeling from strangers all around me. Teary hugs, gruff asides, the simplest expressions of recognition of my daughter.

Every now and then, I glimpse the split-screen images spliced into my interviews: the sweet, rosy face of my baby girl juxtaposed with Tim Armstrong's inhumanly chiseled visage. Suddenly it hardly seems like a fair fight.

I do my best to shift the conversation out of the battle arena. I reply that Tim Armstrong's apology seemed heartfelt and that I forgive him. That my husband is at work and I'm not really worried about retribution. That I haven't talked to a lawyer and I haven't thought about suing.

I explain that my goal is not to vilify anyone, but to point out the injustice that was done to my daughter in the hopes that, going forward, we might be more careful about reducing human lives to dollar figures. I acknowledge that, in a country where so many are forced to do without basic health care, it's important to have a rational discussion about costs—and that as the mother of a baby who spent three months in intensive care, I certainly don't take health care spending for granted.

At the same time, I assert that no individual deserves to be publicly singled out for her medical expenses—let alone a baby.

Throughout the day, journalists continue to write and call—to be fair, including a *Business Insider* reporter, who wants to know if "sources close to AOL management" lied to him about having paid two million dollars "above and beyond." Some reporters say that the public response is so strong that they want to keep the story rolling somehow. They ask if I can think of other angles to pursue.

I'm starting to grasp that the issues involved are much bigger than me and my daughter, and that our story has touched a nerve that runs much deeper than a few callous words from a gaffe-prone CEO, but right now, I just want to rush home to my family.

By the time I finish my last interview, the news cycle is turning anew. In the theater of public apology, my forgiveness has brought closure, and tonight, that's fine with me.

Mila's face has never looked so familiar and unaffected. Leo lays a concerned hand on my shoulder.

"Mama, you feel better?" he asks. "You're all done TV?"

Yes, I assure him, and I hug my babies so tight that they squeal.

59

OVER THE NEXT DAYS and weeks, people stop me in the neighborhood to express their sentiments about my daughter—strangers who recognize us, acquaintances who never knew about Mila's prematurity, friends who did but confess they had no idea what it meant. Even now, I still feel the urge to hide my daughter in my coat and duck my head and flee.

While I've stopped responding to media requests, it's more difficult to ignore the queries from organizations that see in me and my daughter an opportunity to rally for an important cause: congressional committees, nonprofits, support groups. But I'm not one to step onto a soapbox, and I'm not ready to speak for anyone but myself and my daughter, and I don't know what causes we represent, if any.

Most of all, I want life to finally feel normal again.

Then I start to read the messages piled up in my in-box from ordinary people across the country and around the world: fathers, grandparents, aunts, entire families signing off together. They send blessings and prayers to my daughter. They say that they know my love for her from the words that I wrote. They tell me that, one day soon, she'll be proud of me for speaking out.

They acknowledge the anguish of her arrival and the joy she has brought. They congratulate her on her first steps. They celebrate her fierceness, her heroism, even her mischievous grin and the light in her eyes. "Your daughter is beautiful and the world is a better place because she is here," one person writes, and my tears spill over.

People thank me for standing up for them, too, no matter that my motivations weren't quite so selfless. A social worker and teacher who adopted five children with Down syndrome. People who describe themselves as "ordinary workers who don't deserve a bait-and-switch on their 401(k)." One woman simply writes, "For all of us who 'use more than their fair share' of the health-care pie, thank you."

Parents write to me about their own "distressed babies," co-opting the phrase—*I'm also the mother of a "distressed baby" . . . As the proud father of two of my own "distressed babies"*—defiantly, with dignity and wit, yet without denying the pain. Some restrict themselves to bare stats, trusting in our mutual fluency in that unforgettable code: "26 weeks and 2 lbs . . . NICU for 10 weeks . . . [now in] college and playing Division III lacrosse." "25 weeks, 1 lb. 15 oz . . . transfusion, respiratory distress, cardiac arrests, PDA ligations . . . She'll be three in April."

Others write long pages of stunning eloquence and clarity, recounting the sudden bleeding, the water breaking early, the car accident that precipitated the labor, the complicated delivery. The tolls on their careers, their marriages, their other children. Flashbacks, panic attacks, symptoms of PTSD that strike a chord of recognition in me.

Yet what wins out in the end is the gratitude, the wonder, the love. "Our pride and joy." "It gets easier . . . You make new memories that help move the other ones a little further back." "I am writing this from the side of a pool watching my brave girl jump into the deep water—all with her trademark ear to ear grin."

People who were born prematurely and given grim prognoses write to me, too: "I am now a successful professor who teaches statistics and psychology. It's going to be ok; the miracles have only just begun."

Others share tragic stories, or redefine the happy ending. A father who lost three babies to extreme prematurity and never was able to talk to his wife or the doctors about what happened. A Canadian woman who attaches a photo of herself and her husband tan and smiling in Florida and describes herself as, among many other things, a breast cancer survivor and "the mother of a 37-year-old son who suffers from athetoid cerebral palsy with a cognitive function of ten months." A mother who brought home twin girls after three months in the NICU, then lost one of them to SIDS; her surviving daughter is now planning to become a doctor.

This is a birth story, too, they affirm. *It might not be the kind of story most people want to hear, but it's how our children came into this world. We need to tell our stories, too.*

Others write to me without an ending, from the NICU, beside their babies, among ventilators and hand sanitizer and breast pumps.

Some people write to me about babies whose need for medical care had nothing to do with prematurity: a cleft lip and palate; "a twist in his upper intestines"; a common heart defect; a cyst on the brain; "a random massive stroke after birth after a normal, healthy pregnancy"; simple "failure to thrive." All of them could have been labeled "distressed babies," too.

Here is all the support and solidarity that I thought I'd never find. Several readers wryly note that Tim Armstrong couldn't have known the potential power of his coinage, how it would give us a way to connect over traumas that once seemed unspeakable.

"I don't feel so alone suddenly," people write. "I thought I was the only one who felt that way." "I have tried very hard to forget."

One mother who became a "prematurity awareness advocate" thanks me for educating people about the experience of having a premature baby. "I only have one thing to add," she writes. "You did nothing wrong. You did not cause your daughter's pre-term birth. I can't stop you from feeling guilty but remember: you are not to blame."

I find myself reading these words repeatedly, until the tears spill over once again. Now I have no choice but to believe this because I know it is true of all the parents who have entrusted their stories to me. Not one of them is to blame.

One father shares the story of how the premature birth of his daughter—now twenty-four and a thriving composer—bankrupted his formerly affluent family. "I tell you this story not for sympathy. But, to demonstrate a point," he writes. "Somehow, we are perceived as shameless takers, an experience that you have shared recently. Yet, we had no hand in the creation of our circumstances."

One advocate who refuses to accept my polite demurrals is a woman named Deborah Peel, a Texas physician who founded a nonprofit called Patient Privacy Rights. Her numerous e-mails teem with exclamation points and boldface references to "citizens' rights," "personal health data," and "electronic health systems." She includes links to media interviews in which she discussed the broader implications of the "distressed babies" controversy, which she summarizes for me this way:

"Every employer can do what Tim Armstrong did to you."

As she persists in asking to talk over the phone and even meet at my house, I can't help wondering if she might be unhinged. According to Peel, my daughter and I are the embodiment of the insidious perils surrounding the health privacy of all Americans.

Peel tells me that our medical records, complete from birth to death, are continually accessed, bought, and sold by entities such as banks, drug companies, and marketing firms. This data generates billions of dollars of revenue for corporations and is used for a multitude of purposes that have nothing to do with benefiting us and our health.

"This is my life's work," she tells me, "restoring our fundamental constitutional rights to health information privacy."

I finally tell her that I think she has the wrong person. Like most Americans, I consider privacy a fundamental human right in theory. But when privacy experts intone about the supposedly dire threats radiating from every direction now that every aspect of our lives gets recorded and stored and transmitted as troves of electronic data, I tend to shrug.

I appreciate unsolicited reminders about reordering diapers from Amazon. I don't bother adjusting my Facebook settings every time the site announces new privacy policies. I might find it slightly creepy when ads pop up beside my in-box that reference a nugget of personal information from an e-mail, but I also like the convenience of Google's automatic directions to an appointment in my calendar. Even at the doctor's office—before and after my daughter's arrival—I sign those privacy notices without thinking.

The recent uproars surrounding the hacked nude selfies of female celebrities and Edward Snowden's revelations about the NSA were interesting to me as news stories but failed to shock me into doing anything differently. I'm vaguely discomfited by the idea of having my phone records logged or my geolocation tracked or my face scanned by surveillance cameras, but I can't help doubting that such efforts could yield anything of interest to anyone (except maybe my son).

In other words, I've always subscribed to a common stance that privacy experts have long deplored: only those of us who are doing something wrong have any real reason to worry. Even now, as I listen to Peel's passionate disquisitions that range from her baby granddaughter to Nazi Germany, I'm tempted to cling to this fallacy.

Soon, I find myself reading an article titled "Why Privacy Matters Even If You Have 'Nothing to Hide,'" in which the privacy scholar Daniel Solove notes that the metaphor most commonly cited to illustrate the imperiled state of our right to privacy is the Big Brother totalitarian government of George Orwell's *1984*. He argues that a more apt metaphor for America today is Franz Kafka's *The Trial*, which "depicts a bureaucracy with inscrutable purposes that uses people's information to make important decisions about them, yet denies the people the ability to participate in how their information is used." According to Solove, our biggest privacy problems are not those caused by surveillance, such as censorship and conformity, but "problems of information processing—the storage, use, or analysis of data."

Much of our personal data might seem innocuous, but it can quickly accumulate into the kind of information that nearly all of us would consider highly sensitive. "Suppose you bought a book about cancer," Solove writes. "This purchase isn't very revealing on its own, for it indicates just an interest in the disease. Suppose you bought a wig. The purchase of a wig, by itself, could be for a number of reasons. But combine those two pieces of information, and now the inference can be made that you have cancer and are undergoing chemotherapy. That might be a fact you wouldn't mind sharing, but you'd certainly want to have the choice."

Whether we're thinking of a cancer diagnosis, a pregnancy, a prescription for anxiety, a Pap smear, an STD, a mastectomy, depression, sexual impotence, an abortion, incontinence, testing for the Alzheimer's gene, number of sexual partners, family history of mental illness, alcohol use, medical marijuana, a child's ADHD: few of us would shrug at the prospect of others readily accessing such information about us and our families without our knowledge or permission. But that is exactly what happens all the time.

As Peel has warned for years, the health records of all Americans are a hugely lucrative commodity for corporations seeking to develop business tools, target sales pitches—and, perhaps most significantly, evaluate individuals according to their medical expenses.

The data is also used for purposes that we might consider worthwhile, such as identifying public health trends. Our individual right to health privacy might even seem like a small sacrifice to pay for scientific progress. But, as Peel argues to me in the course of our ongoing conversations, the public good is often impeded by a marketplace dominated by corporations whose profits depend upon keeping control over these troves of data.

Our health records are considered up for grabs once details such as names and addresses have been stripped away. But they still contain enough personal information—ages, zip codes, dates of service—that motivated companies can easily unmask patients' identities and trace their complete histories, including the medical conditions and expenditures of their families.

In America today, those companies are increasingly likely to be our employers.

Nearly half of all Americans depend upon an employer for health insurance—approximately 150 million of us. As most ordinary citizens know all too well, over the last few decades, health care costs have risen exponentially—just as most companies have become increasingly fixated on the relentless quest to reduce labor costs and return more wealth to executives and shareholders.

Consequently, many companies have cut out middleman insurance companies to become self-insured. These days, any large company that has more than a thousand employees is likely to be self-insured, and even companies with a few dozen employees are starting to join the trend. These employers directly collect the premiums, pay out claims, and amass employees' health data.

In the midst of the "distressed babies" controversy, many observers surmised that AOL is self-insured, though the company refused to confirm this to reporters. Even the *HuffPost* reporter assigned to the "distressed babies" story was, like most employees, forced to guess.

I happened to already know that AOL is self-insured only because Mila's Early Intervention service coordinator once asked me to find out whether our policy was regulated by New York State. After multiple calls and cagey replies, an insurance rep told me the policy was "funded by the employer." I still didn't understand that the insurance company I'd called hundreds of times wasn't responsible for paying claims, but was contracted only to handle administrative tasks.

Employers that still use outside insurance carriers are also increasingly focused on monitoring employees' health expenditures. Employees are often asked to authorize the disclosure of their health information, and most sign off without much thought—or, perhaps, without feeling they have much choice— the way most of us sign those privacy notices at doctors' offices.

I would like to believe that what happened to my family was an isolated occurrence, and that the vulnerabilities it exposed were largely resolved by my defense of my daughter and Tim Armstrong's public apology. After all, some observers have noted that "distressed babies" is destined to become a business world meme for what not to do.

But Peel tells me, "I can see this happening again and again and again."

I notice that several reports that seek to contextualize my story among other instances of bosses data-mining intimate details of employees' personal health mention a professor of labor and employment law named Matthew T. Bodie. When I contact him, he strikes me as a mild-mannered man who might offer a more dispassionate assessment of the significance of "distressed babies."

"It was a wake-up call at your expense," Bodie tells me.

The hard reality is that the spectacle of a megamillionaire CEO using my daughter as a scapegoat for his cost cutting was only a particularly cringeworthy instance of a dangerous tension that threatens the basic rights of working Americans.

"We hope and we cross our fingers that employers are acting like decent human beings," Bodie says. "But they're not asked to be in other ways. In the system that we have now, the pressures to cut costs are real. We're living in a fool's paradise if we think that employers aren't making these calculations that in this case became explicit."

60

A S I CONTINUE TO sift through the e-mails in my in-box, Deborah Peel's warnings no longer seem overwrought. A striking number of people write to share stories that are devastating not because of their medical outcomes, but because their employers treated them as if they had committed grave offenses for suffering medical crises.

A woman with a Ph.D. and a diagnosis of incurable cancer writes, "I lost my job Dec 20, 2012 (Merry Christmas) over being 'too expensive' for my health insurance," after she pushed herself to work full time through rounds of surgery and chemotherapy. "They kept trying to push me to quit, finally accused me of taking the job just so I'd have insurance." Now that her unemployment benefits are running out, she is confronting the prospect of being homeless. "If it gets out there that I even had cancer to begin with, that info alone might sink my job search."

The mother who lost a twin to SIDS recalls the annual meeting with the insurance representative at the company where her husband worked the year their babies arrived prematurely. "The rep stated, 'Rates are going up because last year someone had the nerve to have twins that cost the company a lot of money.'

To this day, that statement still brings me to tears," she writes. "I want you to know that your experience with corporate shaming is not unique."

For many of these people, this part of the story seems to be the hardest to tell—harder than the medical trauma, the perilous prognoses, even the suffering of their children. What they manage to articulate surfaces again and again in the form of one word: *shame*.

Another mother of twin girls writes of feeling pain midway through her pregnancy, visiting numerous perinatal specialists, being put on bed rest and told that one daughter was unlikely to survive. When her husband told his employer about the situation, "they were initially supportive," she writes. "But as the prognosis grew worse, they suddenly decided to fire my husband—over the phone. After he had just told them that one of our babies was going to die."

Her surviving daughter is now a lovely seven-year-old, but her e-mail ends on a wrenching note. "It was the most horrible day of my life, to be lying in bed with a dying baby, a struggling baby, and now my husband had been fired," she writes. "I've never felt such a weight of guilt and failure—what had I done ... I felt such shame."

For those who write to share stories like these—who appear to span the spectrum of race, gender, class, religion, politics, and geography—this charge of being a burden seems to tear at their basic identity even more than the helplessness that any parent confronts in the face of a sick child. It strikes me that what we Americans share, above all, is how much we cherish our sense of ourselves as hardworking individuals who take personal responsibility for ourselves and our families. The torment of suddenly being viewed, first and foremost, as financial liabilities is what people carry with them long after the crisis has passed.

None of these people have the privilege of remaining complacent about medical privacy—a privilege I've shared with most Americans until now.

"Be well," they tell me. "Stay strong." And: "There are many others that do not have the media access or voice to keep this from happening again."

Even before I spoke out about how Armstrong's disclosure affected my family, many AOL employees and outside observers were viscerally stunned by the spectacle of a CEO publicly spouting such intimate details about any employee. How could such disclosures be allowed? Weren't there protections against what most people instinctively recognized as the kind of violation they would never want to endure themselves?

Almost immediately, reporters scrambled for answers to a question that seemed irrelevant to me and my husband at the time: whether Armstrong broke any laws—specifically, the Health Insurance Portability and Accountability Act of 1996 (HIPAA), the federal law that governs how health care entities may use and disclose individuals' personal medical information.

All the experts agreed that what happened should not have happened, but some debated whether the disclosure was a clear legal violation or primarily a breach of decency and ethics. After all, Armstrong did not name names. The consensus seemed to be: it's complicated.

Now I understand why this question matters. How can ordinary citizens defend our right to medical privacy if we can't make sense of the law?

Even when I call Stacey Tovino, a leading expert on HIPAA, to ask for her assessment of the legality of Armstrong's comments, she initially tells me that she doesn't have enough information to make a determination. But once I explain how Peter's co-workers immediately identified our daughter, she offers a measured elucidation.

Tovino explains (with the understanding that she is not providing legal counsel) that under the law, any company that provides health insurance is responsible for ensuring that employees' health records are accessible only to those whose work directly concerns the health plan—presumably, human resources managers. This information can't be shared with other employees, including the CEO, unless it has been stripped of identifying markers, and unless the disclosure is for a permitted purpose, such as modifying the health plan.

No one but Tim Armstrong and his inner circle know exactly what information he possessed about the "distressed babies," but whatever the scope of that information, he was bound by law not to use or disclose it inappropriately. Though Armstrong didn't name names or any of the other identifying markers outlined by HIPAA, Tovino underscores that a disclosure is permitted only if the information can't be used to identify the individuals in question. In other words, a close reading of HIPAA clearly indicates a legal violation.

After I came forward, some commentators pointed out that if Peter's co-workers already knew that we had a baby in the hospital, then Tim Armstrong's comments exposed only what they already knew. If we set aside the obvious fact that none of them had previously been privy to the extent of our daughter's medical bills, this argument sounds logical enough.

But Tovino stresses, "The HIPAA Privacy Rule makes no exception for already public information." In other words, the law recognizes that employees might reveal their own health information in circumstances under which they see fit to do so: for instance, Peter's taking a week off when Mila arrived, then his paternity leave three months later. Such disclosures are voluntary (and generally unavoidable), and they don't make an involuntary exposure of employees' health information at a companywide meeting any less of a violation.

Of course, you don't need to be a legal expert to grasp the difference—or to understand that the CEO trotting out this information to fend off criticism for his cost cutting doesn't qualify under HIPAA as a "permitted purpose."

Tovino's cautious analysis confirms what Deborah Peel tells me in a more vehement tone: "He outed your family. Maybe he didn't realize what he was doing, within a company of five thousand employees, but you don't have to be a mathematical genius to know that anyone at the company who knew you and your husband would know."

Yet, from Peel's perspective, the question of HIPAA violation is, in some ways, a dangerous distraction from the need to confront a much bigger problem: the stark reality that we are all vulnerable to such exposure.

While one of the original intents of HIPAA was to protect patient privacy, it evolved to become less of a protective barrier than a gaping hole. In 2002, under the administration of President George W. Bush, the Department of Health and Human Services (HHS) eliminated the HIPAA rule that health care providers must obtain consent from individuals before disclosing their health information. This effectively wrested our medical records from our own control and deposited them at the mercy of profit-seeking companies.

"This is what armies of lobbyists can do," Peel explains.

What about those privacy notices at doctors' offices? In fact, Peel tells me, those forms provide nothing more than the illusion that our medical records are private. Generally, a patient's signature simply acknowledges the receipt of the privacy policy. Whether or not we sign, as the official website of HHS confirms, the health care entities that collect our health information— doctors, hospitals, insurers, employers—can largely do what they like with our data, without giving us any notice at all.

"We can't protect ourselves because we don't have audit trails, we don't have accounting trails, there's no record of the chain of custody," Peel says. "These are basic fair information practices that have been enacted in the European Union. In America, there's a streak of denialism."

Peel points me to a chilling survey in which 35 percent of Fortune 500 employers admitted to looking at employees' health records before making hiring and promotion decisions. Clearly, it is no coincidence that HIPAA serves as a distinctly mild deterrent for plenty of cost-cutting employers to target high-cost individuals.

Indeed, one flagrant case that gets aired out now, in the wake of the "distressed babies" controversy, involves none other than Tim Armstrong. Back in 2005, when he was a vice president at Google, a sales director named Christina Elwell became pregnant with quadruplets and told him she was having medical problems that would temporarily prevent her from traveling. According to *Valleywag*, Armstrong soon demoted her. She lost two of her unborn children. Armstrong called her an "HR nightmare" and fired her over the phone. Elwell lost a third baby. After she filed a lawsuit, she eventually received a financial settlement, which barred both parties from publicly discussing the case.

Several people who write to me cite this prior offense of Armstrong's, as well as similarly egregious cases involving other employers, to urge me to sue Armstrong and AOL, in the hope of preventing such injustices in the future.

"Please do not let this story drop," one person writes. "Please consider the important voice you might be for improving corporate empathy for employees who labor for their company's bottom line."

61

B UT THEN THERE ARE OTHERS who write to attack me for my lack of gratitude, my delusion that my daughter was entitled to medical care, my audacity for speaking up at all.

These are a few of the more polite examples:

"Your response could have been a heartfelt thank you for having the coverage to save your daughter. Instead you focused on creating a negative Tim Armstrong image. It is hard to comprehend someone so lucky having such bitterness."

> You know what, Ms. Fei? Your daughter's alive and well thanks to the medical care paid for by your insurance, which is largely paid for by AOL. So Armstrong mentioned distressed babies. So what? . . . Much as you may not like to hear it, you and your daughter's harrowing journey had financial ramifications for your husband's employer . . . An unpleasant reminder of your experience seems a small price to pay in this instance. Appreciate what you have and the corporation that helped make it possible.

Here is one of the less polite examples:

I can't believe you actually have the audacity to write anything but thank you after thank you. You should be on your freakin' hands and knees in front of him thanking him in any way he asked. Bottom line; it affected AOL's finances and there is no way you think you should have been entitled to a million dollars' worth of coverage. All I can say is you gotta be kiddin' me. You are so lucky that your kid lived and I hope it grows up strong and healthy and is someday able to justify such a outrageous cost to keep it alive. I seriously doubt that will happen, so, since neither AOL nor Tim Armstrong can say it, I will; Fuck you and your baby! I honestly hope they shit-can your husband regardless of the backlash and you are left feeding your family on your own.

And this: "Your million dollar baby is ugly you should of let it die instead of being such a burden on everyone."

After I read these messages, I rush to hold my daughter close until I can breathe again. I soak up the light of her eyes and the warmth of her skin until I'm convinced that she is not a mirage.

In truth, there is nothing anyone can say about me and my daughter that I haven't thought to myself. There are no harsher condemnations that anyone can issue than those that I issued from the day of her arrival.

My detractors are dead right in one regard: through everything that happened, from the morning I woke up in pain to the day Tim Armstrong blamed "distressed babies" for his decision to cut employee benefits, I've been blessed. Compared to the parents of children who didn't survive, the people who were fired for having a sick child or getting sick themselves, the ordinary Americans who suffered ordeals similar to mine without attracting any notice from the media—I'm undeniably blessed.

Am I the most pitiable victim of corporate callousness? Of course not. A voice in my head still hisses my own version of my detractors' admonitions: *Keep your head low.*

But that also seems like the most selfish and ungrateful thing that I could possibly do.

I'm tempted to dismiss those who attack me as sociopaths or trolls. But after I'm able to sit down again and peer beneath the malice, it strikes me that the viewpoints they espouse aren't so different from what plenty of decent people might think about situations like mine but might never say directly.

On Twitter, there's a sprinkling of tweets like these:

"sorry about yr baby but econ realities exist. There's limited $."

"Another whinny Liberal Leech expecting a free ride."

"You and your husband can clearly pay your own family's medical bills, so why didn't you? Some people need help with bills."

On Facebook, a high school classmate posts my story with this comment: "How much is too much? Is $1M to save a life worth it?"

Even among the generally sympathetic reactions in the media, a number of journalists readily accept the underlying premise of Armstrong's contention: that employee benefits are zero-sum, and my daughter consumed an outsized share.

Take *Re/code*'s Kara Swisher—lauded as "Tech's Most Powerful Snoop" by *New York* magazine—who regurgitated Armstrong's characterization of my pregnancy as "difficult and costly." This is her interpretation of Armstrong's statement about "distressed babies": "It is entirely clear from this that Armstrong was trying to make a fair point about making choices—and that paying to ensure the health of the babies was more important than the investment plan—and was not using it as an excuse either. What he seemed to be trying to do—not well enough, though—was to explain that the benefits support a lot of different constituencies and there [had] to be difficult choices."

In a column in the *New York Times*, Andrew Ross Sorkin points out that while Armstrong was "impolitic ... there is something valuable to be said about having an honest conversation about a company's expenses and using real-life examples—even when they make people uncomfortable."

The depiction of Armstrong that emerges from these renderings is an appealing one: the truth-telling, spreadsheet-wielding chief executive making bold, tough decisions in the name of balance and accountability and fiscal responsibility. But it doesn't hold up to reality.

This depiction is premised upon a credulous acceptance of Armstrong's dubious accounting. It takes for granted a dangerous distortion of the fundamental concept of insurance. And it overlooks the fact that if AOL's bottom line really was vulnerable to a couple of "distressed babies," that was a direct result of how the company's finances were managed.

In other words, if anyone is responsible for doing something "high-risk" that cost AOL two million dollars, it's not the women who conceived the babies. It's the CEO and management team in charge of the company.

There is some truth hidden behind Armstrong's claims. Health care is indeed a major line item on corporate balance sheets. And AOL employees are undeniably well compensated compared to, say, low-wage workers at Papa John's, for whom any kind of employer-sponsored health insurance must seem like a luxury. Even the restructured 401(k) retirement savings plan that spawned the criticism that led Armstrong to finger those "distressed babies" was still more generous than the plans offered at the old-media companies where Peter previously worked: one might say "above and beyond," as Armstrong told CNBC that morning.

Finally, there is no denying that my daughter's medical care was expensive. So expensive that in some lights, she appears to be the embodiment of a health care system run amok. The ultimate symbol of the uncontainable costs dragging down not only her parent's employer, but the national economy. The million-dollar baby.

Even those who reflexively side with a sick baby over an ultrarich CEO might well recoil at such a number, from conservative types who believe that everyone should pull themselves up by their bootstraps to liberal types who lament the fact that millions of Americans are completely uninsured. At a time when everyone seems to feel financially squeezed one way or another, a million dollars for a single tiny, tenuous life might strike plenty of reasonable people as unfair, imprudent, or just plain excessive—including me.

No one outside the company knows with certainty how much AOL paid for my daughter's care, though it's not for lack of trying. The company refused to provide specifics when asked by a multitude of reporters. The *Atlantic*'s Olga Khazan turned up an estimate of $51,500 for the cost of a premature infant from the National Business Group on Health, but this figure probably assumes a much shorter hospital stay than my daughter's.

The final bill I received from the hospital itself lists a whopping total: $776,743.41. This figure is the main reason I did not take issue with Armstrong's accounting when I initially spoke out. It includes charges of $98,000 for every two weeks of neonatal intensive care, plus substantial fees from the respiratory therapy department, the pharmacy, and various labs. The account summary lists an insurance benefit adjustment of $247,318.19 and insurance payments totaling $474,717.67.

The other substantial bills are from the NICU pediatrics group, which charged an average of $2,486 per day. After adjustments, the insurance payments averaged $355 per day. My daughter spent ninety-one days in the NICU, which adds up to about $32,290. We can also throw in the bills for my cesarean and four days in the hospital, plus stray bills from various specialists, though these charges were relatively routine for any birth. Overall, my best estimate of what AOL might have paid for my and my daughter's care—in conjunction with the thousands of dollars that my family paid in insurance premiums and copayments—is $550,000.

That is a lot of money, and I'm grateful—I'll say it again—that our insurance covered it. But it isn't a million dollars.

Given the complexity of the bills and the fact that I don't have a Ph.D. in health economics, I'm well aware that my estimate might be off. So I consult a number of scholarly articles and health journals, in which one well-regarded 2005 study puts the daily cost of caring for a low-birth-weight baby like my daughter at $2,380 per day in the NICU. By that benchmark, a ninety-one-day stay would run $216,580, or $263,303.84 adjusted for inflation. Another, more recent estimate pegs the cost of an extreme preemie at $3,000 per day in the NICU, which would total $273,000.

Nowhere can I find numbers higher than these except in cases where a baby undergoes a series of complicated surgeries, requires an exceedingly extended stay in the NICU, or remains extremely sick after discharge—none of which applies to my daughter or the other "AOL mom's" baby. The more I look, the more Tim Armstrong's number appears to have been chosen for effect.

But let's give him the benefit of the doubt and assume that AOL was billed a million dollars for each of our babies. After all, this is the American hospital system, where $6 Band-Aids, $11 tissue boxes, and $500 stitches are routine—and where such inflated bills are almost never paid in full. Insurers typically negotiate steep discounts, as my own bills attest.

Health care executives refer to this as the "Saudi sheikh problem" of hospital pricing. As one expert told the *Times*, "You don't really want to change your charges if you have a Saudi sheikh come in with a suitcase full of cash who's going to pay full charges."

If AOL really was charged a million dollars for my daughter's care, why would the company have paid the way only Saudi sheikhs are known to do?

Now another e-mail in my in-box that catches my attention is from a Harvard-educated health economist who works for a private insurer and seems to be the furthest thing from an activist, yet is so appalled by Armstrong's comments that he feels compelled to walk me through the inner workings of health insurance in a situation like mine.

Companies choose to self-insure, he explains, for two main reasons: to avoid government regulations that may require them to cover certain medical services, and to save money. Instead of paying an outside insurer, they keep the money and assume the responsibility for paying out claims themselves. This is considered advisable only if they can afford to handle that risk.

Generally, self-insured companies are expected to set aside money for the purpose of covering high costs in any given year. Most of them also pay for "stop-loss" insurance policies to pick up the bill beyond a capped amount—typically, $50,000 to $100,000 per individual. This form of "reinsurance" serves as a financial backstop if, say, an employee needs heart surgery, or gets hit by a car—or has an extremely premature baby.

You don't need an actuarial degree to know that prematurity is a common medical condition. According to the CDC, in 2012, preterm birth affected more than 450,000 babies in the United States: roughly one in nine. No one knows exactly why the rate is so high or what can be done to lower it. Some risk factors for preterm birth are considered preventable for the individuals in question—smoking, lack of prenatal care—but others are not, such as being African American or contracting a viral infection.

Furthermore, half of all women who experience premature labor have no known risk factors. This statistic is also borne out in my in-box, where plenty write to tell me that their births were as unexpected as mine and remain equally unexplained.

When Mila arrived, Peter and I felt we'd been struck by lightning—and, in the specifics of our situation, we had. But in the context of health insurance, it's the kind of thing that happens.

Anyone who deals in health insurance understands this reality—as should anyone charged with running a company of five thousand employees. If a CEO doesn't want to be on the hook for the unpredictability of such life events, he can choose not to be.

"One of two things happened," the health economist tells me. "Either they reinsured and the CEO is wrongfully attributing the cost to you. They hit the cap and someone else was on the hook for those bills. Or they specifically didn't pay to reinsure and they willingly took on the risk."

Maybe that gamble paid off in previous years. Maybe no one ever had an extremely premature baby during Armstrong's tenure at AOL until we came along. Maybe, during those years, Armstrong and his management team were able to pocket millions that otherwise could have been spent on a solid reinsurance policy or a healthy reserve fund. It almost goes without saying that he never held a town hall meeting to announce that he'd decided to *increase* the 401(k) matching program because zero "distressed babies" were born to AOLers the previous year.

Maybe this chancy approach to insurance enhanced AOL's reported earnings and stock prices. Maybe Peter's own stock options reflected that boost. But none of that makes for a fiscally prudent health care plan.

"They made a bet and lost," Matthew Bodie tells me. "They could have said, *Well, that didn't work out, maybe we shouldn't have done that.* Instead, they said, *You shouldn't have cost us so much money.*"

*   *   *

As much as we all might like to believe otherwise, some version of what happened to my family could happen to anyone. Never mind "distressed babies." Any one of us could suffer a spinal cord injury or wake up with colon cancer or have a child who needs intensive care. This is the fundamental purpose of insurance: pooling the risks that are extraordinary for the individual and utterly predictable in the aggregate.

As individuals, we can do our best to limit our risk. We can wear bike helmets and eat organic kale and drink from BPA-free cups and slather ourselves with SPF 90 lotion. If we're prospective parents, we can go to every checkup, sail through every screening, take prenatal vitamins and yoga classes, abstain from wine and blue cheese and smoked fish.

Still, there is only so much that any of us can do to prevent a medical catastrophe. That is why we pay our premiums into a pool so that we're covered in such an event. Chances are, at some point in our lives, plenty of us will have a turn at being that unlucky person—or, as some would put it, being that burden.

"High-cost claims are what insurance is designed to cover," the health economist tells me. "If it's not for catastrophic claims, then what's it for? Nobody has a million dollars to pay for an event that everyone would want to have covered." Except for those Saudi sheikhs, if not Tim Armstrong and AOL.

Yet another aspect of Armstrong's comments that incensed the health economist was the implication that the company paid those bills "out of the goodness of their hearts."

"That's your business," he points out. "You entered into a contract. Nothing more, nothing less. You offer benefits and this is the benefit."

But what's the point of offering health benefits if you're going to point fingers when employees actually need to use them?

What I still struggle to understand is why anyone at all was blamed for being a drag on the company's bottom line. Hadn't Tim Armstrong announced AOL's "Olympian" financial performance right before he blamed those "distressed babies"?

It turns out that, two days prior to that town hall, the *Washington Post* had drawn attention to a recent tweak in AOL's 401(k) program that most employees hadn't noticed. The subtle restructuring would allow AOL to save millions of dollars that had previously gone toward employees' pay packages.

When Armstrong appeared on CNBC to tout the company's best earnings in a decade, he found himself questioned on the rationale of those cuts. At that point, he blamed Obamacare: "As a CEO and as a management team, we had to decide, do we pass the $7.1 million of Obamacare costs to our employees? Or do we try to eat as much of that as possible and cut other benefits?"

At first, this sounds like one of those bold, tough, data-driven decisions that justify a CEO's salary. But then I reread the quote. One stated option is to pass the costs on to employees. The other is "to cut other benefits"—which also means passing the costs on to employees.

Plenty of other CEOs get away with similar corporate spin. This time, commentators quickly debunked Armstrong's Obamacare numbers as "totally bogus," as one expert told CNBC. And when Armstrong stepped into that town hall meeting, he found himself facing a deeply skeptical audience of his own employees.

Which led him to blame those "distressed babies"—a rationalization that a column in the *New Yorker* assessed as "just a riff on how much higher profits would be if you didn't have to hire human beings."

Amid the public backlash, many observers noted that those babies' medical bills were a pittance compared to plenty of other expenses on AOL's balance sheets: for instance, the $200 million

Armstrong had sunk into Patch, his disastrous pet local news project. Or the $12 million he was paid in 2012.

What I find striking about this number is not how many "distressed babies" it could have paid for, but the fact that, according to *Newsweek*, a large chunk of it consisted of a "special bonus" designed to reward him for his "continuing tight cost controls."

This information finally helps me to understand Armstrong's accounting. There is no inherent reason why health care spending and retirement contributions must be pitted against each other. In this model of corporate accounting, the real zero-sum game is between employee benefits and executive bonuses.

62

FOR ME, COMING FORWARD to defend my daughter allowed me to confront the trauma surrounding her birth and allowed me to say to Tim Armstrong, as Matthew Bodie put it, "Shame on you, not on me." But I still quaked at the prospect of facing Peter's co-workers in person. I couldn't imagine ever shaking Armstrong's hand at another company event or hugging Arianna Huffington at another dinner party.

For my husband, my defense of our family brought a degree of vindication. Plenty of his co-workers—especially women and other parents—asked him to pass on their thanks to me. The media outcry and popular wrath against Armstrong and AOL were so intense that a few co-workers dryly noted that Peter could coast for the rest of his career if he wanted; no one there would dare to touch him. Even so, when he was offered a job at another digital news company soon after the firestorm subsided, he didn't hesitate.

After he resigned, he happened upon a magazine interview in which Arianna, in the midst of promoting her book, implied that she'd supported our family's position. I watched his hands shake from across the room.

We never took steps toward filing a lawsuit. We had no appetite for seeking retribution in a courtroom.

Deborah Peel, who is also a practicing psychotherapist, tells me that most people who suffer medical privacy violations hide from the trauma. The same circumstances that make such disclosures so damaging—the exposure of psychological wounds, the breaching of interpersonal boundaries, the shame and guilt that linger in the aftermath of medical crises, and the power that companies wield over employees whose families depend upon their paychecks and health coverage—tend to make people feel utterly helpless to fight back.

Indeed, among those who wrote to me about being unjustly targeted by their employers, not one of them sought legal recourse, no matter how blatant the violation.

Current legal protections include HIPAA as well as the Americans with Disabilities Act (ADA), the Employee Retirement Income Security Act (ERISA), and state tort laws. But as we entrust more and more of our medical information to the matrix of Big Data, these laws are increasingly outdated and inadequate. And for most ordinary citizens who suffer violations of this nature, justice is likely to be elusive. The government agencies charged with handling complaints, such as the Office of Civil Rights, are chronically underequipped to handle complex issues of health privacy. Courts are often wary of levying substantial penalties for injuries that might seem abstract. Meanwhile, employers have an arsenal of plausibly deniable means of targeting vulnerable employees.

"They can reassign you," Peel tells me. "They can drum up any reason to fire you. They can make you feel like you have no choice but to resign."

The reality that Americans largely depend on employers for their health insurance is the result of a historical quirk: amid a chronic labor shortage during World War II, employers offered health benefits, which were exempt from high wartime taxes, to attract the workers they needed. These days, for most companies, the steep costs of offering those benefits are still outweighed by the tax breaks.

Under Obamacare, more people can buy health insurance from state-run exchanges rather than depend on their employers. Smaller companies that can't afford to provide insurance can send employees onto the exchanges. But the Affordable Care Act also increases tax incentives for employers to provide health insurance. For the near future, most will continue to do so.

At the same time, most companies show little sign of shifting away from short-term strategies to squeeze out profits that accrue to the CEOs and shareholders.

"It's just going to get worse in terms of employers monitoring employees' health and making these sorts of calculations," Matthew Bodie tells me. "There will be increasing tensions, depending on the size and wealth of the company and how much they care to safeguard their reputations. It's not just Tim Armstrong. Across the board, there's an increasing tendency to shift the onus of risk to the individual. Imagine a ten-person company where employees turn against each other: *We all know Joe's been overweight, now he's gone and had a heart attack.*"

How many of us can truly feel protected in such a system?

Health care reform has never been a cause that ignited my personal passions, but I'm struck by the frank bewilderment in the notes I receive from well-wishers in Canada, the United Kingdom, the Netherlands, Finland, and New Zealand: bewilderment at why anyone would begrudge my baby's hospital bills, why my husband's CEO would have any involvement with those bills, and why the bills for that care, which seems to be relatively routine in NICUs around the developed world, are so staggeringly expensive in the United States.

Indeed, among my fellow Americans, even those who describe themselves to me as fortunate to have compassionate employers also describe carrying feelings of guilt, failure, and shame for the medical bills of their babies. This group includes a pediatrician who spent years caring for premature infants and never imagined that she would have one of her own. She writes, "The next year, premiums skyrocketed, placing health insurance beyond the means of many of my husband's fellow employees. It was heartbreaking to think that our little boy's life was causing others so much financial burden."

You don't need to have socialist leanings to notice that such fallout would be nonexistent in a country with universal health coverage—which is to say, every other industrialized nation.

The subject of universal health coverage also becomes unavoidable in my conversations with the experts, no matter if they have no such primary agenda. "If you'd had this baby in Europe, it wouldn't have broken anyone's bank," Peel points out.

Single-payer systems certainly have their own perils: bureaucracy, inefficiency, the entire population's health data in the hands of the government. But they also have a notable advantage beyond the obvious ones of lower costs and universal coverage: no one's boss is motivated to assess employees according to their medical expenses.

"A grown man on a corporate conference call whining about the burden of other people's babies is simultaneously the most un-American and distinctly American scene one can imagine," writes Amy Davidson in the *New Yorker*. "What are we risking as a country when we price a child that way?"

63

IN THE WAKE OF the controversy, as my daughter continues to reveal new facets of the girl who has made the life of our family impossible to imagine without her, the designation is often unavoidable: *miracle child.*

As she walks and runs and snuggles in our laps and stashes pilfered treasures in her secret hiding places, scampers up jungle gyms and throws operatic tantrums and shrugs off winter colds and gobbles cookies faster than her big brother, just about everyone who sees her can't help invoking that word. Our parents, our friends, our doctors, even the laser-eyed specialists. Even Peter, even me.

Of course she is a miracle. We named her Mila, after all.

Of course every minute of heartbreak and fear was worth it. Every call from the NICU, every drop of milk I wrung from my body, every long, dark night that she fought for her life inside her isolette.

Every heroic intervention from the doctors and nurses, every painstaking procedure, every high-tech machine, every delicate instrument. Every puff of oxygen, every IV drip, every transfusion of blood, every tube and wire.

But calling her a miracle also implies that she was a long shot. A huge gamble that, by any laws of probability, shouldn't have paid off.

Which raises some hard questions. If Mila beat the odds, what about all the babies who don't? If we accept that the fundamental purpose of health insurance is to cover everyone in the event of a catastrophe, can we also argue that such attempts to shoot the moon are a wise use of limited resources?

I've come to understand that, in the context of a profitable corporation that was contractually obligated to abide by the terms of our health insurance policy, there was nothing unjust about my daughter's medical expenditures. But what about the broader context of a nation with finite care available to its citizens?

A part of me is still deeply troubled by the charge that my daughter and I didn't deserve the care that she received. That, despite the fact that my family faithfully paid our insurance premiums and copayments, we are still freeloaders of a sort.

Long before Tim Armstrong singled out the medical bills of "distressed babies," premature infants have been labeled with price tags. A typical example is a 2008 *Businessweek* headline that many of us might have guessed: MILLION-DOLLAR BABIES.

This article reports that "the cost of care for preemies is sky-high—some fifteen times the expense of full-term infants and rising," with an estimate of $26 billion per year: half of all hospital spending on the care of newborns. "Factor in the cost of treating all of the possible lifelong disabilities, and the years of lost productivity for the caregivers, and the real tab may top $50 billion."

The book *Too Expensive to Treat?* cites the estimate that low-birth-weight babies (here defined as those born below 1,250 grams) comprise only 7 percent of newborn patients but account for over 90 percent of newborn hospital costs—"a hugely disproportionate share" that the author calls "simply remarkable."

Caring for extremely premature infants is expensive, a fact that anyone who has ever stepped inside a NICU can surmise. But the real question is this: Compared to what?

It seems that the actual human lives saved in NICUs are not enough in themselves to justify their medical bills, which brings us to mathematical analyses of the cost-effectiveness of their existence. The *Businessweek* article acknowledges that "most health-care economists seem to agree that spending on preemies offers a high rate of return for all but the earliest-stage infants. The reason? The money improves both the quality and length of life, which yields big economic benefits." In other words, investing in the care of premature babies is extremely cost-effective because the large majority grow up to become healthy, productive members of society.

Furthermore, the medical innovations that have enabled millions of premature babies to thrive have also improved the care of full-term infants, greatly contributing to a 73 percent drop in the U.S. infant mortality rate between 1960 and 2000.

But what about those "earliest-stage infants" such as Mila? Given their higher rates of death and disability and the formidable costs of their care, policymakers in England, Sweden, and Australia as well as the United States have considered designating a cutoff birth weight—five hundred, six hundred, or even seven hundred grams (five grams less than Mila weighed at birth)—below which babies would automatically be disqualified from treatment. Such grim approaches might sound reasonable from a purely economic standpoint.

But researchers who modeled these approaches found that they resulted in meager savings for the number of potential survivors who would be forfeited: at most, a 10 percent decrease in NICU costs, which could be achieved only with the most draconian cutoff. In other words, cost savings would accrue only if care was categorically denied not just to the babies least likely to survive, but also to those most likely to thrive among extremely premature infants. Such a strategy would seem to be a hard sell even to the most ruthless bean counters.

In fact, NICUs are actually extraordinarily cost-effective once we draw a more logical comparison: not between babies who need intensive care and babies who don't, but between babies and adults who need intensive care. While over 80 percent of ICU resources are spent on adults who go on to die, in the NICU, more than 80 percent of resources are spent on babies who ultimately survive—even among the tiniest babies. This is partly because the babies who will die tend to die quickly, regardless of heroic medical treatment.

Yet NICUs are often depicted as extravagant departments in a way that other high-cost hospital units, such as orthopedics and oncology, are not. Patients who have spinal cord injuries or need coronary bypass surgery are roughly as expensive as the average NICU patient, but we don't generally demand that such categories of people prove themselves deserving of medical care the way we demand that premature infants justify the costs of their existence.

Much of our handwringing over those costs is premised upon the deep-rooted concern that premature infants are basically damaged goods. One ominous title that hits home, *Playing God in the Nursery*, exhorts us to "consider the dismal fate of a disturbing number of 'salvaged' babies." The author uses those ironic quotation marks every time he describes children who survive with impairments and expresses abhorrence for their "pathetic lives." He scoffs at the distinctions between mild, moderate, and severe handicaps, referring to a mild learning disorder as "an inability to learn to read or do arithmetic."

This book was published back in 1985, before significant advances in the field of neonatology. But plenty of more recent accounts also imply that disabled babies are wholesale inventions of the modern NICU. Moreover, these accounts often reveal a propensity to lump all nonmiracle babies together as worst-case scenarios, as if every impairment is a tragic deficit. As if death is clearly preferable to life with a disability.

Many graduates of NICUs survive with some kind of disability. Today, 15 percent of premature babies survive with permanent disabilities, down from 40 percent fifty years ago. In particular, there is a relatively high incidence of cerebral palsy among the tiniest survivors: between 5 and 10 percent.

But it is far from evident that NICUs have contributed to a rise in disability overall. While some babies with impairments wouldn't have survived at all without neonatal care, such care also reduces the incidence of impairments among babies who would have survived in previous eras, too.

Some disabled babies will continue to be discharged by NICUs. This is less a failing of neonatal care than a fact of life.

People with disabilities constitute 15 percent of the American population: the largest minority in the country. At any moment, any one of us could join their numbers. As the disability-rights scholar Tobin Siebers points out, "The cycle of life runs in actuality from disability to temporary ability back to disability, and that only if you are among the most fortunate."

These days, it is widely presumed that until modern times, disabled babies were invariably left to die of exposure, as if nothing could be more natural than the denial of precious resources to such forms of humanity. In fact, many societies granted them as much or more dignity than we do now.

At a four-thousand-year-old burial site in Vietnam, archaeologists recently uncovered the skeleton of a boy, curled in a fetal position, who appeared to have been born with a severe disease that resulted in fused vertebrae and paralysis, rendering him unable to feed or bathe himself. Yet he lived another ten years and was carefully buried. Researchers concluded that the people around him, who likely subsisted by fishing and hunting, must have tended to the boy's every need—and that the boy himself must have had a strong sense of his own worth.

It is striking that in a society as wealthy and advanced as ours, people with disabilities are often described as if they have nothing to offer but an occasion for pity and disgust, as if they are nothing but their afflictions. That a significant faction of people believe that a baby who is given precarious odds at birth might not deserve a chance at all. That faction included, at one point, myself.

I don't mean to minimize the suffering of severely disabled children or their parents. The challenges that many of them face on a daily basis—chronic and debilitating pain, colossal financial tolls, relentless proximity to death—aren't part of my current reality. In this way, too, I'm undeniably blessed.

But was my daughter clearly "worth it" only because she defied the odds? If she receives a worrying diagnosis in a few months or a few years, would the value of her life plummet?

Studies indicate that most people with disabilities express high satisfaction with their quality of life. What often torments them far more than their impairments is being regarded as unfortunate outcomes that should have been averted. And while most of us wouldn't choose to have a disabled child, once that human being becomes a reality, few of us would truly wish the child away.

In the transformative book *Far from the Tree*, Andrew Solomon writes, "Everyone is flawed and strange; most people are valiant, too."

Most of us, if given a chance, would immediately tap into our deepest reserves to provide a loved one with all the care we can muster. Set aside, for the moment, the question of premature infants. Imagine that the person struck by catastrophe is your wife, or your father, or your teenage daughter, or your kid brother, or even your newborn baby.

Once you rushed your loved one to the hospital, you'd probably be overwhelmingly grateful and relieved to see the teams of doctors and nurses and technicians, the flashing monitors and beeping alarms, the nests of tubes and wires. Such care wouldn't seem extravagant at all. It would seem like an appropriate marshaling of the resources at hand for a life that you're desperate to save.

Now imagine the doctors tell you that if they treat your loved one, they estimate a two-thirds chance of survival. And, assuming survival, a two-thirds chance of a mild to moderate disability, or no disability at all: a two-thirds chance of your loved one being generally okay.

Those were my daughter's odds, after all—I just couldn't see them that way.

Would any of us deny our loved one treatment? Would we question their right to such care? Would we wish our loved one out of existence to spare ourselves from the agony of uncertainty, the way that I once did?

64

*L*ET HER GO. *She isn't meant to be here. She doesn't belong in this world.*

I'm still haunted by my own impulse to relinquish my daughter upon her arrival—an impulse amplified by those who argue that she didn't earn her place on this earth. I still struggle with the sense that, in some lights, she is a freak of science more than my child.

That because she exited my body so prematurely and I couldn't hold on to her, her existence today can be attributed only to extraordinary measures on the part of medical professionals, combined with the excesses of modern technology. That I'm the undeserving recipient of a lavish gift that nature did not intend for me to keep.

These fears have tormented me, in some form, since the day of Mila's birth. Even now, what happened still seems so incomprehensible that when I first delve into the literature on premature infants, the shock of recognition is overwhelming.

In *The Lazarus Case: Life-and-Death Issues in Neonatal Intensive Care*, the pediatrician and leading bioethicist John D. Lantos describes the NICU as he first encountered it as a medical student:

The babies themselves did not seem quite real, or at least they did not seem central, except in a mechanical way, to whatever dramas were being enacted there . . . Instead, the professionals focused on the machines and the monitors . . . If they cared well, the numbers would be good and the patterns regular, and they would preserve the baby's health. If they could not make the numbers right or the patterns regular, then the baby's health would slowly wane away, and the baby could not survive.

"The babies seem almost, but not quite, human, almost, but not quite, fetal," Lantos continues.

In their chimerical, half-human, half-machine state they seem not only helpless and pitiful but also exotic, threatening, futuristic, feral, untamed, barbarous. They evoke a strange mixture of sympathy and disgust . . . They shouldn't be there, so vulnerable and so dependent on the machinery and technology of medicine. The babies in the NICU make a claim on our humanity but also challenge the limits of it. We want to respond, but we also want to be free to reject the claim that they make upon us, to imagine them not as our babies, whom we must care for, but as something other, different, unrelated. In their terrible dependency aren't they asking too much? Perhaps more than we can give?

As it turns out, we have grappled with some version of these dilemmas since the dawn of neonatology. And though I had no idea about the history of this highly contested space when I first stepped into the NICU, the question of how we care for the smallest, most vulnerable individuals has always been one that reflects who we are as a nation: what we choose to protect and whom we value.

Two competing images of premature infants grip our collective imagination. One is the perfect baby in miniature who simply needs extra time and love and care. The other is the picture of wretched specimens upon whom hubristic, single-minded doctor-scientists wield unbridled technology. Neither of these images is a fair representation of the reality.

These days, neonatal care routinely saves more than 90 percent of the hundreds of thousands of premature babies born in the United States every year—and most of them survive without long-term health problems. We should be able to celebrate such an outcome without mindlessness or treacle.

For babies born at the edge of viability, such as my daughter, the journey is still radically uncertain. Neonatal care is an inherently messy, perilous, and fraught process—as is the basic enterprise of saving human lives.

As I find myself compulsively unraveling the story of how such care has evolved over centuries into the modern NICU, I finally begin to understand the moment in history when my daughter arrived in the world—and how she made her way home. And, at long last, her journey illuminates for me how children like her not only challenge but ultimately affirm our shared humanity.

From the beginning of civilization, we have harnessed our resources to help our babies survive. At heart, this is not playing God, but an integral part of what makes us human: striving to use the tools at hand to mitigate nature's reckoning.

Implausible as it may seem, babies like my daughter have always been born. We tend to think of cesareans as an invention of the modern medical-industrial complex, but the procedure has been part of human culture since ancient times, referenced in Hindu, Egyptian, Greek, and Roman folklore and depicted in Chinese etchings. Attempts to revive apparently lifeless newborns have also been described since antiquity, when methods of resuscitation included "slapping, pinching, electrocution, immersion in hot and cold water, and insertion of corn cobs and ravens' beaks into the infant's rectum," according to an article in the journal *Neonatology*.

Some version of tube feeding has existed for centuries, particularly among the ancient Egyptians, who used reeds and animal bladders to administer a mix of wine, chicken broth, and raw eggs to patients who were too weak to eat. Similarly, the practice of helping a patient to breathe can be traced back to biblical times, and evidence of mouth-to-mouth resuscitation for newborns has been traced as far back as 1472.

Early efforts at neonatal care were largely unsuccessful until the late nineteenth century, an era when as many as one in five babies born in American cities did not live to see their first birthday, as common causes of infant mortality included tuberculosis, typhoid fever, malnutrition, diarrhea, and hypothermia.

Then, in 1880, a French obstetrician became inspired by a chicken incubator display in the Paris zoo and invented the first infant incubator, according to the article "The Incubator and the Medical Discovery of the Premature Infant," by Jeffrey P. Baker. Soon, another enterprising physician brought "incubator shows" to America intending to demonstrate the potential for technology to save premature infants. He eventually installed his incubator station among ethnic exhibitions and freak shows at Coney Island.

Just as some innovators started to make major advances by setting up incubator stations within hospitals, a fledgling eugenics movement gained considerable traction in calling for measures to eradicate what they considered undesirable specimens of humanity. Harsh restrictions were imposed on immigration, forced sterilization was performed on mentally handicapped people, and public support waned for the treatment of premature infants, who were considered inherently unsound "weaklings" and afflictions of the poor.

From the 1920s to the 1960s, practitioners developed significant innovations in neonatal care: supplemental oxygen, temperature control, treatment of infections, and blood transfusions for the treatment of jaundice. All of these innovations primarily improved the survival of full-term or nearly full-term babies. Most premature infants still died from the inability to draw adequate oxygen and nutrition through their immature systems.

Then, in 1963, a premature baby named Patrick was born to President John F. Kennedy and First Lady Jacqueline Kennedy, delivered via cesarean five and a half weeks early. According to the *Times*, he "weighed a relatively robust 4 pounds 10 1/2 ounces. But he immediately began having trouble breathing." Thirty-nine hours after his birth, Patrick died. A few months later, his death was eclipsed by the assassination of JFK, and is barely remembered today—except among those who know how it sparked a national interest in prematurity.

Within several years, mechanical ventilators, which had come into use during World War II, began to be adapted for infants. Had Patrick Kennedy been born a decade later, he likely would have survived. The second key innovation of the 1960s was the development of a precise formulation and technique for intravenous feeding. These combined breakthroughs quickly yielded stunning progress, with the number of deaths among babies born below 1,500 grams declining by two-thirds by the mid-1970s.

Yet practitioners increasingly struggled with a central tension: Would the babies they saved lead lives worth living?

In 1975, experts developed the first set of guidelines for neonatology, specifying conditions under which medical treatment was harmful to newborns: "inability to survive infancy, inability to live without severe pain, and inability to participate, at least minimally, in human experience." This statement would become a touchstone for clinical ethics judgments ever since, though its tangled implications would take decades to work out.

Through the 1970s, the overwhelming majority of doctors still commonly deferred to parental wishes in terms of allowing certain babies to die—mostly babies born with spina bifida or Down syndrome. These cases were generally handled on an individual basis, quietly and privately, without legal or governmental interference.

For premature babies, aggressive treatment became the norm. Practitioners recognized a strong correlation between extreme prematurity and serious disability, but no one could foretell a baby's long-term odds with any degree of accuracy—particularly not in such murky realms as quality of life or neurological development. Doctors and nurses frequently expressed deep ambivalence about the costs of care for babies with poor prognoses, the burdens those children might impose on their families, and whether they would ever enjoy meaningful participation in society. But the breakneck speed of innovation meant that smaller and smaller babies survived—and thrived—all the time. Doctors and nurses were routinely surprised by positive outcomes among former patients—for instance, babies who'd nearly been "write-offs" walking into NICU reunion parties.

During the 1980s, practitioners developed steroid therapy for women in premature labor to hasten babies' lung development, which was quickly shown to drastically reduce the incidence of respiratory distress syndrome, neonatal deaths, and intraventricular hemorrhages. More broadly, as hospital facilities became better organized, nurses gained experience, and monitoring techniques improved, survival rates steadily increased for babies at every birth weight.

But all of these advancements were hugely overshadowed by a legal case that exploded the delicate workings of the NICU into the public consciousness and still conjures widespread unease today: the case of Baby Doe.

In 1982, a baby with Down syndrome was born in Bloomington, Indiana, suffering a life-threatening blockage in his esophagus that doctors could easily correct with surgery. When his parents refused to authorize the treatment, the hospital filed an emergency petition to override them.

The mother's obstetrician testified that "the possibility of a minimally adequate quality of life was non-existent." The court determined that the parents were within their rights. Appeals were filed. At each stage, the courts ruled for the parents. Baby Doe was given only pain medication, and his parents frequently visited and held him until he died, six days after his birth.

Amid intense media coverage, President Reagan penned an article entitled "Abortion and the Conscience of the Nation," declaring: "The death of that tiny infant tore at the hearts of all Americans because the child was undeniably a live human being—one lying helpless before the eyes of the doctors and the eyes of the nation." In Reagan's portrayal, the courts had ruled that "retardation was the equivalent of a crime deserving the death penalty."

Reagan directed his Justice Department to treat decisions to withhold treatment from disabled newborns as violations of federal civil rights law. While Reagan had a dismal record on civil rights issues such as voting and school segregation, he had been elected with overwhelming support from the religious right, with a mandate to seek to overturn abortion rights while protecting what they considered the sanctity of life.

Soon, "Baby Doe squads" were converging on hospitals to seize records, interrogate doctors, and confront parents in the middle of the night. In several instances, parents who refused treatment for their newborns were forced to give up custody.

The wrenching dilemmas that had long confronted families and doctors in NICUs were suddenly pawns in America's raging culture wars. Conservatives compared the government's action to Orwell's *1984*. Members of the ACLU advocated for parents' right to privacy, but some civil libertarians noted the hypocrisy of ignoring the infants' rights to due process and equal protection. Liberals were surprised to find themselves on the opposite side of disability rights advocates—who, in turn, were surprised to find themselves allied with Reagan and the religious right.

Meanwhile, many NICU practitioners—who had long argued that newborns had a right to medical care like any other citizen—were dismayed by such draconian government intrusions, not to mention the deliberate conflation of the issue of abortion with the care of sick babies.

The Supreme Court ultimately struck down the Baby Doe regulations. Undeterred, Reagan pushed Congress to enact new standards for decision making in the NICU, which remain enshrined in law today. These rules, which represented some degree of compromise, specified situations in which doctors and parents were permitted to withhold or withdraw life-sustaining treatment: if the infant was "chronically and irreversibly comatose" or if "treatment would be virtually futile" in terms of survival and thus inhumane.

Clearly, the Baby Doe standards were concerned only with the perils of undertreating infants, not overtreating; they denied considerations of quality of life. Though the rules did not impose criminal or civil liabilities for doctors or hospitals, they were widely interpreted as mandating maximum intervention in all but the most hopeless cases.

Within a few years, the Baby Doe standards—combined with spreading public awareness that people with Down syndrome and spinal defects could live meaningful lives—virtually extinguished the previously common practice of withholding treatment for babies with such disabilities. But there was still little consensus about how those standards applied to babies born at the edge of viability.

In the most agonizing cases, NICU practitioners sometimes found ways to limit treatment without withdrawing support: for instance, deciding against a medication or a surgical procedure and hoping that the baby would void the next decision. In the wake of Baby Doe, this approach to decision making began to spread across NICUs as a way to navigate inflexible regulations in the face of enormous stakes and relentless uncertainty.

The next major clinical innovation was the formulation of surfactant to help keep the alveoli in the lungs of premature infants from collapsing between each breath. This development greatly lowered the incidence of deaths from respiratory distress syndrome in the United States: from ten to fifteen thousand babies per year in 1960 to fewer than one thousand by the end of the century.

By the mid-1990s, the astonishingly rapid advancements in NICU technology largely came to a halt. While neonatal care continued to be incrementally refined, the survival rates of premature babies at every birth weight leveled off. Over the previous three decades, the general consensus on viability had shifted from twenty-eight to twenty-four weeks of gestation, where it remained.

This slowdown allowed neonatologists to take stock of all the clinical data that had been amassed over the past decades. They could now define categories of babies for whom treatment was either obligatory or inhumane. Babies who weighed more than 875 grams at birth nearly always survived, while babies who weighed less than 500 grams at birth nearly always died.

But between those thresholds lay a contentious gray zone. What was the proper treatment for babies born between 500 and 875 grams—roughly, those between twenty-three and twenty-six weeks of gestation?

Doctors now had a fairly accurate grasp of the odds for survival in the aggregate, but they still couldn't foretell an individual baby's outcome with any certainty. They couldn't predict whether a given treatment on a specific baby would turn out to be effective or futile—especially not when that decision needed to be made in an instant.

Out of this gray zone, another legal controversy burst forth, the first case involving an extremely premature baby to capture the nation's attention. It remains one of the most divisive and ethically challenging cases in recent history: the case of Sidney Miller.

In 1990, in Houston, Texas, a woman named Karla Miller went into labor just twenty-three weeks into her pregnancy. She was diagnosed with a life-threatening infection that necessitated delivering her baby, according to the book *Bioethics and Disability* by Alicia Ouellette. After being informed of the grave risks for such a premature infant, Karla Miller and her husband requested that their baby not be resuscitated upon delivery, but simply placed in her arms while nature was allowed to take its course. Doctors initially agreed—but then, after consulting with hospital administrators, decided they needed to wait to see the baby in order to evaluate her viability.

The Millers refused to authorize treatment. When the father asked how he could prevent resuscitation, he was told that his only option was to check his wife out of the hospital. By then, Karla Miller was critically ill.

Upon delivery, the baby weighed 615 grams, had a heartbeat, and cried spontaneously. She presented no clear evidence of disability. The doctors resuscitated her, intubated her, and admitted her to the NICU.

Baby Sidney initially responded well to treatment. Then she suffered a severe brain hemorrhage, which led to blood clots and hydrocephalus. Over the following weeks, the Millers consented to a series of aggressive interventions. After six months in the hospital, Sidney was released home. At the age of seven, she could not walk, talk, feed herself, use the toilet, or sit up on her own. She suffered from blindness, cerebral palsy, seizures, and severe mental retardation. She required round-the-clock care, and always would.

The Millers sued the hospital, asserting that Sidney had been resuscitated without their consent. In 1998, a jury awarded them $60 million for medical expenses and punitive damages. But the hospital appealed and ultimately won. The Texas Supreme Court ruled that in cases of extreme prematurity, any parental decisions made before birth "would necessarily be based on speculation."

Until now, this decision would have struck me as ideologically driven, wrongheaded, and cruel. But until now, I couldn't fully grasp what was at stake when I staggered into the hospital twenty-five weeks into my second pregnancy.

Any decision I could have made that morning would have failed to account for the potential contained within my daughter's tenuous existence. In the delivery room, the person she would become was well beyond the limits of my imagination.

65

I'M HAVING A MISCARRIAGE.

When my daughter arrived, I didn't know what a NICU was. My idea of a preterm birth was my mother's tale of how I was born: a little early, a little small, a little scary, but just an amusing birth story.

I vaguely recalled ominous reports about the rising levels of prematurity, the high-tech interventions, the astronomical costs, the dicey outcomes. I didn't recall the case of Sidney Miller, though its specter lurked as a parent's worst nightmare. I didn't know the definition of viability, except as a pawn in abortion debates.

But once my daughter arrived, I knew the tough, pulsating, radical, ancient heart of neonatology: the gray zone. The eerie limbo. The ultimate uncertainty.

Not knowing whether she would survive one month, one week, one day—or whether she should. Whether she was my child or a conditional. Whether to hold on or prepare to let go.

That purgatory seemed like the worst possible fate.

When Dr. Kahn told us about comfort care, it was a hypothetical scenario. The potential option of a quick and merciful release that never came to pass. In my darkest moments, I longed for the option, but my daughter's fate was never my decision to make.

The bleed in her brain. Her right lung collapsing. The night she stopped breathing. Every time she was rescued from the brink, I couldn't help wondering if the doctors and nurses were defying her true destiny. In truth, even when I wrote to defend her and described how hard she fought for her life, part of me still wondered if this was a wishful revision of her history.

What if she shouldn't have been saved?

This fear extended even to Mila's drowsiness during her earliest nursing sessions, her incremental weight gain, her slightest developmental delays—struggles that plenty of normal, healthy, full-term babies undergo, many of them more prolonged and arduous than hers. But because my daughter's birth felt like a death, she and I never had that leeway.

Part of me was always desperate for her to prove, once and for all, that she was worth the heroic interventions that saved her life. Only now do I finally allow myself to believe that, as heroic as the doctors and nurses were, so was she.

Two months after "distressed babies," Peter and I attend a dinner organized by a support group for parents of premature babies. As we recount how our babies arrived in the world, all the fathers at the table shed tears, as if they've held back these tears until tonight. We mothers seem a little more inured to reliving the memories.

I'm seated beside Mia Wechsler Doron, a practicing neonatologist and one of the coauthors of *Preemies: The Essential Guide for Parents of Premature Babies*. When Peter and I mention how we were greeted with congratulations in the immediate aftermath of our daughter's delivery, Doron explains that, among many hospital practitioners, this is a deliberate decision, not a thoughtless blunder. That greeting is an intentional acknowledgment that the arrival of a premature baby, no matter how catastrophic, is still the birth of a new baby.

As the plates are cleared, I suddenly find myself confessing to Doron, a kind-faced woman I've just met, something I've never articulated: I still don't know how to make sense of my daughter as a near miss.

How can anyone see her now and think that she wasn't meant to live? But how could she have been meant to live when she left my body long before she was ready?

"Maybe she wasn't meant to stay inside you," Doron says. "But that doesn't mean she wasn't meant to survive."

Doron tells me that the most common misconception of NICUs is that the babies' fates are completely in the hands of the doctors and nurses and machines. "All we can do," she says, "is provide the conditions to give them a chance."

I've recently come across the idea that babies like my daughter "declare themselves." But how can a creature who can't nurse or cry or breathe on her own truly have a will to live?

"We think of will as mental," Doron says. "But if you think of it as physical, it might not be such a weird concept. It can be in every cell of the body."

In fact, the concept of babies' declaring themselves has long been understood among NICU practitioners. It enables them to navigate the momentous perils of their daily work. Allowing babies to die who should have lived and keeping alive babies who should have died. Giving up on a baby too soon. Prolonging a painful existence that few would consider a meaningful life.

Since the mid-1990s, neonatologists have continued to incrementally refine the quality of care in areas such as reducing infants' pain and stress levels and creating a more womblike environment. Meanwhile, the gray zone occupied by babies at the edge of viability has undergone a slight shift. Now the lower

boundary defines babies born before twenty-two weeks of gestation or at less than four hundred grams, for whom treatment is
rarely offered or attempted.

At the upper boundary, babies born at more than 750 grams
or after twenty-five weeks of gestation are now considered
to have good enough prognoses that treatment is obligatory.
Generally, this is true not only in NICUs across America,
where it is legally mandated, but also in NICUs around the
world.

Neonatologists continue to refine their prognostic skills, but
the fact remains that all they can give are probabilities. Among
babies born under 750 grams, such as Mila, roughly half will live
and half will die.

However much society would like to draw a clear line to
define a life worth saving, for babies in this gray zone, doctors
cannot give a more precise prognosis until the baby is born. At
that point, they can evaluate the baby's weight, development,
and vital signs to make an individual determination about
resuscitation—but they have only an instant to make an
irreversible decision.

Thus, for many doctors, resuscitation is the standard protocol
in the delivery room for all but the most hopeless cases. It's the
only way they can continue to individualize their prognoses,
which allows for more ethical decision making in the precarious
course of NICU treatment.

Even with the most aggressive measures, the sickest babies
simply can't be saved. Nearly half of all neonatal deaths occur on
the first day of life. The babies who declare themselves members
of the other half still face an extremely uncertain journey.
They might become more difficult to ventilate, or suffer brain
swelling, or develop sepsis. They might experience organ failure
or seizures. Their condition might worsen despite every
intervention.

When a baby responds well to treatment, doctors and parents don't need to discuss the full range of options. When a baby's prognosis significantly worsens, doctors are obligated to initiate the process of decision making with parents. Generally, the decision to withdraw treatment is reached by consensus. Until consensus is achieved, treatment continues. Doctors and parents might agree to set limits on interventions—for instance, withholding a medication or issuing a do-not-resuscitate order—to give babies more chances to declare themselves. When babies simply can't surmount the formidable obstacles before them, doctors and parents must eventually conclude that further interventions are likely futile—and inhumane.

The process of letting babies declare themselves requires all parties to live in an excruciating limbo, which often ends within hours or days, but can stretch to weeks or months. As parents bond with their babies—and doctors and nurses become more invested in their patients—decisions about treatment options tend to become even more fraught than they might have been in the delivery room.

The process also increases the likelihood that some babies will survive with serious impairments who, given a stricter standard, might never have been resuscitated. This is probably the most damning charge against NICUs today: that they wantonly create babies like Sidney Miller, who are destined to become terrible burdens on their families and society.

To this day, the Millers maintain that the hospital "sentenced" their daughter to her life, and my heart still breaks for them. But the court's final decision reflects the inescapable reality that, in the context of extremely premature babies, an advance directive to withhold treatment can't be anything but speculative. In the delivery room, no one could have known the kind of life that Sidney Miller would live.

What remains most confounding about this case is not that

Sidney was resuscitated against her parents' wishes—a protocol that can vary from hospital to hospital, doctor to doctor, and case to case—but that neither her parents nor her doctors mentioned reevaluating her treatment after she suffered the severe brain bleed and its resulting complications. Generally, such a grave turn of events would obligate doctors and parents t o arrive at a shared decision about the most humane options for treatment.

The process of letting babies declare themselves is a gradual, fluid approach that acknowledges the impossibility of formulating a clear-cut, one-size-fits-all solution. It is centered on each individual baby rather than the hypothetical, hasty debates in a delivery room or the cold, stiff language of government regulations. At this point in time, it has emerged as the most ethical process.

It is not a final answer or a perfect answer. It is a fair reflection of who we are as a society and the messy process by which we continue to progress in our morals as well as our technology.

In the seminal book *Neonatal Bioethics: The Moral Challenges of Medical Innovation*, coauthors John D. Lantos and William L. Meadow write, "Technology does not create a moral imperative for its own use. We can, after all, decide not to use it. But technology does create a moral imperative to choose, to decide whether and how to use it. There is no longer an option to not choose."

Over the last century, neonatology has evolved—through a complex interplay of scientific, ethical, legal, and political processes—to reflect our values as a nation. Most of us can agree that we don't want to revert to the era of simply letting babies with Down syndrome and similar disabilities die. Most of us can also agree that while quality of life might be a slippery concept, it is an important factor in the lives we choose to save, and that the life of Sidney Miller crosses a critical line.

Most of us can agree that a life-and-death decision for a baby should not be the sole right of doctors or parents to make, but one that is ideally reached by consensus. Finally, most of us can agree that when the stakes are life-and-death, and the life in question might well be as full and rich as that of anyone else, we should err on the side of life.

The care of premature infants profoundly challenges us because to accept them as people in their own right means accepting how vulnerable we all are. We want to know where life begins and where it ends. We don't want to contemplate a knife-edge between birth and death. We know there isn't much perfection in the world, but we tend to think that the arrival of a new baby is one moment when it comes to light.

This isn't how life should begin, we can't help thinking. *This isn't like any birth story I've heard.*

We want to believe that in the primordial business of bringing a baby into this world, we know what to expect. But parenthood, like life, doesn't come with any guarantees.

We want to remove such radical uncertainty from this realm of life, but that would necessitate cutting out its heart. Some babies will live and some babies will die and we don't know which will be which.

Mila is a miracle. But I don't know if she'll get a worrying diagnosis when she's five, or twelve, or thirty-six. I don't know if she'll turn out to be a slow reader, or challenged at math, or asthmatic, or depressed. Any one of these could emerge as a direct result of how she arrived in the world—or simply as a matter of chance.

I also don't know if she will slip on an icy sidewalk, or tumble down a staircase, or be struck by a falling tree branch one day. In this way, I'm like every other parent on earth.

Did my daughter defy the odds? Of course she did. She defied the odds by being a person who, by definition, transcends the numbers—like every other child who ever lived.

In the delivery room, I was not asked to make any decision about her treatment. I was in shock and denial. I would have traded anything for the certainty of grief. If I couldn't have my baby girl safe and sound, I wanted her not to exist.

At the time of resuscitation, on the other side of the curtain that was drawn at my waist, my daughter declared herself. Her first Apgar score was 1 on a scale of 10. Weeks passed before I learned that her second score surged to 6.

Throughout her first day, while I wept at her bedside, she declared herself. She was breathing well, feeding well, even punching and kicking.

Then she suffered the intraventricular hemorrhage. The irreversible, invisible, unknowable damage that the cloud of blood would leave in its wake.

Yet she declared herself again. The bleeding resolved on its own. She survived her second day, and then her third.

She lived to see her first week: her most fateful declaration yet.

Her right lung collapsing. The night she stopped breathing. Each setback was also a chance for her to fight back harder. Again and again, she did.

She held on to my hand. Maybe that's only a reflex, but so is the will to live.

66

O N A FRIGID AFTERNOON IN DEEP WINTER, two years after I brought my daughter home, I peek through the window of her preschool classroom. Her face lights up: "Mama!" I open the door and she runs into my arms.

Her eyes widen when I lead her in the opposite direction from home. *"Baobao,"* she says, demanding to be carried. After a few steps: "No, I want to walk." A few steps later: "Mama, *baobao!*" And then: "No, walk."

The roots of her hair continue to grow thicker and darker, but the gossamer ends are the same tendrils I saw on the day she was born. Now they ruffle in the gusts of icy air that announce the arrival of the subway.

On the bridge, I point out the river, the skyscrapers, the setting sun, but she has already lost patience with this mysterious departure from her daily routine. She tells me that she wants her dinner, and a muffin, and a mango. At her two-year checkup, she was suddenly tall for her age.

Above ground, dusk has descended. At last we step into the

light pouring through the revolving doors of the hospital lobby. She has no idea where we are, but she immediately spots a familiar face: "Dada!"

The elevator buttons are still out of her reach. When Peter gives her a lift and the button for the twelfth floor lights up beneath her fingertips, she exults, "I did it!"

Together, we approach the locked steel door of the NICU. Everything is exactly the same, and everything is completely different with our daughter on this side of the glass.

One of the doctors spots us and gapes, then another. A few nurses gather, and a few more. They all feel like family.

"This is Mila," I say, and my voice catches.

We cluster beneath the bright fluorescent lights of the corridor. On all sides of us are the hushed, dim rooms where babies struggle to breathe and grow and make their own way home.

Again and again, Peter and I thank the doctors and nurses. Our words are inadequate, but it hardly matters. Here is Mila in the flesh. They still know her face. They exclaim over her hair, her height, her voice, her eyes.

She refuses to smile or say thank you. She shies away from the fussing of all these women whose ministrations she will never remember. Her face brightens only when she spots the flickering screens of the monitors.

"I want to watch TV," she says.

It's time to take our daughter home, time for the nurses and doctors to return to their duties. The moment Mila learns that we're heading out, she finally beams and blows kiss after kiss.

Back on the ground floor, we pause at the revolving doors to bundle up against the cold. At the first chance, she flings off her mittens. Then she takes our hands and leads us outside, into the fresh, falling night.

ACKNOWLEDGMENTS

I'll never find the words to adequately express my eternal gratitude to everyone who helped my daughter make her way home, everyone who contributed to her care, everyone who supported me in telling her story.

Thank you:

To the doctors and nurses of the NICU at St. Luke's-Roosevelt Hospital, who are the true definition of heroes.

To Dr. Amy Glaser, whose devotion to looking after every aspect of my daughter's well-being extends to our entire family. To Freda Rosenfeld, Dr. Richard Koty, Dr. Scott Rickert, Blimi Grossman, and our Early Intervention therapists, all of whom have helped Mila thrive.

To the friends and family who helped sustain us through times of crisis, especially Maia Merin, Alex Nazaryan, Elise and Arnold Goodman, Leah and Eli Goodman, Emily Goodman, Adam Block, Dafna Linzer, David Segal, Ji Yoon Chung, Vivian Lee, and Vivian Xiuyan Lu.

To the many openhearted people who reached out to embrace Mila's story and to entrust me with their own. The support and solidarity they offered to me was transformative, and I can only hope I've done some justice to them.

To the authors of the following books, which helped me place my daughter's birth in a broader social and historical context: *Neonatal Bioethics: The Moral Challenges of Medical Innovation*, by John D. Lantos and William L. Meadow; *The Lazarus Case: Life-and-Death Issues in Neonatal Intensive Care*, by John D. Lantos; *Far from the Tree: Parents, Children, and the Search for*

Identity, by Andrew Solomon; *Bioethics and Disability: Toward a Disability-Conscious Bioethics*, by Alicia Ouellette; and *Mixed Blessings: Intensive Care for Newborns*, by Jeanne Harley Guillemin and Lynda Lytle Holmstrom.

To Deborah Peel, Matthew Bodie, and Stacey Tovino for helping to illuminate the critical issues surrounding "distressed babies."

To Dana Wechsler Linden, Emma Trenti Paroli, and Mia Wechsler Doron, coauthors of *Preemies: The Essential Guide for Parents of Premature Babies*, a book that lives up to its title.

To Nick Hall of Graham's Foundation for his tireless work on behalf of parents of premature babies. To all the wonderful advocates at March of Dimes for their commitment to giving every baby a fighting chance.

To Nancy Miller and Lisa Bankoff, each of whom recognized the earliest pages of this manuscript as a gift to my daughter before I understood them myself.

To all the dedicated folks at Bloomsbury who guided this book into the world, especially Gleni Bartels, Lea Beresford, Theresa Collier, Marie Coolman, Emily De Huff, Megan Ernst, Callie Garnett, George Gibson, Cristina Gilbert, and Patti Ratchford.

To Diane Chang, whose wisdom and empathy are inspirational. To Frances de Pontes Peebles and Mika Tanner, my soul mates. Their improvements to this book were immeasurable.

To my parents, Mimi Wen-Pi and Donald Li-Tao Fei, whose unwavering love, compassion, and sense of fun are as foundational to my children as they are to me. To my sisters, Michelle and Jessica Fei, who are my guiding lights, as well as superstar aunties.

Finally, to Peter, who rescues me every single day. He is all the superhero I need.

Reading Group Guide

These questions are designed to enhance your group's discussion about *Girl in Glass*.

About the book

When novelist Deanna Fei went into labor at twenty-five weeks, she was forced to confront a parent's worst fears. Her daughter Mila, born at one pound nine ounces, clung to life inside a glass box, tethered to countless devices. Over the next months, Fei held the tiny hand of a baby she could lose at any moment.

A year later, with Mila finally home and thriving, Fei's husband's employer blamed "distressed babies" for employee benefit cuts. The subsequent media firestorm prompted Fei to find a voice to defend her daughter, speak about her birth, and celebrate her astounding determination to live.

For discussion

1. How do you think Fei's background as a novelist influenced this book?

2. Fei spends significant time grappling with maternal guilt that she couldn't "hold on" to Mila for a full term pregnancy. How do you think you would feel in a similar situation?

3. Where do you think the turning point for Fei was in vanquishing her doubts about the heroic measures used to treat her daughter?

4. Fei and her husband learn that the nurse's upbeat response is hospital policy following a premature birth. What are your thoughts on this policy?

5. For you, what was the most frightening prospect facing Mila in her first months? Why?

6. Did *Girl in Glass* influence your views or expectations about prenatal and neonatal care? Why or why not?

7. How has the book altered your perception of pregnancy and parenthood? What can all parents learn from Fei's story?

Suggested Reading: Deanna Fei, *A Thread of Sky*; Andrew Solomon, *Far from the Tree*; Elizabeth McCracken, *An Exact Replica of a Figment of My Imagination*; Anne Lamott, *Operating Instructions*; Paul Kalanithi, *When Breath Becomes Air*